OpenCms 7 Development

Extending and customizing OpenCms through its Java API

Dan Liliedahl

BIRMINGHAM - MUMBAI

OpenCms 7 Development

Copyright © 2008 Packt Publishing

All rights reserved. No part of this book may be reproduced, stored in a retrieval system, or transmitted in any form or by any means, without the prior written permission of the publisher, except in the case of brief quotations embedded in critical articles or reviews.

Every effort has been made in the preparation of this book to ensure the accuracy of the information presented. However, the information contained in this book is sold without warranty, either express or implied. Neither the author, Packt Publishing, nor its dealers or distributors will be held liable for any damages caused or alleged to be caused directly or indirectly by this book.

Packt Publishing has endeavored to provide trademark information about all the companies and products mentioned in this book by the appropriate use of capitals. However, Packt Publishing cannot guarantee the accuracy of this information.

First published: April 2008

Production Reference: 1160408

Published by Packt Publishing Ltd.
32 Lincoln Road
Olton
Birmingham, B27 6PA, UK.

ISBN 978-1-847191-05-2

www.packtpub.com

Cover Image by Karl Moore (karl.moore@ukonline.co.uk)

Credits

Author
Dan Liliedahl

Reviewer
Olli Aro

Senior Acquisition Editor
Douglas Paterson

Development Editor
Nikhil Bangera

Technical Editor
Himanshu Panchal

Editorial Team Leader
Mithil Kulkarni

Project Manager
Abhijeet Deobhakta

Indexer
Rekha Nair

Proofreader
Angie Butcher

Production Coordinator
Shantanu Zagade

Cover Work
Shantanu Zagade

About the Author

Dan Liliedahl is the founder and CTO of eFoundry Corporation, a premier consulting company with expertise in selecting, specifying, and delivering Open Source and commercial content management portal and collaboration systems. Since starting eFoundry in 1998, he has architected and developed Web solutions for Fortune 500 companies such as JPMorganChase, Disney, Sirius Satellite Radio, and AMTRAK. Prior to starting eFoundry, Dan was a principal consultant and architect with FutureTense, a start up commercial CMS product vendor, and Open Market, whose products continue to have a strong market presence under a new company name. In addition to his full-time work, Dan frequently donates his marketplace and technical expertise to selected non-profit organizations. He holds a degree in Electrical Engineering and Computer Science from the University of New Hampshire and has over 20 years of industry experience. In his spare time, he enjoys alpine skiing, ice hockey and coaching his kids' soccer.

I would like to thank the people at Packt who have helped me along the way with this book, especially Douglas Paterson, Senior Acquisition Editor for his initial guidance and ongoing support. Thanks also to Abhijeet Deobhakta for his patience and for putting up with many delays and missed deadlines. Many thanks to Olli Arro and Himanshu Panchal for their time, comments, and helpful suggestions. It is great people like these who have made this book enjoyable to write and seem to go by quickly.

I also would like to thank Alexander Kandzior and his OpenCms team. Beside building an outstanding product, they have always been available for questions and help, despite their busy schedules. I know their schedules are busy because they came out with four versions of the software before this book was completed! Alex's focus, diligence, obsession with quality, and professionalism has made OpenCms and his company great.

Special thanks to my wife for her support and encouragement and for keeping me going on those days I didn't want to. And of course, to my three children for making me laugh and for tolerating the times I couldn't spend with them.

About the Reviewer

Olli Aro hails from Finnish Lapland, but is based now in the north of England. Olli Aro has over 10 years experience in the area of innovation and development of software and web-based applications. In his current role as head of technology and product development for Clicks and Links Ltd, Olli has been responsible for the company's portfolio of Open Source-based solutions. He has been involved in the OpenCms project since 2001 (version 4), contributing various open source modules and bug fixes to the project. Olli was also involved in reviewing the previous version of the OpenCms book. Prior to Clicks and Links, Olli worked for organizations such as Nokia, eMobile Ltd, and CCC Systems Oy. In his spare time, he works on his own social networking site, Breakaway Republix.

Table of Contents

Preface	**1**
Chapter 1: Overview	**7**
The Site Design	**8**
Required Developer Skills	**12**
Basic Site Development	12
Sites Requiring Custom Content Types	13
Sites Requiring Custom Features	14
Bespoke Site Development	14
OpenCms Application Overview	**14**
The OpenCms Directory Structure	15
The Real File System Layout	15
The Virtual File System Layout	18
OpenCms Architecture	19
Extensibility through Modules	20
The OpenCms Web Request Process	20
OpenCms Web Application Packaging	21
Building a Complete Site with OpenCms	21
Summary	**22**
Chapter 2: Developing in OpenCms	**23**
Developing Basic Site Content	**23**
Setting Up an Environment for Creating JSP Code	**24**
Editing Files Using File Synchronization	26
Using WebDAV for Editing	28
Debugging JSP Code in OpenCms	30
Setting Up an Eclipse Environment to Build OpenCms	**33**
Tools Needed to Build OpenCms in Eclipse	33
Step 1: Checkout the Project Source from CVS	34
Step 2: Setting the Classpath for Compilation	40
Step 3: Using Ant to Build a Distribution Package	41
Building OpenCms outside of Eclipse Using Ant	44
Debugging OpenCms in Eclipse	45

Table of Contents

Setting Up an Eclipse Environment without Building OpenCms	**46**
Summary	**47**
Chapter 3: Our First Module	**49**
Understanding OpenCms Modules	50
Common Module Types	50
Module Events	51
Exporting and Importing Modules	51
Creating a Module	**52**
Creating a BlogEntry Content Type	55
Registering the Content Type	59
Additional Schema Features	66
Field Mappings	66
Field Validations	67
Default Field Values	67
Localization	68
Content Relationships	68
Content Previewing	69
Creating Content Using a Model	70
User Interface Widgets	70
Nested Content Definitions	80
Editing Configuration Files with Validating Editors	84
Organizing the Content	87
Summary	**87**
Chapter 4: Developing Templates	**89**
Review of the Page Layout	**89**
Templates in OpenCms	**94**
Creating the Templates	94
The Homepage Template	95
The Blog Content Loop	97
The Sidebar and Footer	99
Common Code Elements	100
Header Code	101
Search Form	102
Advertisements	102
Blog Archives	103
RSS Client and RSS Feeds	105
Footer Section	106
The Supporting Java Bean Class	106
The Blog Template	112
The Content and Template Loading Process	**113**
Expressions in JSP Templates	**115**
Using the Tag Library from JSP	115

Combining Expressions with JSTL	116
Accelerating Template Development Using WebDAV	**117**
Install the Eclipse WebDAV Plug-in	118
Create a Site Within Eclipse for the Server	120
Import Content into the Project	122
Summary	**124**

Chapter 5: Adding Site Search — 125

A Quick Overview of Lucene	**125**
Search Indexes	125
Search Queries	127
Configuring OpenCms Search	**127**
Field Configurations	128
Creating a Field Configuration	130
Creating an Index Source	133
Additional Search Settings	136
Introducing Luke – a Visual Index Tool	137
Writing the Search Code	**140**
A Simple Search Example	140
Subclassing the CmsSearch Bean	143
The Search.jsp Template	145
Summary	**151**

Chapter 6: Adding User Registration and Comment Support — 153

Understanding OpenCms Security	**153**
User, Groups, Roles, and Permissions	154
Organizational Units	157
Setting up Security for Our Site	**158**
Organization Unit and Group Setup	159
Adding the Users	163
Resource Permissions	166
User Login and Registration Code	**169**
Adding Comment Support	**178**
Adding the Comments to the XML Content	181
Publishing the Comments	183
Summary	**184**

Chapter 7: Providing Site Customization Features — 185

What is RSS?	185
Creating the Module	186
The RSS Client Code	187
Displaying the RSS Feed in the Template	189
Adding User Preferences to Accounts	190

[iii]

Updating the Java Code	191
Updating the JSP Templates	193
Hooking up the Account Management Page	196
Summary	**198**

Chapter 8: Extending OpenCms: Developing a Custom Widget — 199

Designing a Custom Widget	199
Designing the Widget	201
The Widget Code	202
Custom Source Interface and Implementations	207
Using OpenCms Message Strings for Localization	212
Registering the Widget with OpenCms	213
Summary	**214**

Chapter 9: Extending OpenCms: Adding RSS Feed Support — 215

RSS Feed Design	215
The RSS Feed Content Type	218
Creating a Supporting Widget	223
The RSS Feed Template and Java Classes	226
Content Wrapper Java Classes	231
Wrapping It Up	236
Summary	**238**

Chapter 10: Extending OpenCms: Adding an Administration Point 239

Administrative Points	239
The Administration View	243
Hooking the Administration Point Up to the Module	245
The RSS Administration Module	246
Leveraging the OpenCms Dialog Classes	250
The Feed Manager Class	259
The New Channel Action	265
Summary	**270**
Index	**271**

Preface

OpenCms can be used by Java developers to create sophisticated add-ons and customizations that extend the power of OpenCms in virtually unlimited directions. Starting by showing how to set up a development environment for OpenCms work, this book moves you through various tasks of increasing complexity. Some of the common tasks covered are building OpenCms, XML asset type development, templating, module development, user and role setup, and search integration. In addition to these common tasks some more advanced topics are covered such as self-registering users, RSS support, developing custom widgets, and extending the administrative interface. All the topics include examples and are presented while building a sample blog site.

This book is a clear, practical tutorial to OpenCms development. It will take you through the development of an example site, illustrating the key concepts of OpenCms development with examples at every stage.

What This Book Covers

Chapter 1 starts out by describing a sample site that will be created to demonstrate OpenCms development concepts. It also provides a description of the developer skills required for OpenCms development, followed by a basic overview of OpenCms architecture. We also provide a basic description of OpenCms configuration files and their file locations.

Chapter 2 sets the stage for coding by providing details on how to set up various OpenCms development environments. The chapter includes a step-by-step procedure for using Eclipse to check out and build OpenCms from the CVS repository. The chapter describes how to build OpenCms using Ant and also how to debug OpenCms itself.

Chapter 3 begins with an explanation of OpenCms modules, including a guide for creating a new module. The module is used to define a new content type, which is another concept covered in the chapter. Included in the content type discussion is a complete, step-by-step guide for designing and creating a new content type used to contain blog entries. All aspects of content type schema files are covered, including schema design, widget usage, field selectors, field validations, nested definitions, and registration. At the end of the chapter, the content type may be used to create new blog entries.

Chapter 4 continues developing the sample site by covering JSP template coding. A set of templates is created to display the blog content, including a complete run through of how they are put together. The example illustrates the use of custom template coding beyond the standard OpenCms tag library by sub-classing Java template classes. Included in the chapter is an overview of the resource and template loading mechanism. Also relating to templates is a description of using expressions and JSTL within template code. Lastly in the chapter is a guide to using WebDAV for template editing in Eclipse.

Chapter 5 covers the usage of Lucene within OpenCms, beginning with an overview of basic Lucene concepts. This is followed by an in-depth guide to creating a search index in OpenCms. The guide provides an example of building a new search index for the blog site example and describes a developer tool, which may be used to perform test queries against the index. The chapter includes a walkthrough of implementing a search form in OpenCms for simple cases and for more advanced situations.

Chapter 6 continues the build out of the sample site by adding support for users and commenting. It starts with an explanation of OpenCms security, including a discussion on Roles, Groups, Users, and Organizational Units. It then proceeds with the set up of the group and role structure for the sample, and shows how they are used within the code.

Chapter 7 shows how easy it is to support user customizations of site pages. It then show an example of this by adding RSS feed support to the sample site, allowing users to specify a custom feed. Included in the chapter is a discussion of integrating third-party libraries into OpenCms.

Chapter 8 describes the custom widget interface, and then shows how to design and create a widget. The widget provides a pluggable data interface that is used to obtain a list of selection values for a select list. The chapter then illustrates how to read XML content fields by creating a list source that gets its values from any content field. Finally, the chapter shows how to localize message strings and how to register and use the custom widget.

Chapter 9 shows how RSS feeds can be generated from OpenCms content. It also shows how wrapper classes can be used around structured content items to make them easier to work with, and then walks through creation of an RSS feed generation module using these concepts.

Chapter 10 discusses how administration points are created in OpenCms, and also how to use OpenCms dialog classes. The chapter also discusses how widgets can be used programmatically. An example administration point is created that ties together topics from previous chapters, showing how to use widgets, dialogs, and multiple screens.

What You Need for This Book

Tools needed and used for this book:

- MySQL database server
- Apache Tomcat web server
- OpenCms 7.0.2 version (New files might have been added in newer version of OpenCms and some files, like jar files, might not be in the book-specified location).
- Sun Java JDK 1.5
- Eclipse WTP 1.5.4
- Apache Ant 1.70
- Sysdeo Eclipse Tomcat Launcher plug-in
- Oracle JDBC Driver

Conventions

In this book, you will find a number of styles of text that distinguish between different kinds of information. Here are some examples of these styles and an explanation of their meaning.

There are three styles for code. Code words in text are shown as follows: "We can include other contexts through the use of the `include` directive."

A block of code will be set as follows:

```
<jsp:useBean id="search" scope="request"
          class="org.opencms.search.CmsSearch">
   <jsp:setProperty name="search" property="*"/>
   <% search.init(cms.getCmsObject()); %>
      </jsp:useBean>
```

When we wish to draw your attention to a particular part of a code block, the relevant lines or items will be made bold:

```
<mappings>
        <mapping suffix=".jsp" />
        <mapping suffix=".html" /> (add this line)
        <mapping suffix=".htm" /> (add this line)
</mappings>
```

Any command-line input and output is written as follows:

```
>ant -propertyfile opencms.properties [target]
```

New terms and **important words** are introduced in a bold-type font. Words that you see on the screen, in menus or dialog boxes for example, appear in our text like this: "clicking the **Next** button moves you to the next screen".

[Important notes appear in a box like this.]

[Tips and tricks appear like this.]

Reader Feedback

Feedback from our readers is always welcome. Let us know what you think about this book, what you liked or may have disliked. Reader feedback is important for us to develop titles that you really get the most out of.

To send us general feedback, simply drop an email to feedback@packtpub.com, making sure to mention the book title in the subject of your message.

If there is a book that you need and would like to see us publish, please send us a note in the **SUGGEST A TITLE** form on www.packtpub.com or email suggest@packtpub.com.

If there is a topic that you have expertise in and you are interested in either writing or contributing to a book, see our author guide on www.packtpub.com/authors.

Customer Support

Now that you are the proud owner of a Packt book, we have a number of things to help you to get the most from your purchase.

Downloading the Example Code for the Book

Visit http://www.packtpub.com/files/code/1052_Code.zip to directly download the example code.

The downloadable files contain instructions on how to use them.

Errata

Although we have taken every care to ensure the accuracy of our contents, mistakes do happen. If you find a mistake in one of our books—maybe a mistake in text or code—we would be grateful if you would report this to us. By doing this you can save other readers from frustration, and help to improve subsequent versions of this book. If you find any errata, report them by visiting http://www.packtpub.com/support, selecting your book, clicking on the **Submit Errata** link, and entering the details of your errata. Once your errata are verified, your submission will be accepted and the errata are added to the list of existing errata. The existing errata can be viewed by selecting your title from http://www.packtpub.com/support.

Questions

You can contact us at questions@packtpub.com if you are having a problem with some aspect of the book, and we will do our best to address it.

1
Overview

This book is a guide for developers interested in building websites using the OpenCms content management system. The book is intended for developers who are familiar with Java, JSP, and building web applications based on the Java J2EE framework.

In this book, we will develop a website designed for a blog writer. In the course of building our site, we will go over these topics:

- The site design
- Overview of OpenCms
- Setting up an OpenCms development environment
- Creating structured content types
- Creating templates
- Utilizing search
- Extending OpenCms
- Allowing online users to contribute site content

We will go over all the steps involved in building a blog website using OpenCms. We will start by describing the features and requirements of our website and will then provide an overview of OpenCms. Next, we will discuss how to create a development environment. We then will go over the steps involved in creating structured content types, to hold our site content. After that, we will cover creation of templates and Java code, to display the content. The site also supports search and user comments;, so we will cover the Lucene search engine as well to show how to provide login support. As the site additionally supports RSS clients and feeds, we will discuss how to add new features to OpenCms.

Before we get into the development details, we will first discuss some of the skills required to develop sites with OpenCms. This will provide us with a basis for understanding the environment and tools, which we will need to do our development work.

Overview

The Site Design

Before the development of any site can begin, there should be an understanding of the site's feature requirements. The feature requirements will often be driven by the actual layout and design of the site. We will design and build a blog website named 'Deep Thoughts'. The design of the site homepage layout looks like this:

The blog site is designed to support the following features:

- Blogs are listed in descending order of date, with the most recent blog appearing at the top.
- Each blog entry is listed in teaser style, with a link to the full blog appearing at the end.
- Blog entries support a list of topics attached to them.
- Archives of previous blogs appear on the righthand side, in descending order.
- Past blog archives can be browsed.
- The site supports contents search with paginated results.
- Ads may be placed on the righthand side.
- Users may self register for the site.
- Registered users may add comments and create a customized RSS feed on their homepage.
- Blogs may be viewed in various RSS formats.

In addition to the features seen in the mockup, we will also support:

- Direct editing of content in preview mode.
- User submitted comments.

There are two additional mockups for the site. The first one shows a detailed view of a blog. This view is shown when a user clicks on a blog from the homepage:

The last mockup shows what the search result screen looks like. Search results are shown in decreasing order of relevance to the search term. The pagination controls at the bottom of the page allow for the results to be scrolled, if necessary:

Required Developer Skills

The level of technology and coding skills required to do site development will vary depending upon the requirements and features of the site. Designing and architecting a site that properly utilizes and leverages OpenCms is an exercise in itself, which we will not discuss in this book. However, we will discuss the development tasks that are involved, once the architecture has been designed. In general, we can think of four different developer levels and skills.

Basic Site Development

OpenCms may be used to manage content right after installation. One way of using it is to import static files into the **Virtual File System** (VFS) and utilize the publishing and version control features to manage them. In this scenario, files from an existing non-content managed website may easily be content managed. Files in the VFS may be created, edited, and previewed in the offline staging area, before they are published to the online file system. When published, versions can be taken to allow for roll back, if necessary.

Files in the VFS may also be exported to the **Real File System** (RFS) and served statically or by a web server. In this way, the website can operate in exactly the same way it did, prior to being placed into OpenCms, except for the fact that it is now version controlled. The following illustration shows how OpenCms can be used in this fashion:

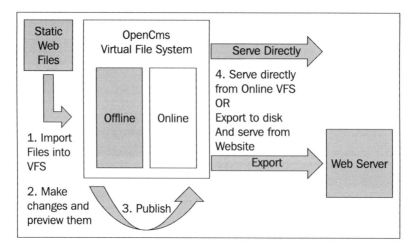

Utilizing OpenCms this way is straightforward, needs little, if any development effort, and probably doesn't require use of this book! However, it is worth mentioning here that there are a number of sites that can take advantage of this.

For this developer audience, the skill levels will include the following:

- Operational understanding of the use of OpenCms
- Operational knowledge of Application, Web, and Database servers
- HTML coding capabilities

OpenCms also provides a sample site called TemplateOne, packaged as a module. This module contains structured content types and templates. Although somewhat complex and confusing, content types and templates provided with TemplateOne may be used to construct sites without requiring development work. The documentation for these templates may be downloaded from the OpenCms website and installed into OpenCms.

Sites Requiring Custom Content Types

After looking at the TemplateOne samples, we may soon realize that it does not quite address our site requirements. Perhaps, the template layouts are not what we desire or the structured content types do not contain the fields necessary to hold our data. In this case, we will want to develop our own JSP code and extend or create our own custom content types. This level of development will require some understanding of Java, JSPs and XML.

This type of development involves working within the framework provided by OpenCms, to define the templates, content types, and JSPs, and also perhaps java classes that we need. Developing, at this level, does not require us to utilize a development environment such as Eclipse or Netbeans. But we will probably want to use a nice editor for our JSP and XML code.

Before undertaking this task, we will want to understand the feature and content requirements of our site in detail. This will allow us to properly design the templates and custom content types, which our site will need. This is a design exercise which will not be touched upon in this book. However, we will discuss the specific tasks required in implementing templates and the custom content types once they have been designed.

For this type of development, the developer requires first level skills plus:

- Understanding of OpenCms modules
- Basic Java and JSP coding skills
- Understanding of OpenCms configuration
- Understanding of OpenCms content types

Sites Requiring Custom Features

There are different types of projects that require integration of features which are not provided with OpenCms. For example, we may need a feature that automatically imports data from a back office application into a structured content type. Or perhaps we need to create a content type that we can easily use to define RSS feeds from articles in our site. For these types of projects, we will want to code in Java, using a development environment. We will also probably want to build OpenCms for ourselves, so that we can step through the source and gain a better understanding of how our own code will need to work. We will discuss how to do these, in the later chapters of this book.

Developing custom features in OpenCms will require the second level skills, plus:

- Advanced Java coding skills
- Understanding of OpenCms Java interfaces

Bespoke Site Development

The last type of development level is custom development, where OpenCms is used as a base framework or platform, and a custom site interface is built on top of it. This type of development might be suitable where the Workplace Explorer is too general, and a more task-specific user interface is required.

Developing, at this level, requires the third level skills, plus:

- Knowledge of OpenCms architecture and
- Familiarity with OpenCms code

This type of development is not covered in this book.

OpenCms Application Overview

Before undertaking development, it will be helpful to understand the basic design of OpenCms. OpenCms is structured as a typical J2EE web application conforming to a 3-tier web application architecture:

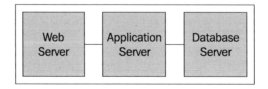

A web server on the front-end tier services incoming requests. The requests are passed through to an application server in the middle tier, where the OpenCms application runs. The OpenCms application utilizes the database on the third tier to read and store its content.

For production, using an array of web servers will typically distribute load to the application server tier. A common choice is to use the Apache web server, utilizing the `mod_jk` plug-in to distribute load. For development purposes, using a web server is optional, and instead the application server container may be accessed directly. OpenCms supports a wide variety of application servers, including commercial servers such as IBM Websphere and BEA WebLogic. It also supports open source servers such as Tomcat and JBoss. A popular choice among developers is the Apache Tomcat server. We will be using the Apache server for our development environment.

On the back end, OpenCms supports a variety of databases, including Oracle, Postgreas, and the popular open source database, MySQL. The OpenCms installation setup procedure provides a wizard interface guiding the user through the creation of the database schema. Optionally, it allows for manual creation of the database schema through provided scripts.

This wide variety of choices makes it easy to install and run OpenCms in many mixed environments. It also allows for easy integration with other technologies, such as portals, CRM systems, and document management systems. Next, let's take a look at the file structure of an installed environment.

The OpenCms Directory Structure

OpenCms must be installed into the application server as an exploded Web Application Resource (WAR) file, due to the way OpenCms JSP files are handled. We will discuss more of this, in the later chapters. After extracting the WAR file and completing the setup process, the file directory structure should look something like this:

The Real File System Layout

The web application directory structure should be familiar to anyone who has looked at or developed a web application.

```
OPENCMS_WEBAPP_NAME/
```

- `WEB-INF`
- `META-INF`
- `export`
- `setup`
- `resources`

Overview

These directories are explained in detail here:

- `WEB-INF`: This path contains the `web.xml` deployment descriptor, and other files used by the application. There are a number of sub-directories located here:
    - `classes`: This should also be a familiar directory. It contains all class files and property files used by the application that are not packaged into JAR files.
    - `config`: This directory contains configuration files. Some settings in these files are exposed through the Workplace Administrator and may be changed there. There are many other settings which must be managed manually. However, we will cover some of the settings in the later chapters but many of them are for advanced customizations and are not covered in this book. Here is a summary of the configuration files:

`opencms.properties`	This file contains the configuration information for connecting to the database. The setup program will automatically populate this file, based on the input selections.
`opencms.xml`	This is a master configuration file containing the names of classes used to configure a system area. Each class implements the `I_CmsXmlConfiguration` interface and is called upon, at startup, to parse its configuration and initialize its area. This file will rarely need alterations.
`opencms-system.xml`	This file contains core system settings such as locales, cache and site definitions. Most of the settings must be changed manually.
`opencms-vfs.xml`	This file contains settings related to the virtual file system. This file needs to be edited when adding a new resource type, and this is covered in a later chapter.
`opencms-workplace.xml`	This file contains settings related to the Workplace Explorer interface. This file also needs to be edited when adding a new resource type.
`opencms-search.xml`	This file contains settings related to searching and search indexes. Most of the settings in this file can be managed though the Workplace Administrator.
`opencms-importexport.xml`	This file controls the behavior of importing and exporting files from the VFS.
`opencms-modules.xml`	This file contains a registry of modules and is managed by the Module Manager within the Workplace Administrator. Settings in this file should not be modified manually.

- imageCache: This directory contains a cache of images that have been served from the VFS. All content including images is saved in the database. As images may take a long time to read and retrieve, they are cached here upon first retrieval.
- index: This directory is where search indexes are built and maintained.
- jsp: This directory contains JSP files that originate in the VFS. In order to run a JSP file from the VFS, it must first be exported to the disk and made accessible to the web application. This is the default location for these files. As JSPs must be written to the file system, the application must be deployed as an exploded WAR file.
- packages: This directory contains files that have been exported by OpenCms with the intention of importing to another system. Exported files may include VFS database extraction files as well as exported modules.
- setupdata: This directory contains a script file used by the installer. It may be deleted after the setup process is complete. Note also that this script may be altered, before a setup is run to customize an installation.

- META-INF: This is a standard web application directory.
- export: This directory contains files and resources that have been exported from the VFS to the real file system. If a file in the VFS has been marked for export, then it will be exported to this location. The actual time it gets exported is dependent upon the export configuration. URLs within the VFS that reference this file will be updated accordingly.
- setup: This directory contains the setup application. After OpenCms has been successfully installed, this directory may be removed.
- resources: This directory contains resources, such as images, that are used frequently by the application. OpenCms will export frequently accessed items from the VFS into this directory. Items should not be placed here manually, but should rather be managed within a module. This is covered in more detail, in later chapters.

The Virtual File System Layout

Now let's look at the layout of the files in the virtual file system, where the bulk of the application structure exists. To view the entire virtual file system, we must be logged in as `Admin` and have the root site (/) selected. Underneath the root, there are two main branches:

- `sites`: Each directory located underneath this branch represents a site in OpenCms, and is the mechanism used to segregate site content. The title property of each folder appears in the 'Site' pull-down of the Workplace Explorer. Adding a site entry is a two-part manual process. First a new folder must be created in the VFS. Then a site entry must be added to the `opencms-system.xml` configuration file. Each added site entry must have a unique domain name or IP address. When a request is made originating from the assigned domain or IP address, OpenCms will set the site context so that a request for a file appears to be relative to the site root. For example, if the site `http://www.mysite.com` is mapped to `/sites/mysite/` then a request for `index.html` coming from that domain will appear to be located at `/`.

- `system`: This directory contains files that comprise the bulk of the OpenCms Workplace Explorer application. There are a number of sub-folders under this directory, which are used by the application. Here is a summary of the folders:

    - `categories`: This folder is used to define categories that may be applied to a resource. The hierarchy of folder items in this location determines the available categories that may be applied. New categories may be added by creating folders in this location.

    - `galleries`: This folder is used as a shared repository for content galleries. Galleries created here can be made available to all sites.

    - `handler`: This folder contains templates used as the handlers for 404 and 500 site error messages.

    - `login`: This contains the default OpenCms login page template.

    - `lost-found`: This folder is used to place resources that have conflicts during import or export operations.

    - `modules`: This folder contains sub-folders with modules and corresponding module resources.

    - `orgunits`: This folder contains folders used to maintain Organizational Unit structures.

- `shared`: This folder contains resources that may be shared.
- `workplace`: This folder contains resources that are used by the Workplace Explorer interface.

The level of development required will determine if any resources within these locations need modifications.

OpenCms Architecture

OpenCms has a modular architecture centered on a VFS. The file system is considered virtual as it resides inside a database and not on a hard disk. The VFS is similar to a real file system that supports folders, file types, and permissions. Access permission masks on the files and folders, and controls access that users and groups have to the files. The OpenCms VFS also provides a feature very similar to symbolic links in a Unix file system. A link is a directory entry that contains meta-information which is kept separate from the file contents.

The core also provides support for basic features such as publishing, access control, and revisions. Layered above this are application level features such as configuration, the user interface, and module support. Module support is a key feature of OpenCms, providing the ability to extend and modify it. Module support is layered on top of OpenCms. A logical view looks like this:

MODULE	Your Content
MODULE	Your Delivery Framework
MODULE	3rd party frameworks (Struts/JSF/Velocity)
MODULE	User extensions (Widgets, Caching, etc)
MODULE	CMS Feature Support (Photo Albums, FCKEditor, etc)
MODULE	User Interface/ End user CMS Application

Module Management/System Extensibility

Virtual File System
Base Repository API (Revision/ACL/History/Publishing/etc)

It is interesting to note that although OpenCms is a web application, it comes with a shell application that provides an interpretive interface to the API from a Java command line interface! Furthermore, it is possible to script this interface to install content into the VFS.

Most of our development will center around using, or extending these core features. While working on our project, we will strive to work within the framework that OpenCms provides, rather than modify any OpenCms source code.

Extensibility through Modules

Modules are a key aspect of the OpenCms design. They provide a way to package together necessary components that may be easily plugged into OpenCms. Modules are the way that new content types, templates, or web capabilities are added to OpenCms. Later in this book, we will go into the details of creating an administration module for OpenCms.

The OpenCms Web Request Process

It would be useful to understand how a request made to OpenCms results in the display of content. The structure of a typical OpenCms URL looks like:

`http://[server]:[port]/[context]/[servlet]/[parameters]`

For example:

`http://mydevserver:8080/opencms/opencms/system/logon/index.html`

Server: mydevserver

Port: 8080

Context: opencms

Servlet: opencms

Parameters: /system/logon/index.html

The request will invoke the opencms servlet with the parameter `/system/logon/index.html`. When the servlet runs, it goes through the following sequence:

1. Uses the passed in parameter to locate the item in the virtual file system
2. Determines its access permissions, and see if it can be accessed by the requestor
3. Determines its file type
4. Based on its file type, locates a resource loader for that type
5. Invokes the resource loader to load the file

There is a bit more going on; but for our discussion we will consider only the previous steps. It can be seen that after permission has been established, a resource loader is utilized to load the file. Resource loaders are responsible for encapsulating the knowledge required to load and execute items requested from the VFS. There are several types of resource loaders provided by OpenCms, and there is a one-to-one mapping between an OpenCms file type and a resource loader.

Most site content is structured XML, and the assigned loader for this type is the `CmsXmlContentLoader`. When this resource loader is invoked, it examines the properties assigned to the resource, specifically looking for the **template-elements** property. This property must contain the full path to a template used to render the XML content. The resource loader passes control to the template. When the template runs, it takes the responsibility of parsing the original XML resource, and displaying it. Most templates will be JSP files, but they are not restricted to this type. In fact, when a template is invoked, it follows the same loading process, resulting in its corresponding resource loader being invoked. This allows for new template languages to be plugged into OpenCms, by writing and adding new resource loaders.

As resource loaders act on file types, the extension of a file in the VFS is not significant. This means that a file with an HTML extension in the VFS may, in fact, be run as a JSP file, or vice versa. A useful way to leverage this, is to create a file with a .CSS extension that is in fact a JSP file. The JSP could then dynamically generate the CSS based on browser type. We will discuss resource loaders in more detail in a later chapter.

OpenCms Web Application Packaging

Although OpenCms is distributed in a standard WAR file it must be exploded when it is deployed into the application server. This is because, in order to execute a JSP stored in the OpenCms virtual file system, the JSP must be written to the real file system first. As the web application writes to the file system, it cannot be run as a WAR file.

Building a Complete Site with OpenCms

In this book, we will build a sample blog site using OpenCms. The site will have the following features:

- We will be able to create blog entries easily.
- The site will have search capabilities.
- The site will provide an archive view of our blogs.

- The site will provide the ability to import RSS feeds from another news site.
- The site will be able to serve our blog entries as an RSS feed.

Summary

We now have a basic understanding of the architecture of OpenCms and how the various pieces fit together. The following chapters will delve into the details of developing with OpenCms.

2
Developing in OpenCms

In this chapter, we will discuss how to set up different types of environments for OpenCms development. The topics we cover will be useful, as we progress later through the development of the Deep Thoughts site. We also will go over the various techniques we can use to be more productive in these environments. We'll start with a very basic approach to editing the JSP files. We will then go over the techniques to use more advanced editing tools in OpenCms. We will cover how to check out and build OpenCms from the source repository. Finally, we will discuss how to debug OpenCms application code and JSP code.

Developing Basic Site Content

As described in the first chapter, it is not necessary to create a development environment for basic OpenCms sites that consist of static HTML pages. For a site such as this one, we can use the Extended HTML Import feature to import our site into the OpenCms VFS. After we have imported our site, we will be able to edit it in the VFS, and then publish it. OpenCms will manage the different versions of our content, as we publish it. An additional advantage of using the Extended HTML Import utility for static content is that it separates our content neatly into Image, Link, and Document galleries. The Import utility creates references, automatically, inside the imported HTML, to these content items.

Once imported, we can edit our site pages with an in-site editing feature. The feature is accessible by clicking on the icon in the upper right of a content-editable region of the page we are previewing. Alternatively, we may navigate to the HTML page, using the Workplace Explorer. Once we locate it, we can use the '**Edit page**' action to make our changes.

Developing in OpenCms

Setting Up an Environment for Creating JSP Code

Moving beyond this very basic type of editing, we will want to create an environment for developing JSP code. Although we can always use the Workplace Explorer to edit JSP files in the VFS, it is not well suited for development tasks. While there are many excellent code editors available that are better suited, there is no way to link any of these editors into the Workplace Explorer. Before we do this, lets create a JSP file in the VFS, first. From the Workplace Explorer, select the **Offline** project and ensure that the default site is selected. The default site appears in the **Site** pull-down menu as **/sites/default**. Then use the **New** button to create the JSP file:

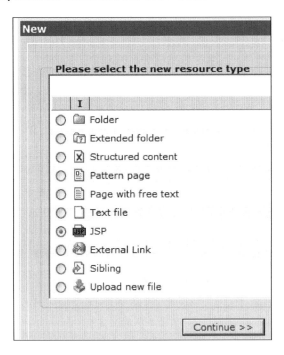

Name the file **Hello.jsp** and uncheck the **Edit properties of the new file** option:

After clicking on **Finish**, the new file will exist in the VFS. To add code to the file after it has been created, the **Edit sourcecode** command is used.

As mentioned already, the source editor is sufficient for quick and dirty changes. But for full development, a more productive editor is preferred. There are three approaches that we can take, to use an external editor.

- Cut and paste from an external editor
- Editing via file synchronization
- Editing directly via WebDAV

The first approach is simple, and allows the use of any editor that we may be familiar with. However, this approach can be cumbersome and difficult when making changes to many files. While the second approach is a little better, it requires the server machine to be locally accessible. The last approach is the most useful, as it allows any editor and many files to be edited, and may also be accessed remotely. Let's take a look at the last two approaches.

Editing Files Using File Synchronization

The first approach is to utilize the OpenCms File Synchronization feature. This feature allows a location on a disk to be chosen, where files in the VFS will be mirrored to. Once the files have been mirrored, they can be edited directly from within a developer IDE. Synchronizing the changes causes the VFS to be updated with the disk file changes. To configure file synchronization, select the **Synchronization Settings** icon from the within **Administration** view, located under the **Workplace Tools** icon.

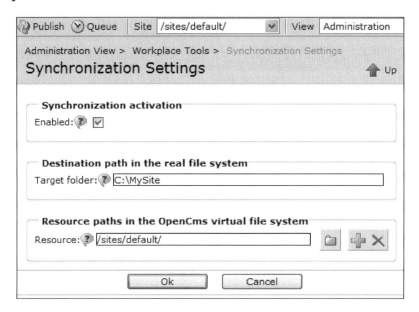

Enable this feature by selecting the **Enabled** checkbox. The **Target Folder** field contains the folder location in the real file system, where the files from the VFS should be mirrored to. The **Resource** option allows for multiple VFS source file locations to be selected. Each Resource or path added will have a corresponding sub-folder located underneath the Target folder path. Let's walk through an example:

For the target folder, first create a folder on the hard drive and then enter the path: **C:\MySite**.

For the resource, click the **plus** icon and enter the path: **/sites/default/**

Click **OK** to save the entries.

After selecting **OK,** use the **Reload** icon in the upper right of the Workplace Explorer. This will refresh the Workplace Explorer and cause the '**Synchronize folder**' icon to appear in the toolbar area. Select the icon, and then press **OK** to begin the synchronization process.

The synchronize action will always take the most recent file from each location and update the other location with it. Any files recently updated on disk will get put into the VFS, and any files updated more recently in the VFS will get updated on disk.

Any new files created on disk will get created in the VFS during the next synchronize action. However, this will only work after an initial synchronization has been done. While doing this, don't forget that OpenCms file extensions do not necessarily reflect their OpenCms file types. When OpenCms writes a file from the VFS to disk, it writes the file on the disk to match the extension it has in the VFS. However, when going the other way round, OpenCms determines the VFS file type, based on the file extension on the disk. This means that a new JSP file created on disk with an HTML extension will get created in OpenCms with a type, 'plain'.

The Workplace Explorer may always be used to change the file type using the **'Change type'** command. But it would be better to create the correct type, to begin with. This is possible by changing the file extension mappings. The mappings of file extensions to OpenCms file types are controlled in the `opencms-vfs.xml` configuration file. This file is located at:

```
<opencms_install>\WEB-INF\config
```

To configure file mappings, locate the resource type to map a file extension to, and then add mappings to that resource type. Keep in mind that there may be only one file extension per resource type. For our example, if we wanted to ensure that files with the .html extension get set to JSP in the OpenCms VFS, we would make the following changes:

```
<type class="org.opencms.file.types.CmsResourceTypePlain"
      name="plain" id="1">
    <mappings>
        <mapping suffix=".txt" />
        <mapping suffix=".html" /> (remove this line)
        <mapping suffix=".htm" /> (remove this line)
    </mappings>
</type>
<type class="org.opencms.file.types.CmsResourceTypeJsp" name="jsp"
      id="4">
    <mappings>
        <mapping suffix=".jsp" />
        <mapping suffix=".html" /> (add this line)
        <mapping suffix=".htm" /> (add this line)
    </mappings>
```

The `.html` and `.htm` mappings have been removed from the `plain` file type and have been moved to the `jsp` file type. A restart of OpenCms is required for these changes to take effect. The next time OpenCms imports a file from disk with a `.html` or `.htm` extension, it will appear as a `jsp` file type in the VFS. While making this change, we should also keep in mind that if we want to import an actual HTML file, we may have to revert our changes.

Using WebDAV for Editing

The previous approach works, but involves two steps and requires local access to the disk that the server is installed upon. Another approach to editing files is to access them directly, using the newly provided WebDAV support in OpenCms 7. WebDAV is an extension to the HTTP protocol that allows users to edit and manage files remotely. OpenCms provides access to its VFS, using WebDAV, by pointing a web browser at the URL:

```
http://servername:8080/opencms/webdav
```

The OpenCms login credentials may be used in the authentication dialog. The browser may be used to navigate and view the files in the VFS. However, in order to edit and create files, a WebDAV client is needed. Most current operating systems provide a built-in WebDAV browser. Windows XP has one built into the Explorer, which can be accessed through the browser. To access it from the browser, select **File->Open...** and enter the previous URL. Ensure that the **Open as web folder** option is checked. After supplying the login credentials, the Windows Explorer will open up into the VFS:

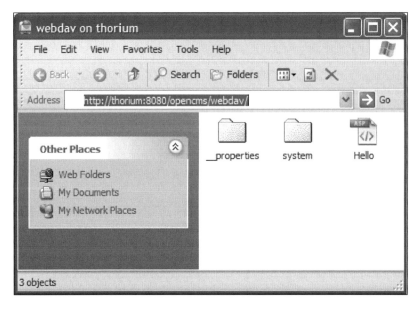

Although Windows Explorer supports WebDAV, the file editor will also need to support it, to be able to edit and write files. Let's open Windows Notepad and place this code into it:

```
<%@ page pageEncoding="UTF-8" %>
<%@ page import="org.opencms.jsp.*" %>
    Hello World - My First JSP<br>
    <%
        CmsJspActionElement jsp = new
        CmsJspActionElement(pageContext, request, response);
        String strRoot = jsp.getCmsObject().getRequestContext().
        getSiteRoot();
        out.write("The site root is:" + strRoot);
    %>
```

This code should be saved into the **Hello.jsp** file that was just created. Unfortunately, Windows Notepad does not support WebDAV and thus the file cannot be saved directly to the VFS. To get around this save the file locally, open the WebDAV location using Explorer, and then drag and drop the local file into it.

A workaround for editors that do not support WebDAV, is to use a free utility created by Novell that allows mounting a WebDAV location as a local drive. Information from Novell about this utility may be found here:

http://www.novell.com/coolsolutions/qna/999.html

After installing NetDrive, any editor may be used to edit files directly in the VFS. As soon as the file is saved from the editor, it can be clicked on in the Workplace Explorer to view the changes.

We now have two methods to create and edit application code that resides in the OpenCms VFS. Any JSPs that we create will have full access to the OpenCms Java API. To fully leverage the features of OpenCms, templates can be created to control the layout and functionality of the site. The template code is kept separate from the site content, to allow non-technical personnel to update the site.

Creating a template in OpenCms is simply a matter of creating a JSP file in the right location in the VFS. OpenCms requires that templates be placed into modules, and that the JSP code be placed into the templates directory of a module. Later on in this book, we will go into more details on templates.

Developing in OpenCms

Debugging JSP Code in OpenCms

Developer tools such as Eclipse and NetBeans have rich environments that provide support for creating and debugging web application and JSP code. It is possible to use these environments to debug JSP code. But this requires that the project be set up in a specific way. We will show how this is done, using the Eclipse developer environment. But before doing this, it is first helpful to understand how OpenCms handles the execution of JSP files from the VFS.

The first time a JSP file in the OpenCms VFS is served, it is written to the real file system, so that it can run as a normal JSP file would be run by the application server container. The location of the JSP file is configurable, and by default will appear underneath the WEB-INF directory of the OpenCms application, in a folder named jsp. Once the JSP is on the real file system, the OpenCms servlet will dispatch to it as a normal JSP file. If a breakpoint is set in the JSP file, the debugger must be able to match up the source with the compiled java class. The debugger will be able to locate the JSP source only if the project has been setup, with this in mind.

Now let's go through how to do this in Eclipse. We must first create the JSP within the OpenCms VFS. The JSP may be created anywhere, but for this example, we will use the **Hello.jsp** file we have just created. We first have to ensure that the JSP gets written to disk, by clicking on it within the Workplace Explorer. Remember that OpenCms will write the JSP to disk and then execute it, displaying its output in the browser.

We now can set up the project in Eclipse. Using the New Project Wizard, expand the Java node and select Tomcat Project:

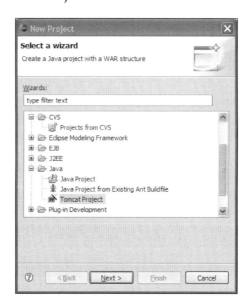

[30]

Provide a name for the project and click **Next**. On the next screen, provide a context name and web application root that matches the OpenCms web application installation. The default is **/opencms**, as shown in the following screenshot:

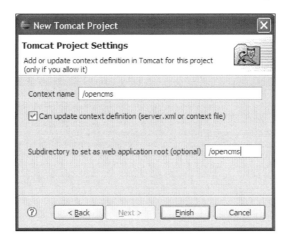

Click **Finish** to create the project.

Once the project has been created, the JSP files may be added to it. We want to add the JSP files that were written to disk by OpenCms. To do this, open the project, navigate to the web application directory, and then select the **WEB-INF** folder.

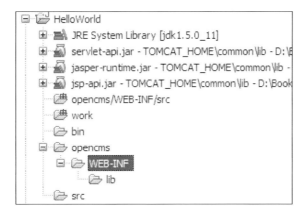

Developing in OpenCms

The JSP files under this node may be added by right-clicking on it and selecting **New > Folder**. In the New Folder dialog box, open the **Advanced** option and check **Link to folder in the file system**.

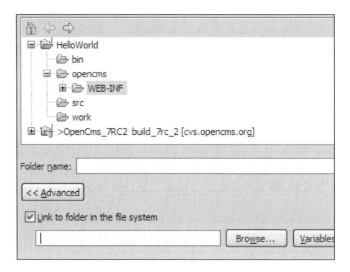

The **Browse** action can then be used to navigate to the existing folder. The folder to add is the location where OpenCms has placed the JSP files. The default location is:

    <opencms_install>\WEB-INF\jsp

Navigate to this location, and click **OK**. On returning to the project, the **jsp** subfolder can be expanded to locate the **Hello.jsp** file. The file can be found at:

    <project>\opencms\WEB-INF\jsp\sites\default\offline\Hello.jsp

After locating the JSP file, open it in Eclipse and double-click on the left gutter to set a breakpoint:

```
String strRoot = jsp.getCmsObject().getRequestContext().getSiteRoot();
```

Now open your browser and run **Hello.jsp** by clicking on the **Offline project** from the Workplace Explorer. Eclipse will switch to debug view and will stop at the file source.

If Eclipse cannot locate the source of the file, the **Edit Source Lookup Path** button can be used to add the project path. In the **Edit Source Lookup Path** dialog box, click the **Add** button and select **File System Directory**. Then browse to the location where OpenCms is installed and click **OK**. For Tomcat, the default location is:

```
<tomcat_install_location>\webapps\opencms
```

After doing this, breakpoints can be set within the JSP code, and it may be walked through!

It is important to remember that although this method allows JSP code to be debugged, it is a one way trip, meaning that JSP files opened in Eclipse cannot be edited. Recall how the JSPs get written from the VFS to the disk. To make changes to the JSP file, one of the previously mentioned methods will need to be used.

It is also worth mentioning that best practices should be followed while writing JSP code. Although it is possible to write application logic in JSP code, it is better to encapsulate that code into Java beans or objects that the JSP uses. The majority of JSP code that makes up the OpenCms user interface, is written in this fashion. Following this convention will allow breakpoints to be set within Java classes, instead of debugging JSP code. It also allows for changes to be made directly to the loaded Java files.

Setting Up an Eclipse Environment to Build OpenCms

Moving ahead, JSP editing usually requires creating new Java classes that extend OpenCms. Although it is not necessary to build OpenCms in order to develop new code, it is often extremely useful to step through the OpenCms web application. In this section, we will cover the steps necessary to build OpenCms using Eclipse. Before starting, we will need to install some tools.

Tools Needed to Build OpenCms in Eclipse

Sun Java JDK 1.5: The JDK is needed for us to build the OpenCms application. Although the older 1.4 JDK is supported, the default version and the one we are going to use, is the 1.5 JDK.

Download from: http://java.sun.com

Apache Ant 1.70: For building outside of an Eclipse environment, OpenCms provides ant build.xml scripts. Ant build scripts allow us to automate the process of building our Java projects. As Eclipse provides support for Ant build scripts, this tool only needs to be installed, if builds are to be done outside of Eclipse.

Download from: http://ant.apache.org/

Eclipse WTP 1.5.4: We may want to download and install the Web Tools Platform (WTP) version of Eclipse as it provides support for J2EE based web applications. After installing Eclipse, it should be configured to use the JDK that was installed.

Download from: http://download.eclipse.org/webtools/downloads/

Sysdeo Eclipse Tomcat Launcher plug-in: This is an Eclipse plug-in which provides us the ability to start and stop our Tomcat application server.

Download from: http://www.eclipsetotale.com/tomcatPlugin.html

Oracle JDBC Driver: The Oracle driver is optional, but is recommended. It may be needed if you intend to build OpenCms for an Oracle distribution, or if you want to eliminate all errors from your build. The ojdbc14.jar file needs to be downloaded and placed into a directory.

Download from: http://www.oracle.com/technology/software/tech/java/sqlj_jdbc/index.html

Step 1: Checkout the Project Source from CVS

We start by creating a new project in Eclipse using the **New Project Wizard**. In the Wizard, locate the **CVS** option, select **Projects from CVS** and press the **Next** button.

In the **Checkout from CVS** dialog, provide the following information:

- **Host: cvs.opencms.org**
- **Repository Path: /usr/local/cvs**
- **User: anon**
- **Password: anon**
- **Connection Type: pserver**
- **Save password: you may enable this, if desired**

Pressing the **Next** button will bring us to the **Select Module** screen. Here, we have to check the **Use specified module name** option, and provide the value **opencms**.

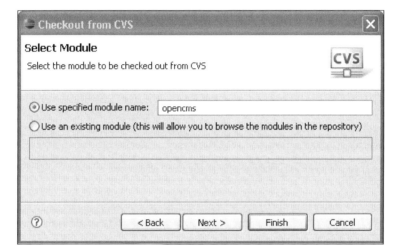

Developing in OpenCms

After pressing the next button, we are asked how we would like the project to be checked out. We will take the default to use the New Project Wizard, and ensure that the **Checkout subfolders** option is checked.

Pressing the **Next** button will allow us to specify which version we would like to check out. At the **Check Out As** dialog box, we can use the **Refresh Tags** action to retrieve the list of available versions, we may check out.

Expanding the **Versions** tree will reveal the list of available versions we may check out. To find out which version label to use for a particular OpenCms release is as easy as visiting the OpenCms website and looking at the associated release information. The version label is specified in the release notes. At the time of writing this book, the most recent release is OpenCms 7 RC2, with a version label of **build_7rc_2**. Select the version you wish to check out and click **Finish**. This will bring us to the **New Project** wizard, as we had previously specified.

Developing in OpenCms

We now have to select **Java Project** and click **Next**. The **New Java Project** dialog box will appear next.

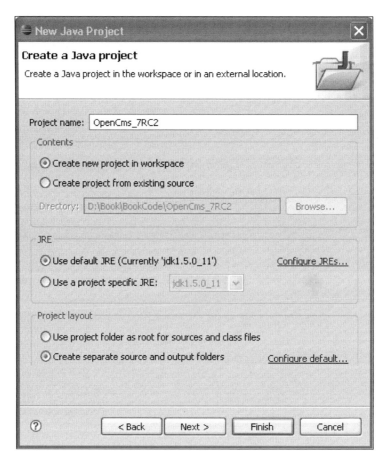

Chapter 2

The project name will contain the name of the Eclipse project that we will create. It is good practice to use a project name that indicates the version of OpenCms, rather than just the generic name of OpenCms. This will allow other versions of OpenCms to be built, if necessary. For the Project Name, fill in: **OpenCms_7RC2**. For the JRE, we should use the JDK that was installed previously. For our project, we can use separate folders for our source and our output. To do this, select the **Configure default...** option.

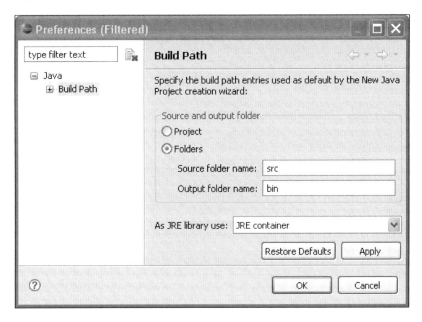

Ensure that the **Folders** option is selected, accept the default values of **src** and **bin**, and click **OK**. Clicking the **Finish** button will begin the process of checking out the project from the OpenCms source code repository.

Step 2: Setting the Classpath for Compilation

The checkout operation may take a while to complete. But when it is finished, Eclipse will attempt to compile the project immediately. OpenCms utilizes several other open source class libraries, which we must specify on the build path, in order to build successfully. We do this by right-clicking our newly checked out Eclipse project and selecting **Properties**.

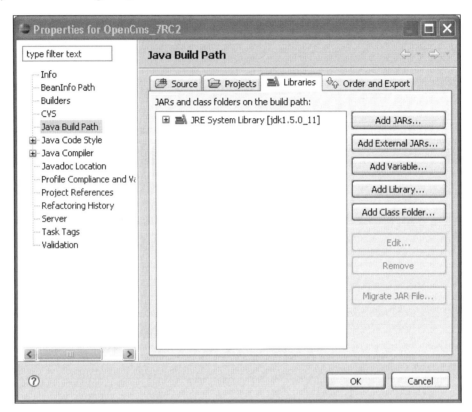

In the project properties dialog box, select **Java Build Path** on the left, and then the **Libraries** tab. We then select the **Add JARs...** button and add all the jars in, from the following locations:

- OpenCms_7RC2/webapp/WEB-INF/lib
- OpenCms_7_RC2/modules/org.opencms.frontend.templateone.form/ resources/system/modules/org.opencms.frontend.templateone.form/lib/

After specifying these libraries, Eclipse will once again compile the project. All errors will be removed except for the Oracle Database support. To remove these errors from the project we use the **Add External JARs...** button to locate the `ojdbc14.jar` file and add it to our project build path.

Step 3: Using Ant to Build a Distribution Package

We have now successfully checked out and built OpenCms within the Eclipse Development Environment. The project settings will compile the java files in the project for us, and will allow us to debug the OpenCms web application. This will be discussed in more detail, later on. However, if we want to build a distribution of OpenCms we will need to create jar files, zip files, and documentation. OpenCms provides an Ant build script to handle all this for us, and Eclipse provides support for executing an Ant build file.

The OpenCms build file uses some custom Ant build tasks, which are defined in jar files included in the source download. We must first configure the Ant environment to pick these jar files up as well as other jar files needed by the build file. From within Eclipse, select **Windows > Preferences**, expand the **Ant** option and select the **Runtime** node.

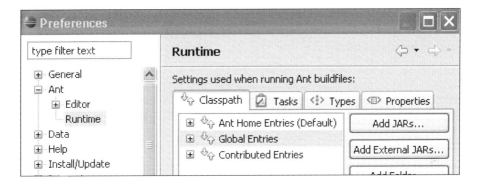

In the **Classpath** tab, select the **Global Entries** item and click the **Add JARs...** button:

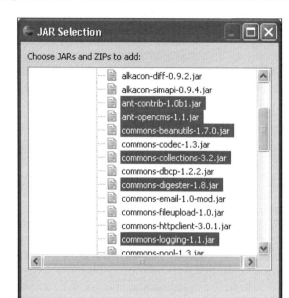

In the dialog box, expand the **OpenCms_7RC2/webapp/WEB-INF/lib** node and select the following jar files.

- **ant-contrib-1.0b1.jar**
- **ant-opencms-1.1.jar**
- **commons-beanutils-1.7.0.jar**
- **commong-collections-3.2.jar**
- **commons-digester-1.8.jar**
- **commons-logging-1.1.jar**

Click **OK** to add the jar files.

The Ant build environment allows for property files to contain settings that are specific to each build platform. OpenCms takes advantage of this, by referencing the property values in its build script. We must set these property values within Eclipse according to our particular environment.

The **Properties** tab is where we will add these values. Select this tab and click the **Add Property...** button. We will need to add the following properties:

- `tomcat.home`: This property value sets the location of our Tomcat installation. The OpenCms build script also supports JBoss, in which case, you must set the `jboss.home` value.
- `jboss.home`: The OpenCms build script also supports the JBoss application server. If you are using JBoss, you may set this property value to the JBoss installation location.
- `app.name`: This property value contains the context name of the web application. The default value is 'opencms' but you may change this, if you decide to use a different context name.
- `opencms.output`: This property value contains the location that the compiled class and jar files will be placed into.
- `opencms.input.externlibs`: This property value contains the location of any external libraries that may be required. It is used by the build file to specify the location of the Oracle `ojdbc14.jar` file.
- `modules.common.selection`: When the build script creates a distribution, it allows for control over which optional modules get included. How the modules to be included get specified, is controlled by this property value. The possible settings are:
  - `interactive`: If set to this value, then the build script will present a dialog box, where the user may select the modules to include in the build. This is the default setting.
  - `selection`: If set to this value, then the modules to be included are specified by another property value: `modules.common.selection`
  - `all`: If set to this value, then the modules to be included are specified by the `all-modules.properties` file. This file is located in the 'modules' subdirectory of the project source code.

We now can enable the Ant Window within Eclipse, by going to the menu and selecting **Window > Show View > Ant**. When the Ant build window appears, select the **Add Buildfiles** icon:

Developing in OpenCms

In the dialog box, expand the project **OpenCms_7RC2** and select the `build.xml` file. The Ant window will show the build file with the target tasks inside it. If we plan on working on more than one version of OpenCms, we should edit the **build.xml** file to change the project name from **OpenCms** to **OpenCms_7RC2**. This will prevent our multiple OpenCms build scripts from having the same name of **OpenCms** in the Ant build window.

There is also a separate Ant build file for the OpenCms modules contained in the distribution. This build file is called from the main build file, but is provided to allow individual module builds, if necessary. To add this build file, select the **Add Buildfiles** icon again, and this time add the `build.xml` file located in **OpenCms_7RC2/modules/**.

We now can use the Ant build utility to build OpenCms from within Eclipse. There are several Ant tasks available, out of which, here are the most useful:

- **bindist**: This build target creates a complete OpenCms distribution along with all the modules. It is the same distribution that would be downloaded from the OpenCms web site.
- **clean**: This build target is used to clean up the build. All compiled classes and jars from a previous build are removed.
- **jar**: This target creates the `opencms.jar` file
- **tomcat.copy**: This target copies the newly built `opencms.jar` file into the Tomcat application server directory.
- **jboss.copy**: This target copies the newly built `opencms.jar` file into the Jboss application directory.
- **war**: This target builds a `opencms.war` file that contains all the components selected for the distribution.

Building OpenCms outside of Eclipse Using Ant

If we want to build OpenCms from a command line, outside of the Eclipse environment, we just have to provide the property values for the build. To do this, we can create a text file containing the build properties and specify it on the Ant command line. For example, the **opencms.properties** file might look like:

```
app.name = opencms
tomcat.home = D:/apache-tomcat-5.5.20
opencms.output = D:/AntBuild
opencms.input.externlibs = D:/libs
modules.common.selection = all
```

The build can then be run with the Ant command:

```
>ant -propertyfile opencms.properties [target]
```

Debugging OpenCms in Eclipse

Now that we can build OpenCms from source, we will be able to run it in a debugging environment. Although we do not want to modify the OpenCms source code, running through a debugger is a great way of getting a better understanding of how OpenCms works. This will help us when we create our own java classes that extend OpenCms. In order to debug, we may want to control our application server, from within Eclipse.

There are a number of Eclipse plug-ins available, that allow us to control the Tomcat application server. We will use the Sysdeo plug-in, which can be downloaded from the following location:

```
http://www.eclipsetotale.com/tomcatPlugin.html
```

The installation is very straightforward and the instructions are found on the web site. Now that we have everything we need, the steps to debug OpenCms are simple:

1. Install OpenCms according to the OpenCms distribution instructions. After it has successfully installed, stop the application server.
2. Use the **jar** Ant build target to build a debug version of the `opencms.jar` file.
3. Use the **tomcat.copy** Ant build target to copy the jar into our OpenCms installation directory.
4. Start the Tomcat server using the Sysdeo plug-in.
5. Set a breakpoint in the OpenCms code and step through it.

We now will be able to peek into the inner workings of OpenCms using the Eclipse development environment.

Setting Up an Eclipse Environment without Building OpenCms

As mentioned earlier, it is not necessary for us to build OpenCms if we just want to develop code. In this case however, we want to create a library that allows us to easily reference the OpenCms java files. To do this within Eclipse, we must first go to the **Window > Preferences** screen and expand the **Java > Build Path > User Libraries** node:

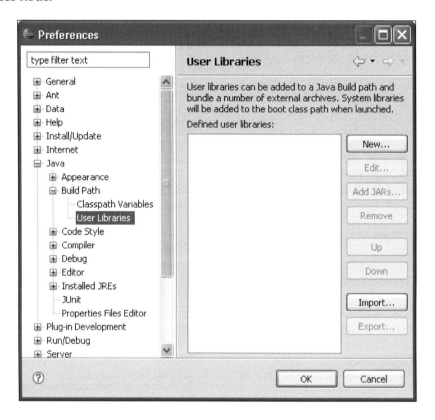

Click the **New...** button and enter the name of our new library, OpenCms_7RC2, and then click **OK**. We now specify the jar files we want to put into our library, by using the **Add JARs...** button. In the dialog window, navigate to the OpenCms installation and select the opencms.jar file. Any new project we create will be able to add this Library to the build path and use the OpenCms API.

Summary

We have discussed different types of development environments that are suitable for different levels of development. We have now understood how WebDAV can be utilized to improve the way we interact with the OpenCms VFS. We now have the basics we will need to develop our site. Later on, we will utilize these development environments while building our site code.

3
Our First Module

Now that we have set up a development environment we can begin the process of developing the site. However, before we can actually start coding, there are some tasks that we need to complete. The first task is to design and create our content types. While doing this, we have to make sure we can easily package up our efforts. This will make it easier for us to manage and distribute the code to other systems. As we have already touched upon, support for this is provided through modules. In this chapter, we will create a module and discuss the following:

- Understanding OpenCms modules
- Creating an OpenCms module
- Creating a structured content type for a blog entry
- A close look at rules for creating OpenCms schema files
- Registering a content type with OpenCms
- A tour of the User Interface Widgets and their options
- Nesting Content Definitions
- Using Validating XML editors for editing configuration files
- Organizing content for the blog site
- Using Eclipse for module development

At the end of the chapter, we will have a content type that will be used to contain the site data. We will build on this in the following chapter, by developing site templates. We will also have a module to contain the content types and templates.

Understanding OpenCms Modules

The module framework is a flexible mechanism both for packaging resources together and extending OpenCms. Resources placed within a module package may be easily managed and distributed to other OpenCms installations. There is no restriction on the types of resources that may be part of a module. They usually consist of things such as JSP code, java libraries, class files, property files, and images.

Apart from being used as a container to hold things, a module may be used to extend OpenCms. OpenCms provides support for this by looking for certain module attributes and sending event notifications that may be acted upon. A module may use or ignore these things, based on what it is intended to do. Let's look at some of the types of modules that may be created and at how they must be constructed.

Common Module Types

Due to the flexibility of the module mechanism, there is no specific attribute that is used to determine a modules type. However, here are some examples of typical module types one might find:

- **Content Type Module:** This type of module contains XML data type definitions and resources that allow for new resource types to be introduced to OpenCms.
- **Template Module:** This module type contains templates for a site. The templates are based upon the requirements of a given site and are tied to specific content types. Thus, the module is usually dependant upon a Content Type Module.
- **Content Module:** This module type may contain site content. Although the database export feature may also be used to manage site content, it is sometimes advantageous to use a module for this.
- **Extension Module:** This type of module contains class files and jar files that add new features or change existing features.
- **Integration Module:** This type of module contains JSP, class files, and jar files that integrate a third party technology. For example, a struts module may be used to add struts support to OpenCms.
- **Admin Module:** This type of module contains class files and JSP files that add an administrative interface.

These module types are based on how they are structured and what they contain. There is no hard and fast rule that governs what is in a module, or how it is structured. Often, a single module may be used to contain all these things. However, higher reuse can be achieved by using a granular module structure as described above.

Module Events

Modules may take advantage of advanced OpenCms features through module events. Module events are sent from OpenCms during the lifecycle of a module and can be acted upon with a Java class. The Java class is usually contained within the module and is thus installed along with it. To receive the module events, the class must implement the `org.opencms.modules.I_CmsModuleAction` interface, and must be specified as the Action class in the module definition. This can be done via the Module Management interface.

Module events allow for a setup or termination procedure to be performed, as well as any actions that should take place during publish. A module may also register itself as an event listener, if it needs to act upon any resource-change-events that occur. These types of events are sent using the `I_CmsEventListener` interface, from which module events are derived. Though we will not cover module events in more detail, we may inspect the `I_CmsModuleAction` and `I_CmsEventListener` interfaces, if a better understanding is needed.

Exporting and Importing Modules

After a module has been created, it can be exported using the Workplace Administration Module Management interface. When a module is exported, all the resources contained directly within its folder and any external resources it references are extracted and placed into a `.zip` file. The file is written to disk in the `WEB-INF\packages\modules` directory on the server that OpenCms is running on. This zip file may be transported to another system and then imported using the same administrative interface.

When a module is imported the following things will occur:

1. The module directory structure is created.
2. Resources in the module directory are imported.
3. Resources outside the module directory are imported.
4. The module is published.
5. Any resources marked as export points (described a little later on) are written to disk in the appropriate location.

The important things to take note of are that resources outside of the module directory are retained in their original locations, and that any export points are written to disk. By retaining resources outside of the module directory, a module may be used to manage any resources in the VFS. We will make use of this in the later chapters when we create other module types. Also, the fact that marked resources are written to the disk allows us to place properties, jar files, web configuration files, and classes in the module. We will also take advantage of this, later on.

Now that we have a better understanding of modules, we'll go through the process of creating one.

Creating a Module

The first JSP we created in Chapter 2 was a standard JSP page. While it is possible to build a site using just JSP pages and Java Beans, such a design would require content authors to understand JSP code. To get around this, we will instead use a design that uses site templates to separate content from presentation. The template code is responsible for controlling the presentation and features of the site, while the content resides elsewhere and may be edited by non-technical people. OpenCms requires that templates be placed inside modules.

Let's create a module by clicking the **Module Management** icon in the Administrative View of the Workplace Explorer. When we click on the **New Module** icon, we are presented with these entry fields:

- **Package Name**: This field contains the name of the module. Modules within OpenCms should follow the Java naming convention used for packages.

- **Module Name**: This is a human readable name for the module. It is for documentation purposes.

- **Module Description**: This may contain a description of the module. It is for documentation purposes.

- **Module Version**: This contains a version number for the module. The version number is a serial number that gets incremented at the time of editing or exporting the module. As such, care should be taken while using the version number for serious tracking purposes.

- **Module Group**: Module group names are used to collate modules together in the Administrative view.

- **Action class**: This field is provided to allow our module to hook into OpenCms events. If used, the field must contain the name of a java class implementing the `I_CmsModuleAction` interface. The interface is called during certain module actions, allowing the module to initialize or register as an event listener. We will go over this in more detail, later in this book.

- **Author name**: This field provides for the module author's name and is for the purpose of documentation only.

- **Author email**: This field provides for the module author's email and is for the purpose of documentation only.

The next group of fields control whether or not folder locations will be created for the module:

- **Create Module folder**: If checked, OpenCms will create a folder in the VFS to hold our module. The folder name will match the **Package Name** field and will reside underneath the /system/modules/ folder.
- **Create templates subfolder**: If checked, a subfolder within our module will be created with the name of templates. This folder is used by OpenCms to contain templates.
- **Create elements subfolder**: This subfolder is used to contain additional code that may be utilized by templates, or our module.
- **Create resources subfolder**: This folder can contain resources that the module may use, such as images.
- **Create classes subfolder**: The classes folder may contain java classes or property files. We will go over this folder in more detail, in a later chapter.
- **Create lib subfolder**: This folder may contain any Java Library (.jar) files that are to be included with our module.

Let's create a new module using the following values:

Module information	
Package name:	com.deepthoughts.templates
Module name:	Deep Thoughts Templates
Module description:	This module contains the definitions for our content types and the templates for the deepthoughts.com site
Module version:	0.1
Module group:	DeepThoughts
Action class:	

Author information	
Author name:	Your Name
Author email:	Your eMail

Module folders	
Create Modulefolder:	✓
Create templates subfolder:	✓
Create elements subfolder:	✓
Create resources subfolder:	✓
Create classes subfolder:	✓
Create lib subfolder:	✓

Our First Module

Make sure all the options are selected in the **Module folders** section and click **OK** to create the module. A location will get created for us in the VFS for our module. Switch to the Explorer view and make sure the root (/) site is selected, and then navigate to the /system/modules location. We should see the newly created folders for our module:

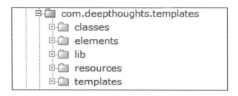

Now we can proceed with creating a content type definition and then building a template for it.

Structured Content Types

Support for structured content is a key feature of OpenCms. Structured content types allow different templates to be used to re-skin a site, or to share content with other sites that have a different look. Structured content types are defined by creating XSD schemas and placing them into modules. Once a new content type has been defined, the Workplace Explorer provides a user interface to create new instances of the content and allows it to be edited. There are some sample content types and templates that come with the Template One group of modules. These content types are very flexible and allow a site to be built using them right away. However, they may not fit our site requirements. In general, site requirements and features will determine the design of the structured content types and templates that need to be developed.

For example, the Deep Thoughts site design requires a content type to contain blog entries. The BlogEntry type will require these fields:

- **Blog Title:** Text String containing the title of the blog
- **Date:** Date field with the creation date of the blog entry
- **Image:** Optional image to be used with our blog
- **Alignment:** Alignment control for our image
- **Blog Text:** HTML editable text of the blog
- **Categories:** Selection of categories that we can assign to the blog

Creating a BlogEntry Content Type

Once we understand the data requirements, we can go ahead and define the XML schema. Our first task is to map the data fields to data types that OpenCms supports in structured content. The data types are summarized here:

Datatype	Description
OpenCmsString	This is suitable for containing string data that is not meant to contain formatting.
OpenCmsHtml	This type is meant to contain user editable HTML markup.
OpenCmsLocale	The locale type stores Locale information.
OpenCmsVfsFile	This data type contains the path to a resource in the VFS.
OpenCmsVarLink	This is a new data type for version 7 that allows storage of either an internal or external URL.
OpenCmsColor	This data type contains a hexadecimal color value stored in HTML format.
OpenCmsDateTime	This data type contains a date/time value.
OpenCmsBoolean	The data type contains either true or false. The default value of the field, if empty, is false.

Using these data types we can create an XSD schema file for the content type. Although the XSD follows the standard rules for XML stylesheets, there are certain rules that must be followed for use within OpenCms.

Required Code for Creating XSD Schema Files

To be recognized by OpenCms, the XSD file must follow certain naming conventions and ordering rules. These rules are listed here:

1. The first line must define the namespace declaration. This line of code is the same for all OpenCms XSD files, and is required! This is how the first line will look:

   ```
   <xsd:schema xmlns:xsd="http://www.w3.org/2001/XMLSchema"
     elementFormDefault="qualified">
   ```

2. The next line defines the location of other schema files used by this schema file. At the very least, it must include a reference to the OpenCms data types. More complicated XSD schemas may include other schema references, but a typical reference would look like this:

   ```
   <xsd:include schemaLocation=
                  "opencms://opencms-xmlcontent.xsd"/>
   ```

> The location of the file is prefixed with `opencms:` and not `http:` as one might normally expect. This is because the type is resolved internally rather than by using an actual file. We'll talk more about this later.

3. The next line must define a name that will be used as the root element for the content type. The root element is the containing element name that is used when an instance of this content is created. The format looks like this:

   ```
   <xsd:element name="[NAME]s" type="OpenCms[NAME]s"/>
   ```

   where NAME is the element name of the content item. Most importantly, note that the type attribute is prefixed with `OpenCms` and suffixed with `s`.

4. After this is a section that defines the complex type that was declared as the root element. The format is always the same:

   ```
   <xsd:complexType name="OpenCms[NAME]">
      <xsd:sequence>
         <xsd:element name="[NAME]" type="OpenCms[NAME]"
                      minOccurs="0" maxOccurs="unbounded"/>
      </xsd:sequence>
   </xsd:complexType>
   ```

   Again NAME must be the element name of the content item being defined.

5. Following this is a complex type definition section, which contains the actual field definitions of the content type. The type attribute of each defined field may be chosen from the previous table, or may be a reference to another XSD schema type. By referencing another schema type, it is possible to create nested type definitions. This will be covered a little later on.

6. Within the complex type definition, a locale attribute definition is required even if other locales are not to be used within the content type. This line always looks like this:

   ```
   <xsd:attribute name="language" type="OpenCmsLocale"
               use="required"/>
   ```

7. Finally there is an optional annotations section, which can contain additional information used by OpenCms while editing or pre-populating the content type. We will also cover this section in more detail later on.

Chapter 3

Putting all this together, we will create a schema file for the BlogEntry content type, which looks like the following:

```xml
<!-- ========================================================
     Content definition schema for the BlogEntry type
     ======================================================== -->
<!-- 1. Root Element -->
    <xsd:schema xmlns:xsd="http://www.w3.org/2001/XMLSchema"
            elementFormDefault="qualified">
<!-- 2. Define the location of the schema location -->
    <xsd:include schemaLocation="opencms://opencms-xmlcontent.xsd"/>
<!-- 3. Root element name and type of our XML type -->
    <xsd:element name="BlogEntrys" type="OpenCmsBlogEntrys"/>
<!-- 4. Definition of the type described above -->
    <xsd:complexType name="OpenCmsBlogEntrys">
        <xsd:sequence>
            <xsd:element name="BlogEntry" type="OpenCmsBlogEntry"
                minOccurs="0" maxOccurs="unbounded"/>
        </xsd:sequence>
    </xsd:complexType>
<!-- 5. Data field definitions -->
    <xsd:complexType name="OpenCmsBlogEntry">
        <xsd:sequence>
            <xsd:element name="Title" type="OpenCmsString"
                        minOccurs="1" maxOccurs="1" />
            <xsd:element name="Date" type="OpenCmsDateTime"
                        minOccurs="1" maxOccurs="1" />
            <xsd:element name="Image" type="OpenCmsVfsFile"
                        minOccurs="0" maxOccurs="1" />
            <xsd:element name="Alignment" type="OpenCmsString"
                        minOccurs="1" maxOccurs="1" />
            <xsd:element name="BlogText" type="OpenCmsHtml"
                        minOccurs="1" maxOccurs="1" />
            <xsd:element name="Category" type="OpenCmsString"
                        minOccurs="0" maxOccurs="10" />
        </xsd:sequence>
<!-- 6. locale attribute is required -->
        <xsd:attribute name="language" type="OpenCmsLocale"
            use="required"/>
    </xsd:complexType>
<!--optional code section -->
    <xsd:annotation>
        <xsd:appinfo>
<!-- Mappings allow data fields to be mapped to content
    properties -->
```

Our First Module

```xml
            <mappings>
               <mapping element="Title" mapto="property:Title" />
               <mapping element="Date" mapto="attribute:datereleased" />
            </mappings><!-- Validation rules for fields -->
         <validationrules>
            <rule element="BlogText" regex="!.*[Bl]og.*" type=
                  "warning" message="${key.editor.warning.BlogEntry.
                     dontallowblog|${validation.path}}"/>
         </validationrules>
<!-- Default values for fields -->
            <defaults>
               <default element="Date" value="${currenttime}"/>
               <default element="Alignment" value="left"/>
            </defaults>
<!-- user interface widgets for data fields -->
         <layouts>
             <layout element="Image" widget="ImageGalleryWidget"/>
             <layout element="Alignment" widget="SelectorWidget"
                     configuration="left|right|center" />
             <layout element="Category" widget="SelectorWidget"
                     configuration="silly|prudent|hopeful|fearful|
                              worrisome|awesome" />
             <layout element="BlogText" widget="HtmlWidget"/>
         </layouts>
<!-- UI Localization -->
          <resourcebundle name="com.deepthoughts.templates.workplace"/>
<!-- Relationship checking -->
          <relations>
             <relation element="Image" type="strong" invalidate="node" />
          </relations>
<!-- Previewing URI -->
          <preview uri="${previewtempfile}" />
<!-- Model Folder for content models -->
             <modelfolder uri="/system/modules/com.deepthoughts.templates
                              /defaults/" />
         </xsd:appinfo>
      </xsd:annotation>
</xsd:schema>
```

We can now use this definition file although it must be registered with OpenCms, first. OpenCms does not require the file to reside in any particular location; in fact it may be placed anywhere in the VFS. However, as we want to create a reusable content type, we will place it into a module, where it is managed. To do this, we'll create a new folder in the module named **schemas** and place the schema file in there. We will name the file: `blogentry.xsd`.

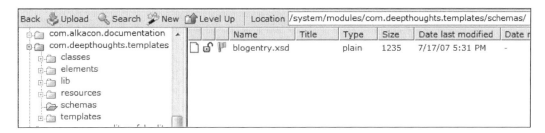

Now we need just to register the schema file with OpenCms.

Registering the Content Type

To register the schema file with OpenCms, we need to add an entry into the module database. Modules are defined in an XML configuration database maintained by OpenCms. For most items, we want to let OpenCms manage the contents of this file by using the Administrative interface, as no interface has been provided for adding new content types. We thus have to edit the OpenCms module database file directly. The module database file can be found at:

<opencms_install>/WEB-INF/config/opencms-modules.xml

Let's edit this file and add the resource type corresponding to the structured content type we've defined. It is possible to register resource type definitions in either the **opencms-vfs.xml** or the **opencms-modules.xml** configuration file. However, by defining resource types in a module, we can ensure that the definition is easily transported. As our content type will be placed into our module, we have to search the **opencms-modules.xml** file for our module name: `com.deepthoughts.template`

We should find the following:

```
<module>
    <name>com.deepthoughts.templates</name>
    <nicename><![CDATA[Deep Thoughts Templates]]></nicename>
    <group>DeepThoughts</group>
    <class/>
    <description><![CDATA[This module contains the definitions for our content types and the templates for the deepthoughts.com site]]></description>
    <version>0.1</version>
    <authorname><![CDATA[Your Name]]></authorname>
    <authoremail><![CDATA[Your eMail]]></authoremail>
    <datecreated/>
    <userinstalled/>
    <dateinstalled/>
```

Our First Module

```
        <dependencies/>
        <exportpoints>
          <exportpoint uri="/system/modules/com.deepthoughts.templates
                            /lib/" destination="WEB-INF/lib/"/>
            <exportpoint uri="/system/modules/com.deepthoughts.templates
                              /classes/" destination="WEB-INF/classes/"/>
        </exportpoints>
        <resources>
            <resource uri="/system/modules/com.deepthoughts.templates/"/>
        </resources>
        <parameters/>
    </module>
```

Note that the elements in the module definition coincide with the data provided earlier in the Administrative interface. We will not go over the format of this file in detail, as the OpenCms DTD file for this XML file is documented. The DTD file may be consulted if more information is needed on the elements. To define the new content type, we need to add two new entries. The first entry defines the new resource type and goes into the `resourcetypes` element:

```
<resourcetypes>
    <type class="org.opencms.file.types.CmsResourceTypeXmlContent"
        name="blogentry" id="3000">
        <param name="schema">/system/modules
               /com.deepthoughts.templates/schemas/blogentry.xsd
        </param>
    </type>
</resourcetypes>
```

This entry should be inserted right after the `<parameters/>` element, and has the following fields:

- `type`: This element defines a new resource type

    ◦ `class`: The attribute specifies a Java class that must implement the `I_CmsResourceType` interface. For structured XML content types, we should always use the `CmsResourceTypeXmlContent` class.

    ◦ `name`: The name attribute refers to the name of our new resource type.

    ◦ `id`: This attribute refers to a unique id that is used to identify the type of our resource. The value should be carefully chosen as it should not conflict with other resource ids. Resource ids should never be changed once instances have been created.

The second entry we need to create is a menu definition. This allows users to create a new instance of the resource from the Workplace Explorer. This entry goes within the `explorertypes` element:

```
<explorertypes>
    <explorertype name="blogentry" key="fileicon.blogentry"
                icon="xmlcontent.gif" reference="xmlcontent">
        <newresource uri="newresource_xmlcontent.jsp?
                newresourcetype=blogentry" order="25"
                info="desc.blogentry"/>
        <accesscontrol>
            <accessentry principal="ROLE.WORKPLACE_USER"
                                    permissions="+r+v+w+c"/>
        </accesscontrol>
    </explorertype>
</explorertypes>
```

The fields for this entry are:

- `explorertype`: This element defines how the Workplace Explorer presents a user interface for our resource
    - `name`: This is the name of our resource type.
    - `key`: This attribute refers to an entry in a properties file (described later) that contains label text for the UI. Placing the text into a properties file allows the user interface to be localized.
    - `icon`: This attribute refers to the name of an image resource used by the Workplace Explorer for our resource type. For now, we will use an existing image: `xmlcontent.gif`.
    - `reference`: This attribute is used for content types that are derived from other content types. All XML structured content types should refer to the base XMLContent type and should thus use the value `xmlcontent`.
- `newresource`: This element defines how the Workplace Explorer will create instances of our resource.
    - `uri`: This refers to the URI that is called to instantiate a new instance of our resource. For most resource types, we can use one of the default JSP files in the `/system/workplace/commons` folder. For all XML structured content types, we can use the `newresource_xmlcontent.jsp` file and set the `newresourcetype` parameter to our resource name.

Our First Module

- ◦ `order`: This attribute sets the order in which the item will appear in the Workplace Explorer. Items with lower numbers will appear before the ones with higher numbers.
- ◦ `info`: This attribute refers to an entry in a properties file that contains a description of the content type for the UI.
- `accesscontrol/accessentry`: These elements allow access control to be applied to the resource type
  - ◦ `principal`: This is the principal to which we want to apply a permission.
  - ◦ `permission`: This is the permission mask that the given principal will have.

After adding the code and saving the file, the application server must be restarted. We can then go into the Workplace Explorer and create a new instance of the data type. However, when we do this, we will see the following error:

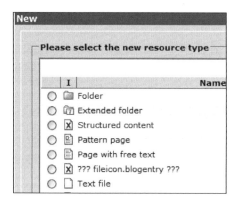

The error occurs when OpenCms cannot find the definition of the property surrounded by the **???** characters. The Workplace Explorer looks for property definitions in a `workplace.properties` file stored under the `<opencms_install>\WEB-INF\classes` directory. Each module, containing a content type definition, may have its own properties file. Placing the string definitions in the properties file allows for the user interface to be localized.

The properties file must be stored in a subdirectory, with a name that matches the module name. The entries in the property file consist of name-value pairs. The Workplace Explorer retrieves a string value from the properties file, using the key, and displays the corresponding string. The `explorertype.key` and `newresource.info` elements described previously are examples of references to this property file.

The properties file may also contain text labels and help text for each field appearing on the editing form of the content type. The editing form is automatically built by OpenCms when an instance of the content type is edited. Normally, each form field has a label that corresponds to data field name. However, it is possible to change the label and also have a help bubble displayed next to it with some information text to aid data entry. These are added by creating property file entries with the following format:

```
label.[CONTENT_TYPE].[FIELD]=FIELD_LABEL
```

CONTENT_TYPE is the name of the structured content type, FIELD is the particular field name, and FIELD_LABEL is the label for the field. The help text has a similar format:

```
label.[ [CONTENT_TYPE].[FIELD].help=FIELD_HELP_TEXT
```

Adding this entry will cause a help bubble icon to appear next to the entry field. Hovering over the icon will cause the text to appear in a tooltip.

Localizing messages strings in properties files

Property values in message strings are easily localized in OpenCms. When a property file is loaded, OpenCms attempts to locate a locale-specific version of it by combining the locale in the filename. For example, the German locale name is de. In this case, OpenCms will look for a file named workplace_de.properties to contain the localized strings. If a locale specific version cannot be found then the default filename without a locale suffix will be used. A common practice is to have several locale files present:

workplace_de.properties – German strings

workplace_en.properties – English strings

A sibling is then created for the one to be used as the default:

workplace.properties → workplace_en.properties - sibling

This way the default locale can be easily set and changed if necessary.

This is what the file looks like for the BlogEntry content type:

```
#
# This property file contains the localized strings for
#   the BlogEntry XML type
#

# text used to display the type of content being created
fileicon.blogentry = Blog Entry
```

```
# description of the content type
desc.blogentry=A Blog Entry is our daily blog content

# User Interface Labels per field
label.BlogEntry.Title = Title
label.BlogEntry.Date = Blog Date
label.BlogEntry.Image = Image (optional)
label.BlogEntry.Alignment = Image Alignment
label.BlogEntry.BlogText = Blog
label.BlogEntry.Category = Category
label.BlogEntry.Comment = User Comment

# Help Icon text per field
label.BlogEntry.Title.help = Enter a Title for the Blog Entry
label.BlogEntry.Date.help = This contains the creation date for the
blog. It gets automatically set when first created and should not need
changing.
label.BlogEntry.Image.help = Enter an optional Image
label.BlogEntry.Alignment.help = Set the image alignment
label.BlogEntry.BlogText.help = Enter the blog text here
label.BlogEntry.Category.help = Apply some categories to the blog
label.BlogEntry.Comment.help = User Comments go here

# text used in a validation rule
editor.validate.BlogEntry.dontallowblog=Text in {0} must not contain
"blog" or "Blog"
```

The original error in the Workplace Explorer may be resolved by creating the properties file in the required directory, and then restarting OpenCms. However, the problem with this is that we would need to remember to do this again when the module is distributed to another machine. Fortunately, OpenCms provides a solution to this through module export points.

A module export point is a module setting that allows a resource in the VFS to have a corresponding export location on the real file system. When the module is published, all defined export points will get copied to the real file system. This feature allows resources to be managed from within a module, but allows them to be placed onto the real file system upon import. Note that because OpenCms is a web application, exported files may only be placed underneath the installed location of the OpenCms web application.

Now let's create the properties file. From the Workplace Explorer, select the root folder and then navigate to the module. Expand the **classes/com/deepthoughts/templates** subfolder, and create a new text file named **workplace.properties**. Place the property definition code into the file, and save it. To support localization, we would just need to create additional properties files with localized definitions. One file would have to be created per locale, and would be named according to the locale it supports. For example, in German, a file named **workplace_de.properties** would have to be created.

Next we have to ensure that the file gets exported. Adding it as an export point is done through the **Module Management** panel of the Administrative interface. Locate the module, click on it to edit it, and then use the **Module exportpoints** icon to add the export point. Notice that the **classes** folder is already specified as an export point. This is because the option to create the **classes** folder was clicked when the module was created. OpenCms automatically recognizes this folder as an export point and adds it for us. This means that, in fact, there is nothing for us to do; the resource will automatically get exported.

The only thing left to do is to **Publish** the module. This will cause the new content types to become available to the Online project. It will also cause the properties file to get exported to the WEB-INF/classes folder. After publishing, remember to restart OpenCms. After this, new instances of the Blog Entry data type can be created by using the **New** button in the Workplace Explorer:

The new resource dialog will appear and will contain the new content type as a choice. Remember that if the order needs to be changed, it can be done by modifying the order attribute in the explorertype section of the XML configuration file.

Additional Schema Features

As mentioned earlier, there are a rich variety of options available when designing a structured content type. OpenCms provides support for these features through use of the `xsd:annotation` section of the schema file. The following sections provide detailed information about additional features that may be used, when designing content types.

Field Mappings

Mappings allow for data fields to be mapped to a property or attribute.

```
<mappings>
    <mapping element="Title" mapto="property:Title" />
    <mapping element="Date" mapto="attribute:datereleased" />
</mappings>
```

This is a useful feature to collate content based on fields contained inside the XML. OpenCms provides API support for filtering items based on values of properties, but not for values of XML fields. This is because doing something like that would require opening each XML resource, and parsing it. However, by mapping a data field to a property value, this is easily accomplished. If a data field is mapped, then the corresponding property value is updated whenever the XML content is saved. Data field values only get copied to property values, and this occurs only if the XML content editor is used to make the content change. If an XML content field is updated programmatically, then no update will be made to the property file. Moreover, if the corresponding property value is changed, there will be no update made to the XML data field. In other words, the change is unidirectional. The syntax for creating a mapping value is:

```
<mapping element="FIELD" mapto="TYPE:[SCOPE]:NAME" />
```

- FIELD: This is the name of the data field we are mapping.
- TYPE: There are three types of mappings:
    - `attribute`: There are only two available attributes: `datereleased` and `dateexpired`
    - `property`: This maps the field to a property value. If the specified property value does not exist it will get created.
    - `propertyList`: This allows for multiple instances of the same field to get mapped to a single property value. It should be used for data fields that repeat, such as the Category field in our BlogEntry schema. Multiple values will get placed into the property field separated by a vertical bar character.

- SCOPE: This is an optional scope field which allows individual or global property values to be mapped. The possible option values are:
  - individual: Map to an individual property (Default if not present).
  - global: Map to a global property.

For the BlogEntry content type, we have mapped the Title field to the Title property and the Date field to the datereleased attribute.

Field Validations

OpenCms supports basic validation rules for data fields. The validationrules element allows these rules to be defined through regular expression syntax checking:

```
<validationrules>
    <rule element="BlogText" regex="!.*[Bl]og.*" type="warning"
         message="${key.editor.warning.BlogEntry.dontallowblog|
                   ${validation.path}}"/>
</validationrules>
```

If a match is found on the syntax rule, then the message is displayed. The message text is defined in a properties file. There are two levels of error checking: warning and error. The warning level will present a warning message to the user if the save action is pressed, but will allow the content to be saved. The error level will present an error message, and will not allow the content to be saved. For our BlogEntry content type, we have included a validation rule that provides a warning message if the word 'Blog' is used in our blog.

If more complex validation is required it is possible to create a custom validation handler by adding a Java class that implements the I_CmsXmlContentHandler interface.

Default Field Values

Data fields may have a default value assigned to them by setting the defaults element. Each entry contains the field name along with the default value. For example, the blog entry date field is populated by default with the current time. This is done by using the ${currenttime} macro, another feature of OpenCms. There are several macros that may be used both from within schema files and templates. For a complete listing of the available macros the org.opencms.util.CmsMacroResolver java file should be examined.

```
<defaults>
    <default element="Date" value="${currenttime}"/>
    <default element="Alignment" value="left"/>
</defaults>
```

Localization

OpenCms provides localization support for the content editor form. As described earlier, the field labels may be placed in a properties file. The location of the properties file may be specified in a `resourcebundle` element:

```
<resourcebundle name="com.deepthoughts.templates.workplace"/>
```

The name attribute contains the name of the folder containing the properties file. For the blog content type the properties file is located at:

<module_location>\classes\com\deepthoughts\templates\workplace.properties

The format of the properties file is as described earlier.

Content Relationships

OpenCms Version 7 introduces a new content relationship engine that maintains relationships formed between content items. There are two general classes of relationships that may be formed: **strong links** and **weak links**. A strong link is formed when the existence of the linked child item is crucial to the function or display of the containing parent. An example of a strong link is a stylesheet, where the page does not display properly if the stylesheet is missing.

A weak link occurs when the child item is not crucial to the parent. An example of this might be a contained link that is displayed on the page. The page can still be displayed, but the link will not appear.

Content relationships may be formed either implicitly or explicitly. A content relationship is formed implicitly whenever a content item is inserted into an unstructured field using an OpenCms editing form. For example, consider an image that has been selected from an image gallery and inserted into an HTML field of a content item. In this case, a relationship will automatically be added from the content item to the image. If a user attempts to later delete the image in the Workplace Explorer, then a warning message appears informing the user where it is used, and that broken links will occur. At the time the relationship is formed, OpenCms will parse the child item and decide whether it should be a weak or a strong link.

Explicit content relationships may only be formed programmatically or may be declared from within a content type definition. When links are formed this way, it is up to the programmer to decide the type of link and how it should be handled. To support link declaration in structured types the `relation` element may be used in the XSD file:

```
<relations>
    <relation element="[ELEMENT]" type="[TYPE]"
              invalidate="[INVALIDATE]" />
</relations>
```

The options for the tag are:

- ELEMENT: This is the name of the data field the relation applies to.
- TYPE: This is the type of relationship.
    - `weak`: Relationship is a weak link.
    - `strong`: Relationship is a strong link.
- INVALIDATE: Determines how validations are handled.
    - `false`: Disable link checking.
    - `true/node`: Invalidate just this node if broken.
    - `parent`: Invalidate the entire parent node in nested content.

The INVALIDATE attribute may only be used for elements that are optional, and is used to control the link checking behavior of that element. If set to **false**, then link checking will be disabled. If set to **true**, then link checking will be enabled. A third option of **parent** may be used to cause a parent node to become invalid if the link is broken. This feature is useful for a compound content type where a broken child item should cause the entire included type to become invalid. For example, consider the following content structure:

```
<BlogEntry>
    <Title>
        <BlogComment>
            <Image>
            <Description>
        </BlogComment>
</BlogEntry>
```

Here, the `BlogComment` element is an optional item that may appear multiple times. It is a nested content type which consists of an `Image` and a `Description`. In this case, we might define a relationship and set the invalidate type to `parent` so that if the `Image` is missing, the entire `BlogComment` will get ignored.

Content Previewing

The structured content editor has a preview action allowing editors to preview content before saving. By default, this action is not enabled for structured content types, but may be turned on by adding the `preview` element:

```
<preview uri="${previewtempfile}" />
```

> Although the blog entry schema file is using the `<preview>` element, an error will occur if we try to use it. This is because a template is necessary to preview the content. In the next chapter, we will perform that step.

When content is edited, a temporary copy of the file is created and the changes are made to it, instead of the original. The temporary file has the same name as the original file but is prefixed with the '~' character. When the content is saved, the original is overwritten with the temporary copy. A macro is provided to resolve the name of the temporary file in the schema definition.

Creating Content Using a Model

It is often useful to be able to create a new content item from an existing model. This is easily supported with the `modelfolder` element:

```
<modelfolder uri="/Blogs/Default/" />
```

The specified folder contains the location of content types that may be used as a model. Each instance may have the data fields pre-filled, as desired. When a new instance of the content type is created, one of the models can be chosen:

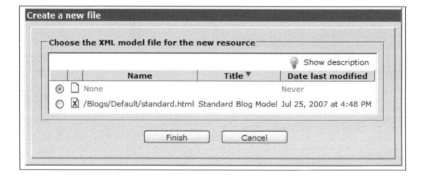

Choosing one of the items will copy it to the new instance, having pre-filled the field.

User Interface Widgets

The editing form for content types is built automatically by OpenCms. By default, each data field has an entry field for entering the field data. Each entry field may be customized by specifying a user interface widget to be used.

There are several default widgets available to choose from. If the default widgets are not suitable, then custom ones may be built. Widget definitions are provided through Java classes that implement the I_CmsWidget interface, and are registered in the opencms-vfs.xml configuration file. In a later chapter, we show how to create a custom widget class. The default widgets available are detailed next.

DateTimeWidget

This widget provides a popup date/time picker allowing the user to select a date and a time.

The resulting value is stored as a string in the format: **07/19/2007 05:05 PM**. The syntax for using this widget is:

```
<layout element="FIELD_NAME" widget="DateTimeWidget"/>
```

BooleanWidget

The Boolean widget provides a simple checkbox.

The resulting value is stored in the data field as a string and is either true or false. This is the default widget for the OpenCmsBoolean data type. There are no configuration options for this widget, and its syntax is:

```
<layout element="FIELD_NAME" widget="BooleanWidget"/>
```

ColorPickerWidget

This widget provides a popup window allowing the user to select a color or to enter a hexadecimal value directly.

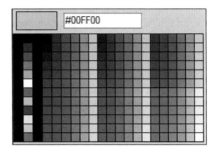

The resulting value is stored as a string in HTML hexadecimal format. This is the default widget used for the OpenCmsColor data type and has no configuration options. Its syntax is:

```
<layout element="FIELD_NAME" widget="ColorpickerWidget"/>
```

DownloadGalleryWidget

This widget provides an interface allowing a user to enter a filename, or to browse to a download gallery, and select a resource from it.

This widget may be used for either the OpenCmsString or the OpenCmsVfsFile data types. If used for the OpenCmsString data type, then the value returned is a string containing the path to the selected resource. If the widget is used for an OpenCmsVfsFile data type then the returned value is added as a reference. By adding the item as a reference, the content relationship engine will ensure the integrity of the link if it is moved later. There are no configuration options for this widget, and its syntax is:

```
<layout element="FIELD_NAME" widget="DownloadWidget"/>
```

HtmlGalleryWidget

This widget is similar to the DownloadGalleryWidget except in that it allows the user to select a snippet of HTML from a gallery.

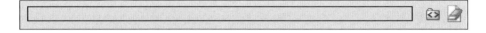

HTML galleries are useful for creating boilerplate HTML that is used often. Items selected from an HTML gallery are always inserted by value, and never by reference. The returned value is a literally inserted copy of the selected HTML gallery item. There are no configuration options for this widget, and its syntax is:

    <layout element="FIELD_NAME" widget="HtmlGalleryWidget"/>

ImageGalleryWidget

This widget is similar to the `DownloadGalleryWidget`, except in that it browses image galleries for images.

It returns data in the same manner depending on which OpenCms data type it is used for. There are no configuration options for this widget, and its syntax is:

    <layout element="FIELD_NAME" widget="ImageGalleryWidget"/>

LinkGalleryWidget

This widget provides an interface for the user to enter a link, or to browse to a link gallery and select a link.

It behaves the same way as other gallery widgets do in that it returns a string or a reference, depending on which data type it is used for. There are no configuration options for this widget, and its syntax is:

    <layout element="FIELD_NAME" widget="StringWidgetPlaintext"/>

TableGalleryWidget

This widget provides an interface for the user to browse to a table gallery and select a table.

The widget always inserts a literal copy of the selected table item. There are no configuration options for this widget, and its syntax is:

    <layout element="FIELD_NAME" widget="TableGalleryWidget"/>

VfsFileWidget

This widget provides the user with a means of browsing for files in the VFS, and selecting them.

The returned value is a string containing the path to the selected file. The widget may be used for both the `OpenCmsString` and `OpenCmsVfsFile` data types. If used for the `OpenCmsVfsFile` data type, then a reference is kept to the selected resource. The configuration for this widget allows specification of the starting location and whether to enable the site selector:

```
<layout element="Element" widget="VfsFileWidget"
    configuration="startsite=/sites/default/
    somepath|hidesiteselector" />
```

HtmlWidget

This widget provides a mini WYSIWYG HTML editor. This is the default widget used for the `OpenCmsHtml` data type, and is implemented using the open source FCKeditor (www.fckeditor.net). The widget may be configured by setting the configuration attribute to a list of configuration options separated by a comma. The available options are:

- anchor: This option adds the anchor button allowing a user to enter a link.
- css:/vfs/path/to/cssfile.css: This allows CSS styles to be rendered in the WYSIWYG editor. The path should contain the absolute path in the VFS to a CSS stylesheet. Content within the editor is displayed according to the stylesheet.
- formatselect: This presents a selector for using common formatting options.
- fullpage: This causes the editor to be displayed as a full page.
- imagegallery, downloadgallery, htmlgallery, tablegallery, linkgallery: Provides a button to bring up the specified gallery to allow a user to select an item.

- height:${editorheight}: This allows the height to be specified in pixels or %, for example, 400px.
- image: This option shows the image dialog button.
- link: This option shows the link dialog button.
- source: This option shows a button allowing editors to toggle between source and WYSIWYG mode.
- stylesxml:/vfs/path/to/stylefile.xml: This option allows a set of custom styles to be used in the editor. The path must be the absolute path to a file containing style definitions. The style definitions must be an XML file that is formatted like:

```
<?xml version="1.0" encoding="utf-8" ?>
<Styles >
    <Style name="My Image" element="img">
        <Attribute name="style" value="padding: 5px" />
        <Attribute name="border" value="2" />
    </Style >
    <Style name="Italic" element="em" />
    <Style name="Title" element="span">
        <Attribute name="class" value="Title" />
    </Style >
    <Style name="Title H3" element="h3" />
</Styles>
```

  More details on options for configuring styles can be found by consulting the FCKeditor site.
- table: This option presents a button that brings up a dialog for creating a table.

Although it is certainly possible and also tempting to use this widget for editing an entire page, using it in this fashion should be avoided. This is because it limits content reuse and also encourages non-uniformity of pages. This widget may be used for either the OpenCmsString or the OpenCmsHtml data type.

> Inserted links and content items will be maintained only as references when used for the OpenCmsHtml data type.

ComboWidget

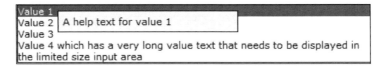

The `ComboWidget` is an interesting user interface widget presenting the user with a choice of items and a corresponding help text for each item. The help text appears as an item is hovered over with the mouse. This widget is configured by setting the configuration attribute to a delimited string of option values and help text. Each option value and help text pair is delimited with a vertical bar:

```
<layout element="FIELD_NAME" widget="ComboWidget"
configuration="value='Value 1' help='Value 1 Help'|value='Value 2'
help='Value 2 help'" />
```

The list of options for this widget is specified using the `configuration` attribute. This attribute is commonly used by all multi-option select type widgets to specify the value settings. The `CmsSelectWidgetOptions` class located in the `org.opencms.widgets` package can be consulted to obtain details of the syntax used for the configuration settings. All multi-value select widgets are limited, and so the list options are static and must be defined within each individual XSD file. In a later chapter, we will develop a custom widget to show how to get around this limitation.

SelectorWidget

This widget presents a list of choices in a drop-down select box.

The selected value is returned as a string. The configuration options for this widget must contain a list of options, delimited by a vertical bar, to display:

```
<layout element="Selector" widget="SelectorWidget"
        configuration="Option 1|Option 2|Option 3|Option 4" />
```

MultiSelectWidget

This widget presents a list of choices as a multi-select list box.

The selected values are returned as a string delimited by commas. The configuration options for this widget must contain list of options, delimited by a vertical bar , to display:

```
<layout element="Selector" widget="MultiSelectorWidget"
        configuration="Option 1|Option 2|Option 3|Option 4"  />
```

StringWidget

This widget provides a basic text input box for entering string data.

The content is not checked or filtered before it is saved, allowing it to contain HTML mark-up or code. There are no configuration options for this widget, and its syntax is:

```
<layout element="FIELD_NAME" widget="StringWidget"/>
```

StringWidgetPlaintext

This widget is similar to the `StringWidget` except in that the content is filtered before it is saved. Any HTML code is stripped out to leave only the plain text behind. It is useful for data entry fields where one is required to be sure that no HTML mark-up is present. There are no configuration options for this widget, and its syntax is:

```
<layout element="FIELD_NAME" widget="StringWidgetPlaintext"/>
```

TextareaWidget

This widget is similar to the `StringWidget` except in that it uses a text area field for input.

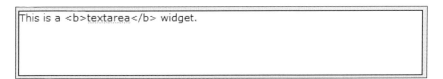

Content may be entered unfiltered as in the `StringWidget`. The number of rows may be specified in the configuration field:

```
<layout element="FIELD_NAME" widget="TextareaWidget"
        configuration="ROWS"/>
```

TextareaWidgetPlaintext

This widget is similar to `TextareaWidget` except in that it strips out any HTML mark-up before saving, leaving only plain text. The number of rows may be specified in the configuration field:

```
<layout element="FIELD_NAME" widget="TextareaWidgetPlaintext"
        configuration="ROWS"/>
```

DisplayWidget

The display widget is a read-only output widget that displays a field value on the entry form.

> Value that is simply displayed and not editable.

Since the field is read-only for editors, it must be populated by using the `default` attribute, as shown in the following XSD code listing. It is possible to use HTML as long as XML entity values are used instead of angle brackets. For example, using this default setting will populate the data field when a new instance is created:

```
<default element="FIELD_NAME" value="This is read only, &lt;b&gt;non-
editable&lt;/b&gt;text with HTML.&lt;br&gt;This is another line of
text."/>
```

There are no configuration options for this widget, and its syntax is:

```
<layout element="FIELD_NAME" widget="DisplayWidget"/>
```

GroupWidget

This widget presents an interface for selecting a group name defined in the OpenCms **Group Administration** screens.

The returned value is the name of the selected group. There are no configuration options for this widget, and its syntax is:

```
<layout element="FIELD_NAME" widget="GroupWidget"/>
```

UserWidget

This widget presents an interface for selecting a user name defined in the OpenCms **User Administration** screens.

The returned value is the name of the selected user. There are no configuration options for this widget, and its syntax is:

```
<layout element="FIELD_NAME" widget="UserWidget"/>
```

Additional Widgets

There are a few other available widgets which are not enabled by default. They are easily enabled, by editing the `WEB-INF/config/opencms-vfs.xml` file and adding these lines of code to the `<widgets>` section:

```
<widget class="org.opencms.widgets.CmsRadioSelectorWidget"
        alias="RadioSelectWidget"/>
<widget class="org.opencms.widgets.CmsPasswordWidget"
        alias="PasswordWidget"/>
<widget class="org.opencms.widgets.CmsPrincipalWidget"
        alias="PrincipalWidget"/>
<widget class="org.opencms.widgets.CmsOrgUnitWidget"
        alias="OrgUnitWidget"/>
```

After restarting OpenCms, we will have a few additional widgets available to choose from:

RadioSelectWidget

This widget provides a selection of options using a radio button interface.

The selected value is returned as a string. The configuration options for this widget must contain list of options to display, delimited by a vertical bar:

```
<layout element="Selector" widget="RadioSelectWidget"
        configuration="Option 1|Option 2|Option 3|Option 4" />
```

PasswordWidget

This widget presents a text input area that will contain asterisks when data is input. It is useful for password entry fields.

There are no configuration options for this widget, and its syntax is:

```
<layout element="FIELD_NAME" widget="PasswordWidget"/>
```

PrincipalWidget

This widget is similar to the `CmsGroupWidget` except in that it allows for selection of a Principal.

There are no configuration options for this widget, and its syntax is:

```
<layout element="FIELD_NAME" widget="PrincipalWidget"/>
```

OrgUnitWidget

This widget is also similar to the `CmsGroupWidget` except in that it allows for selection of an OrgUnit.

There are no configuration options for this widget, and its syntax is:

```
<layout element="FIELD_NAME" widget="OrgUnitWidget"/>
```

Nested Content Definitions

Sometimes it is necessary to create a content definition that includes another definition. For example, let's say we want to support the ability for users to add comments to blog entries. For each comment, we'd want to capture the following fields:

- User name: This would contain the name of the user making the comment. We would want to only allow registered users to add comments
- Date: The date and time of the comment
- Comment: The comment

- Approved: This would provide us some control over the comment appearing on the site

The resulting schema file might then look like this:

```
<!-- =======================================================
     XSD content definition file for the BlogComment type
     ======================================================= -->
<xsd:schema xmlns:xsd="http://www.w3.org/2001/XMLSchema"
    elementFormDefault="qualified">
    <xsd:include schemaLocation="opencms://opencms-xmlcontent.xsd" />
      <xsd:element name="BlogComments" type="OpenCmsBlogComments"/>
      <xsd:complexType name="OpenCmsBlogComments">
        <xsd:sequence>
           <xsd:element name="BlogComment" type="OpenCmsBlogComment"
                      minOccurs="0" maxOccurs="unbounded"/>
        </xsd:sequence>
      </xsd:complexType>
      <xsd:complexType name="OpenCmsBlogComment">
        <xsd:sequence>
           <xsd:element name="User" type="OpenCmsString"
                      minOccurs="1" maxOccurs="1" />
           <xsd:element name="Date" type="OpenCmsDateTime"
                      minOccurs="1" maxOccurs="1" />
           <xsd:element name="Comment" type="OpenCmsString"
                      minOccurs="1" maxOccurs="1" />
           <xsd:element name="Approved" type="OpenCmsBoolean"
                      minOccurs="1" maxOccurs="1" />
        </xsd:sequence>
        <xsd:attribute name="language" type="OpenCmsLocale"
                      use="optional"/>
      </xsd:complexType>
</xsd:schema>
```

This content type defines a blog comment. As each blog would need to have multiple comments attached to it, the blog content type needs a new field allowing multiple instances of the comment. The updated BlogEntry schema file looks like:

```
<!-- =========================================================
     XSD file for the BlogEntry content type with comments
     ========================================================= -->
<!-- Root Element -->
<xsd:schema xmlns:xsd="http://www.w3.org/2001/XMLSchema"
      elementFormDefault="qualified">
    <!-- Define the location of the schema location -->
    <xsd:include schemaLocation="opencms://opencms-xmlcontent.xsd"/>
```

```xml
<xsd:include schemaLocation="opencms://system/modules/com.
deepthoughts.templates/schemas/blogcomment.xsd"/>
    <!-- Root element name and type of our XML type -->
    <xsd:element name="BlogEntrys" type="OpenCmsBlogEntrys"/>
    <!-- Definition of the type described above -->
    <xsd:complexType name="OpenCmsBlogEntrys">
       <xsd:sequence>
          <xsd:element name="BlogEntry" type="OpenCmsBlogEntry"
                       minOccurs="0" maxOccurs="unbounded"/>
       </xsd:sequence>
    </xsd:complexType>
    <!-- Data field definitions -->
    <xsd:complexType name="OpenCmsBlogEntry">
       <xsd:sequence>
          <xsd:element name="Title" type="OpenCmsString"
                       minOccurs="1" maxOccurs="1" />
          <xsd:element name="Date" type="OpenCmsDateTime"
                       minOccurs="1" maxOccurs="1" />
          <xsd:element name="Image" type="OpenCmsVfsFile"
                       minOccurs="0" maxOccurs="1" />
          <xsd:element name="Alignment" type="OpenCmsString"
                       minOccurs="1" maxOccurs="1" />
          <xsd:element name="BlogText" type="OpenCmsHtml"
                       minOccurs="1" maxOccurs="1" />
          <xsd:element name="Category" type="OpenCmsString"
                       minOccurs="0" maxOccurs="10" />
          <xsd:element name="Comment" type="OpenCmsBlogComment"
                       minOccurs="0" maxOccurs="10" />
       </xsd:sequence>
       <xsd:attribute name="language" type="OpenCmsLocale"
                      use="required"/>
    </xsd:complexType>
    <!-- Annotations are used to define additional settings for our
         content type -->
    <xsd:annotation>
       <xsd:appinfo>
          <!-- Mappings allow data fields to be mapped to content
               properties -->
          <mappings>
             <mapping element="Title" mapto="property:Title" />
             <mapping element="Date" mapto="attribute:datereleased" />
          </mappings>
          <!-- Validation rules may be create for field entry -->
          <validationrules>
             <rule element="BlogText" regex="!.*[Bl]og.*"
```

```
                    type="warning" message=
                    "${key.editor.warning.BlogEntry.dontallowblog|
                    ${validation.path}}"/>
            </validationrules>
            <!-- Default values can be set for each field type -->
            <defaults>
                <default element="Date" value="${currenttime}"/>
                <default element="Alignment" value="left"/>
            </defaults>
            <!-- This section controls which widgets are used to edit
                the data fields -->
            <layouts>
                <layout element="Image" widget="ImageGalleryWidget"/>
                <layout element="Alignment" widget="SelectorWidget"
                    configuration="left|right|center" />
                <layout element="Category" widget="SelectorWidget"
    configuration="silly|prudent|hopeful|fearful|worrisome|awesome" />
                <layout element="BlogText" widget="HtmlWidget"/>
            </layouts>
        </xsd:appinfo>
    </xsd:annotation>
</xsd:schema>
```

The changes are highlighted in the code. The total number of comments has been arbitrarily limited to ten. After making these changes, the user interface form will have the additional comment fields in them:

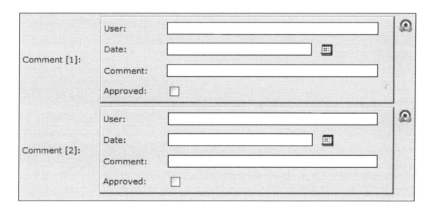

Site visitors would not use the content editor that blog editors would use, as this is available only in the Offline project. To support comment additions, we will also need to create a series of screens for user registration and comment posting. To support comment posting, we will need to write some code that populates the fields. Later on in this book, we will go over how to accomplish this.

Editing Configuration Files with Validating Editors

As mentioned earlier, both OpenCms XML configuration files and XSD structured content schema files use internal URI references:

XML File DTD

```
<!DOCTYPE opencms SYSTEM "http://www.opencms.org/dtd/6.0/opencms-vfs.dtd">
```

Schema File XSD

```
<xsd:include schemaLocation="opencms://opencms-xmlcontent.xsd"/>
```

When these files are parsed, the references are resolved internally with memory based resolvers. This makes it difficult to edit the files using external validating XML editors such as XML Spy, Oxygen XML, or Stylus Studio. However, we can easily get around this by creating local files with the type definitions. For XSD files, we can use this schema file:

```
<!-- this schema file defines the OpenCms Data types available
    for use with content definition XSD files -->
<?xml version="1.0" encoding="UTF-8"?>
<xsd:schema xmlns:xsd="http://www.w3.org/2001/XMLSchema" elementFormDefault="qualified">
    <xsd:simpleType name="OpenCmsString">
       <xsd:restriction base="xsd:string" />
    </xsd:simpleType>
    <xsd:simpleType name="OpenCmsVfsFile">
       <xsd:restriction base="xsd:string" />
    </xsd:simpleType>
    <xsd:simpleType name="OpenCmsBoolean">
       <xsd:restriction base="xsd:boolean" />
    </xsd:simpleType>
    <xsd:complexType name="OpenCmsHtml">
       <xsd:sequence>
          <xsd:element name="links" type="OpenCmsLinkTable" />
          <xsd:element name="content" type="OpenCmsHtmlContent" />
       </xsd:sequence>
       <xsd:attribute name="name" type="xsd:string" use="optional" />
       <xsd:attribute name="enabled" type="xsd:boolean"
                      use="optional" />
    </xsd:complexType>
    <xsd:complexType name="OpenCmsHtmlContent">
       <xsd:simpleContent>
```

```
            <xsd:extension base="xsd:string">
                <xsd:attribute name="enabled" type="xsd:string"
                                use="optional" />
            </xsd:extension>
        </xsd:simpleContent>
    </xsd:complexType>
    <xsd:complexType name="OpenCmsLinkTable">
        <xsd:sequence>
            <xsd:element name="link" type="OpenCmsLink" minOccurs="0"
                         maxOccurs="unbounded" />
        </xsd:sequence>
    </xsd:complexType>
    <xsd:complexType name="OpenCmsLink">
      <xsd:sequence
        <xsd:element name="target" type="xsd:string" />
        <xsd:element name="anchor" type="xsd:string" minOccurs="0" />
        <xsd:element name="query" type="xsd:string" minOccurs="0" />
      </xsd:sequence>
      <xsd:attribute name="name" type="xsd:string" use="required" />
      <xsd:attribute name="type" type="OpenCmsLinkType"
                     use="required" />
      <xsd:attribute name="internal" type="xsd:boolean"
                     use="required" />
    </xsd:complexType>
    <xsd:simpleType name="OpenCmsLinkType">
        <xsd:restriction base="xsd:string">
            <xsd:enumeration value="A" />
            <xsd:enumeration value="IMG" />
        </xsd:restriction>
    </xsd:simpleType>
    <xsd:simpleType name="OpenCmsLocale">
      <xsd:restriction base="xsd:string">
          <xsd:pattern
            value="[a-z]{2,3}(_[A-Z]{2}(_[a-zA-Z0-9]){0,1}){0,1}" />
      </xsd:restriction>
    </xsd:simpleType>
    <xsd:simpleType name="OpenCmsDateTime">
        <xsd:restriction base="xsd:decimal" />
    </xsd:simpleType>
    <xsd:simpleType name="OpenCmsColor">
       <xsd:restriction base="xsd:string">
         <xsd:pattern
           value="#(([a-f]|[A-F]|[0-9]){3}(([a-f]|[A-F]|[0-9]){3})?" />
       </xsd:restriction>
    </xsd:simpleType>
</xsd:schema>
```

We can then temporarily change the reference in the XSD schema file we need to edit so that it references the local schema file. This allows the validating editor to resolve the reference. After editing the file, remember to change the line back to reference the internal definition.

OpenCms XML configuration files can be edited in a similar fashion. While these files are easily editable with a text editor, it is sometimes useful to use a validating XML editor. In this case, we don't need to create our own definition file as all the DTD files for OpenCms configuration files can be found in the source code at this location:

```
<opencms_source>/src/org/opencms/configuration/*.dtd
```

To use a validating editor for configuration files, this procedure can be used:

1. Copy the DTD files from the source directory to the WEB-INF\config directory

2. Edit the copied DTD files, changing all internal DTD references to local ones. For example:

    Change this:

    ```
    <!ENTITY % opencms-explorertypes SYSTEM "http://www.opencms.org/dtd/6.0/opencms-explorertypes.dtd">
    ```

    To this:

    ```
    <!ENTITY % opencms-explorertypes SYSTEM "opencms-explorertypes.dtd">
    ```

3. To edit an XML configuration file, temporarily change the DTD reference to the local DTD. For example:

    Change this:

    ```
    <!DOCTYPE opencms SYSTEM "http://www.opencms.org/dtd/6.0/opencms-modules.dtd">
    ```

    To this:

    ```
    <!DOCTYPE opencms SYSTEM "opencms-modules.dtd">
    ```

4. The file can be edited with most XML editors. After finishing with editing, don't forget to revert the change performed in step 3, or OpenCms will fail to start.

Organizing the Content

Now that we have a content type to hold the site content, we can start creating new blog entries. However, before getting too far into this we should give some thought as to how the content should be organized. We will want to do this in a way that makes it easy for the content editors to locate the blog entries, as the volume of content keeps increasing with time. We also want to ensure that it is organized in a way that lends itself to how it should be displayed. We also want to take into consideration any special requirements of the site for displaying the content. For example, the blog site design features an archive listing on the right hand side used for browsing past blogs:

It is easy to support all these requirements in the case of the blog site, by using a folder structure that is organized according to date:

We will use the **Title** property of each folder as the display text. By organizing blog entries into subfolders, we also limit the number of blog entries that will appear in one location. Now we are ready to start creating some blog entries. Let's go ahead and create a few sample entries so that they are available for use in our Chapter 4.

Summary

In this chapter, we've discussed the concept and structure of modules, and shown how a module is created. We then covered structured content types and created one using the BlogEntry content type for the example website. We went over the rules for creating a structured type, and discussed how it is best to place it within a module. The steps necessary to register a content type were also covered, and we looked at options for using widgets. We also talked about ways to use external editors for schema and configuration files. Finally, we talked about designing folder structures for our content, to support our site design. In the next chapter, we will go over templates and will create a template to display our blog entries.

4
Developing Templates

In this chapter, we will create templates to display the blog content for which we have just finished creating a content type. During the template development, we will also go over these topics:

- A review of the site design page layout
- Understanding how templates get loaded
- Using the template API
- Extending and using OpenCms beans in template code
- Using JSTL tag library
- Template caching
- Understanding resource collectors
- Discussion of the Template One module and template

We will not implement all the site features in our template in this chapter, as some of them will be completed in the later chapters. However, at the end of this chapter, we will be able to use the templates to display the homepage and individual blog pages.

Review of the Page Layout

We'll start off by going back and looking again at the site requirements. From the design we see that we need a homepage template, a blog template, and a search template. We also see that we need to support the direct editing feature, which allows previewed content in Offline mode to be edited directly. On each mockup, we can see where the data fields from the BlogEntry content type will need to go. To make the site easier to update, we will also make these common page areas editable:

- The page header
- The page footer
- The text advertisements on the right panel

Developing Templates

Although these content items are part of each page, they are not blog entries; so we will need to use some other content type to store them in. These items also appear on every page of the site, so they need to be shared somewhere. A good place to put the content is the **index.html** file of the site. This file will represent the homepage and can be easily found by other pages needing to reuse its content. But we still need a content type to store the pieces into.

Rather than designing a new content type just for a single instance of content, we can use the xmlpage content type. The xmlpage content type is designed to be used with the TemplateOne sample code that comes with OpenCms, but is also suitable for other uses. It appears as the **Page with free text** choice while creating a new piece of content from the Workplace Explorer. This content type is a good choice, because its design accommodates an arbitrary number of ad hoc content fields which are of CmsXmlHtmlValue type. This works out perfectly for our site as we need to have three user editable HTML fields: Header, Footer, and Ads.

Let's go ahead and create the content. Select **Page with free text** from the Workplace Explorer to create a new **xmlpage** resource:

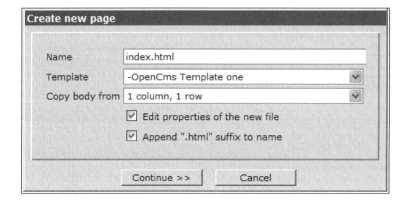

As we intend to use this content for the homepage, it will be named **index.html**. The BlogHomepage.jsp template has not yet been created. So, for now, we can choose the default template **–OpenCms Template one**. Note that the **Copy body from** drop down presents a list of options that can be used to create the content. Each item in the list comes from an **xmlpage** instance that is used as a model. Remember that we had mentioned this in the previous chapter. As there is no model for the homepage content let's choose the **1 column, 1 row** model, and then click **Continue**.

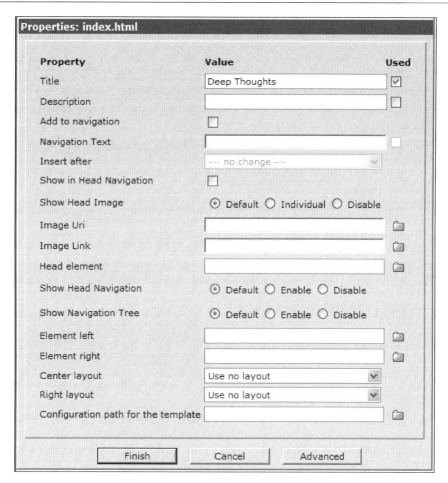

Since we are not using the **xmlpage** content type as it was designed for TemplateOne use, we can ignore most of the property fields. However, we do want to make use of the **Title,** which we will use as the page title. Make sure the **Title** field contains **Deep Thoughts,** and click **Finish**.

Developing Templates

Now, we need to manually edit the XML content, to put in the fields we want, rather than the ones that came from the model we have selected. Remember that the **xmlpage** content type allows for ad hoc fields. So, we are able to add our own field names. This is unlike most other content types, which have strict requirements for field names according to their schema design. To edit the XML, click on the resource in the Workplace Explorer, and select the **Edit controlcode** option from the **Advanced** menu:

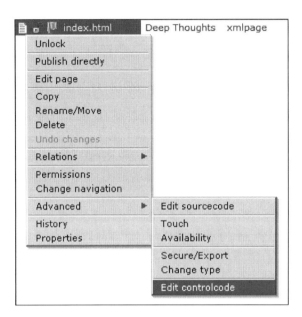

This will bring us to the text editor, where the raw XML content of the file is displayed.

```
<?xml version="1.0" encoding="UTF-8"?>
<pages xmlns:xsi="http://www.w3.org/2001/XMLSchema-instance" xsi:noNam
espaceSchemaLocation="http://www.opencms.org/dtd/6.0/xmlpage.xsd">
    <page language="de">
      <element name="text1">
        <links/>
        <content/>
      </element>
    </page>
    <page language="en">
      <element name="text1">
        <links/>
        <content/>
      </element>
    </page>
</pages>
```

The model we selected for the content has a single data field named `text1`, and defines it for two locales. For our use, we will replace this with our own definitions. This is easily done by replacing the `text1` field with our field name. We then add the additional fields that are needed, ending up with this:

```
<?xml version="1.0" encoding="UTF-8"?>
<pages xmlns:xsi="http://www.w3.org/2001/XMLSchema-instance" xsi:noNam
espaceSchemaLocation="http://www.opencms.org/dtd/6.0/xmlpage.xsd">
    <page language="de">
      <element name="Header">
        <links/>
        <content/>
      </element>
      <element name="Footer">
        <links/>
        <content/>
      </element>
      <element name="Ads">
        <links/>
        <content/>
      </element>
    </page>
    <page language="en">
      <element name="Header">
        <links/>
        <content/>
      </element>
      <element name="Footer">
        <links/>
        <content/>
      </element>
      <element name="Ads">
        <links/>
        <content/>
      </element>
    </page>
</pages>
```

Notice the three elements that have been added: Header, Footer, and Ads. These elements have been added for the German (de) and English (en) locales after saving the file, we can use the edit page command to bring up the HTML WYSIWYG editor. Go ahead and do this, and add some content for each of the three page areas: Header, Ads, and Footer.

Now we should have an `index.html` page for the homepage and some blog entries for the site. This should be enough content for us to create some templates, so let's move on to that step.

Templates in OpenCms

We've gone over how to create instances of structured content in OpenCms and are now ready to start creating templates. In general, a template is written in JSP, and contains code to take a structured content type and display its data onto a page. When the JSP file runs, it needs to access the content item being viewed and may also need to access other content in the VFS. Several JSP tag libraries are available for doing this. The use of the tag libraries is straightforward and is well documented in the OpenCms documentation set. So, we will not cover that topic in this book. Instead, we will take a step further by looking at how to access the template API from JSP code and custom Java beans.

Creating the Templates

We probably want to ensure that content editors are not able to access the template code, and also that the templates are easily installed on other machines. This is easily accomplished by placing the template code into our **com.deepthoughts.templates** module. In fact, it is necessary for templates to reside inside a module, as the Workplace Explorer dialog box used to create new content populates the template field by scanning the templates folder of all modules.

We start out with two templates, one for the homepage and the other for individual blog entries. To do this, first navigate to the module's **templates** folder in the Workplace Explorer and then create the new JSP resource there. The value of the title field is how the template will appear in the drop-down list. So let's use the following names:

After adding these entries, the two templates will appear in the **templates** drop-down whenever a new xml resource is created. Next, we have to add the template code.

The Homepage Template

We'll start by adding the code for the homepage template, which is in the `BlogHomepage.jsp` file. At the top of the JSP file are some declarations and import classes that are needed:

```
<%@page session="true"
        import="com.deepthoughts.templates.*"%>
<%@taglib prefix="cms"
        uri="http://www.opencms.org/taglib/cms"%>
```

Notice that the **com.deepthoughts.templates** package is imported. Later, we'll create a Java package that contains custom code to support the template. By putting support code into Java classes, we reduce the amount of scriptlet code in the JSP file and isolate functionality to the Java code. The OpenCms tag library is also included, as we want to take advantage of its features. The OpenCms documentation should be consulted to get a more detailed understanding of the tag library. Next, we declare and instantiate a Java bean in the template:

```
<%
// create the bean
BlogJspTemplate blog=new BlogJspTemplate
            (pageContext, request, response);
// get all the blogs in the specified folder
    blog.getBlogsInFolder();
// allow edit mode for offline previewing
    blog.editable();
%>
```

The `BlogJspTemplate` class is a custom Java bean, which we will cover in more detail, a little later on. For now, we should note that after being instantiated, a call is made to the `getBlogsInFolder` method. This method exists in a custom Java class and is responsible for gathering a list of blogs in the current folder. In a little while, we will go over the Java class in detail.

Another thing to note here is the call to the `editable` method, which provides support for the direct edit feature. Normally, we would just use the `<cms:editable/>` tag for this. However, the tag library generates HTML code for the direct edit buttons, which disturbs the layout of the page. Fortunately, OpenCms once again provides an easy way to change this behavior by allowing us to specify our own HTML for the direct edit buttons. This is done in the custom Java code and is also covered later on.

Developing Templates

After the initial code comes the HTML for the head content:

```
<!DOCTYPE html PUBLIC "-//W3C//DTD XHTML 1.0 Transitional//EN"
"http://www.w3.org/TR/xhtml1/DTD/xhtml1-transitional.dtd">
<html xmlns="http://www.w3.org/1999/xhtml">
<head>
    <meta http-equiv="Content-Type"
          content="text/html; charset=utf-8" />
    <title><cms:property name="Title" /></title>
    <link rel="stylesheet"
          href="<cms:link>/styles/global.css</cms:link>"
          type="text/css" />
    <script language="JavaScript"
            src="<cms:link>/script/today.js</cms:link>">
    </script>
</head>
```

Here the `<cms:property>` tag from the tag library is used to retrieve the `title` property value from the content.

> The `<cms:link>` tag is used around all linked resources. This ensures that the application context and site context are accounted for correctly. It also ensures that the links get resolved correctly, if later the page is statically exported.

Following the head section is the HTML body:

```
<body bgcolor="#C0DFFD">
  <%-- Include the user editable header content --%>
  <cms:include file="/index.html" element="Header" editable="true" />
  <%-- include the standard header code --%>
  <cms:include file="../elements/common.jsp" element="header" />
  <%-- Table, 7 cells across --%>
  <table border="0" cellspacing="0" cellpadding="0" align="center"
         width="100%">
```

It begins by using the `<cms:include>` tag to include the `Header` data field from the `index.html` content file we have created earlier. This tag is very flexible and is used to dynamically include other files from the VFS. The OpenCms tag library documentation provides full details. One nice aspect of this tag is that it provides for inclusion of only a section (or element) of a file rather than the entire file. This can be used for structured XML content files, and even for JSP template files. In the next line of code, we take advantage of this to include the `header` element of the `common.jsp` file. The `common.jsp` file is shared between templates and more will be covered on this later on.

[96]

Chapter 4

The Blog Content Loop

After this, comes the section used to display the blog content. It uses a loop to iterate through all the blogs it finds in the current folder:

```
            <!-- Content Row -->
            <tr align="left" valign="top">
               <%-- Left Rail --%>
               <td class="leftRail" align="left"></td>
               <%-- Para spacer left side --%>
               <td class="spacer" align="left"></td>
               <%-- Content --%>
               <td colspan="2" valign="top" align="left"><img
                   src="<cms:link>/images/spacer.gif</cms:link>" alt=""
                   eight="1" border="0" /> <br />
                  <table border="0" cellspacing="0" cellpadding="0"
                       width="100%">
<%-- Load all blogs in the most recent folder and display them --%>
               <% while (blog.hasMoreBlogs()) { %>
               <tr>
                <td width="100%"
                    class="blogHeadline"><%=blog.getField("Title")%>
                    <cms:editable mode="manual" />
                </td>
               </tr>
               <tr>
                  <td class="blogTimestamp"><%=BlogJspTemplate.formatDate
                     (blog.getField("Date"), "dd.MM.yyyy")%>
                  </td>
               </tr>
                <tr>
                   <td class="bodyText" valign="top">
                      <div class="photo">
                         <%=blog.getBlogImage(120)%>
                         <%=blog.trim(blog.getField("BlogText"), 700)%>
                             
                         <%=blog.linkToCurrentItem("more...")%>
                      </div>
                   </td>
                </tr>
                <tr>
                   <td class="blogCategories"><br />
                      <span class="label">TOPICS: 
                      </span>
                      <%=blog.showTopics()%>
```

Developing Templates

```
            </td>
          </tr>
          <tr>
            <td class="postDivider"> 
            </td>
          </tr>
                  <% } %>
            </table>
            <br />
        </td>
        <td width="10">
          <img src="<cms:link>/images/spacer.gif</cms:link>"
              alt="" width="10" height="1" border="0" /></td>
```

Recall that at the beginning of the template, the `getBlogsInFolder` method was used to get a list of blog entries. This list is now iterated over to display each item. Within the loop, the `getField` method is used for displaying each blog title. This method improves upon the `<cms:element>` tag by returning a null string if the field has no value entered. This is also supported in the tag library by using the `<cms:contentcheck>` tag.

Next to the code displaying the title, there is a call to the `<cms:editable>` tag. This tag generates HTML code for a direct edit button to appear during Offline previewing. Recall that we want to override the default behavior of this tag. To do this, we just need to ensure that our override takes place using the `mode="manual"` attribute on the tag.

Next, we get the date field from the content and format it using the `formateDate` bean method. This method takes the date field, which is stored as a long integer, and uses a format string to return a human readable date.

Recall from the data design that each blog had an optional image associated with it. To make it easier to display the image, we've added a `getBlogImage` method to our bean. The method determines if an image exists, and also takes care of sizing it properly. Following the image is the text of the blog:

```
<%=blog.trim(blog.getField("BlogText"), 700)%> 
<%=blog.linkToCurrentItem("more...")%>
```

The `trim` method trims text to an arbitrary size on the nearest word boundary. We use it to provide a teaser type display of the blog entries. A link to the full blog entry is generated with the `linkToCurrentItem` method.

The content display loop ends with a call to the `showTopics` method. This method returns a list of topics that have been assigned to each blog entry. The next section of the template deals with the displays on the righthand side and bottom of the page.

The Sidebar and Footer

The code sidebar and footer page areas are common to the homepage and the blog pages. Code for these common areas has been placed into a single JSP file named `common.jsp`. This JSP file is placed into the **elements** folder of the module, and included in the template where needed. The sidebar section of the template does this:

```
            <%-- Sidebar --%>
            <td valign="top">
                <div id="sidebar">
                <ul>
                    <%-- Search Form --%>
<cms:include file="../elements/common.jsp" element="search_form" />
                    <%-- Ads --%>
<cms:include file="../elements/common.jsp" element="ads" />
                    <%-- Archives --%>
<cms:include file="../elements/common.jsp" element="archives" />
                    <%-- RSS Client --%>
<cms:include file="../elements/common.jsp" element="rss_client" />
                    <%-- RSS Feed --%>
<cms:include file="../elements/common.jsp" element="rss_feed" />
                </ul>
                </div>
            </td>
            <td> </td>
        </tr>
        <%-- Footer --%>
        <tr bgcolor="#CCFF99">
            <td> </td>
            <td colspan="5" class="pageFooter">
                <cms:include file="../elements/common.jsp"
                        element="footer" />
            </td>
            <td> </td>
        </tr>
    </table>
</body>
</html>
```

We finish up the template by including another common code section for the footer area. This completes the code for the homepage template. Next, we'll take a look at the common code elements.

Common Code Elements

Anytime HTML or JSP code logic is repeated, it is a good idea to factor it into common code fragments which can be reused. This makes it easy to manage, and allows changes to be made in one place. We've identified common code in the homepage and blog pages, and placed it into a common code element in our module.

The common JSP file we've created for the blog site contains these template sections:

`Header`: Contains the header HTML.

`Search Form`: Contains the search form.

`Advertisements`: Contains the advertisement inclusions.

`Archives`: Displays the blog archives.

`RSS Client`: Contains logic for the RSS client feeds.

`RSS Feed`: Contains links to the RSS feeds.

`Footer`: Contains the footer HTML.

Each includable JSP section is demarcated using the `<cms:template>` tag. The template code starts out with some declarations: .

```
<%--
This template contains common JSP code.  The element is
divided into sections that can individually be included
into a parent JSP via the OpenCms 'include' API.
--%>
<%@ page pageEncoding="UTF-8" %>
    <%-- include necessary imports --%>
        <%@ page import="java.util.*,
        org.opencms.file.*,
        com.deepthoughts.templates.*" %>
    <%-- include necessary taglibs --%>
        <%@ taglib prefix="cms"
        uri="http://www.opencms.org/taglib/cms" %>
<%
    // create the bean
    BlogJspTemplate blog =
        new BlogJspTemplate(pageContext, request, response);
%>
```

Chapter 4

As in the homepage template, some java imports and the tag library are included. After the declaration, an instance of the Java bean is created, as it will be needed later, in the code sections. The code sections appear next.

Header Code

The first section of the common template declares an element named `header`, which is declared using the `<cms:template>` tag:

```
<%-- Header --%>
<cms:template element="header">
    <%-- Header Divider --%>
    <table cellspacing="0" cellpadding="0" width="100%"
          align="center" border="0">
       <tbody>
            <%-- Date Bar --%>
            <tr bgcolor="#ccff99">
            <td id="dateformat" colspan="7" height="25">  
          <script language="JavaScript"
               type="text/javascript">document.write(TODAY);
          </script> 
            <%= blog.getCurrentFolderName() %>
            </td>
            </tr>
        <%-- Thin spacer --%>
            <tr>
              <td bgcolor="#003366" colspan="7"><img height="1"
                  alt="spacer.gif" width="1" border="0"
                  src="<cms:link>/images/spacer.gif</cms:link>" />
              </td>
            </tr>
       </tbody>
    </table>
</cms:template>
```

This section is used by all page templates, and contains common HTML in the header. First, there is some JavaScript code used to write the current date. The JavaScript is assumed to be included in the calling template.

Developing Templates

After the JavaScript code, there is a call to the `getCurrentFolderName` method of the Java bean. This method returns nothing if the current folder is the most recent blog folder. Otherwise, it returns the folder name. It is used to indicate that an archive folder is being browsed against a current list of blogs. When a current blog list is being browsed, the header area appears like this:

> August 16, 2007

But when an archive has been selected for browsing, the header area is modified to contain the archive name to provide additional context feedback:

> August 16, 2007   - Archive: July 2007

As we want this feature on all the pages, it is encapsulated into the header logic.

Search Form

Next in the template, is a section for the search form code:

```
<%-- search form --%>
<cms:template element="search_form">
    <li class="widget widget_search" id="search">
        <form action="<cms:link>/system/modules/
                com.deepthoughts.templates/elements/Search.jsp
                </cms:link>" method="post" id="searchform">
            <div>
                <input type="text" size="15" id="s" name="s" /> <br />
                <input type="submit" value="Search" />
            </div>
        </form>
    </li>
</cms:template>
```

The action of the form is targeted towards the `Search.jsp` file which is located in the **elements** folder of the module. We will cover this in a later chapter. So, searching will not work yet, but the required framework will be in place.

Advertisements

Recall that we created an element in the `index.html` named `Ads`. This element is used to contain user-editable HTML for advertisements that can be put onto the page. The `ads` section contains the code responsible for inserting the element onto the page:

```
<%-- Advertisements --%>
<cms:template element="ads">
    <li class="widget widget_text" id="text-4">
       <h2 class="widgettitle"></h2>
       <div class="textwidget">
          <cms:include file="/index.html" element="Ads"
                       editable="true" />
       </div>
    </li>
</cms:template>
```

The feature is easily supported by using the `<cms:include>` tag and referencing the element name `Ads`. Content editors can then edit the content and the template takes care of inserting it onto the page.

Blog Archives

Archives of past blogs are accessed from the homepage and the blog pages on the righthand panel. The panel contains a list sorted in descending order with a count of entries for each month:

The `archives` code section takes care of generating the HTML for this:

```
<%-- Blog Archives --%>
<cms:template element="archives">
    <li class="widget widget_archives" id="archives">
       <h2 class="widgettitle">Archives</h2>
       <ul>
          <%
          // get the list of blog folders, in descending date order
             List lstBlogs = blog.getBlogFolders();
             Iterator i = lstBlogs.iterator();
          // for each folder...
             while (i.hasNext()) {
                CmsResource res = (CmsResource) i.next();
             // count blogs in it
                String strCount =
                        Integer.toString(blog.getBlogCount(res));
             // get the title
```

Developing Templates

```
            String strTitle =
                blog.getCmsObject().readPropertyObject(res,
                CmsPropertyDefinition.PROPERTY_TITLE, false).getValue();
                // build a uri parameter to it
                String strLink = blog.getCmsObject().getSitePath(res);
                // link to the home page with a folder switch
            String strI =
                blog.link("/index.html").concat("?uri=").concat(strLink);
             %>
             <li><a title="<%=strTitle%>"
                 href="<%=strI%>"><%=strTitle%></a> (<%=strCount%>)
             </li>
                <% } %>
            </ul>
        </li>
    </cms:template>
```

The code starts by retrieving a list of blog folders by calling the `getBlogFolders` method on the Java bean. This returns blog folders in the descending order of date. The code then iterates over the list, using the `getBlogCount` method to obtain the number of blog entries in each folder. The Title property on each folder is used for the displayed name.

Next, a link is constructed for each archive folder. Archives are displayed using the same template as the homepage. To display the blogs in an archive folder, the code just needs to know to retrieve blogs from a past archive folder rather than the one with the most recent date. This is accomplished by using a parameter containing the archive folder to be viewed. Whenever the homepage template code retrieves a list of blogs, it looks for this parameter. Recall that the Java bean on the homepage template makes a call to the `getBlogsInFolder` method. This is the method that takes the parameter into account. So in this code, we need to ensure that the parameter gets created.

The link for the homepage is `/index.html`. We just have to add the additional parameter to this URL. The resulting link will look like this:

opencms/opencms/index.html?uri=/Blogs/2007-06/

When generating this URL, the `link` method is used with the path to the index file. This ensures that the web application and servlet context are accounted for in the URL.

RSS Client and RSS Feeds

These sections will be developed in the later chapters. But for now, stub code is used in their place. In the RSS client section, a dummy link placeholder is used:

```
<%-- RSS Client --%>
<cms:template element="rss_client">
    <li class="widget widget_archives" id="archives">
       <h2 class="widgettitle">Feeds</h2>
       <ul>
       <li><a title="" href="http://www.somelink.com">Feed goes
                        here</a> (16:50)</li>
       </ul>
    </li>
</cms:template>
<%-- RSS Feed --%>
<cms:template element="rss_feed">
    <li class="widget widget_text" id="text-6">
       <h2 class="widgettitle">Subscribe</h2>
       <div class="textwidget">
       <br/>
          <ul>
             <a type="application/rss+xml"
                rel="alternate"
                title="Subscribe to my feed"
                href="/RSS?type=RSS0.91">
                <img style="border: 0pt none ;"
                alt="RSS" src="<cms:link>/images/xml.gif
                    </cms:link>"> RSS 0.91 Feed
             </a>
          </ul>
          <ul>
             <a type="application/rss+xml"
                rel="alternate" title="Subscribe to my feed"
                href="/RSS?type=RSS1.0">
                <img style="border: 0pt none ;" alt="RSS"
                    src="<cms:link>/images/xml.gif </cms:link>">
                     RSS 1.0 Feed
             </a>
          </ul>
          <ul>
             <a type="application/rss+xml"
                rel="alternate" title="Subscribe to my feed"
                href="/RSS?type=RSS2.0">
               <img style="border: 0pt none ;"
                alt="RSS" src="<cms:link>/images/xml.gif</cms:link>">
```

Developing Templates

```
             RSS 2.0 Feed
          </a>
        </ul>
        <ul>
          <a type="application/rss+xml"
             rel="alternate" title="Subscribe to my feed"
             href="/RSS?type=atom">
            <img style="border: 0pt none ;"
            alt="RSS" src="<cms:link>/images/xml.gif</cms:link>">
             ATOM 0.3 Feed
          </a>
        </ul>
      </div>
    </li>
</cms:template>
```

Likewise, for the RSS feed area, we use stub links. Anticipating that the RSS feeds will support multiple formats, URL parameters have been used to specify a feed type. Later, we will discuss developing RSS feeds for the site content.

Footer Section

To complete the common template, there is an element used to include the footer element from the `index.html` content:

```
<%-- Footer --%>
<cms:template element="footer">
  <%-- Include the footer content --%>
  <cms:include file="/index.html" element="Footer" editable="true" />
</cms:template>
```

That completes the common element. We can see how placing the elements into the `common.jsp` file makes it easier to make central changes that affect all the pages of the site.

The Supporting Java Bean Class

The bulk of the work done in the template is accomplished by a Java bean. The `BlogJspTemplate` Java bean subclasses the OpenCms provided `CmsJspXmlContentBean` class. The OpenCms class provides a Java analogue to the features provided by the XML content tag library. This bean has been subclassed in order to provide methods specific to our template, and also to override some of the base bean behavior. The usage pattern for the bean is similar to that of the tag library and its base class:

- Load content from some VFS location into a collection.
- Iterate the content items in the collection.
- Display each content item with the ability to edit it using direct edit.

The beginning of the custom class file looks like this:

```
public class BlogJspTemplate extends CmsJspXmlContentBean {
    // useful constant
    protected final static String NULLSTR = "";
    // path to our blog respository, blogs are arranged by month and
    // year
    protected final static String CONTENT_PATH = "/Blogs/";
    // fieldnames in our blogentry content type
    protected final static String FIELD_IMAGE = "Image";
    protected final static String FIELD_ALIGNMENT = "Alignment";
    protected final static String FIELD_TOPIC = "Category";
    // the resource type id for our BlogEntry resource
    protected final static int BLOG_RESOURCE_TYPEID = 3000;
    // container for the currently loaded list of blogs
    I_CmsXmlContentContainer m_iContent;
    /**
     * Empty constructor, required for every JavaBean.
     */
    public BlogJspTemplate()
    {
        super();
    }
    /**
     * Constructor, with parameters.
     *
     * @param context the JSP page context object
     * @param req the JSP request
     * @param res the JSP response
     */
    public BlogJspTemplate(PageContext context, HttpServletRequest
                                    req, HttpServletResponse res)
    {
        super(context, req, res);
    }
```

The file starts out declaring some useful constants that will be used later on, including the location of the blog repository and the resource type id for the BlogEntry data type. Constructors are provided to use the class either as a bean or with parameters. The next method overrides the direct editing feature.

As mentioned earlier, OpenCms provides direct editing support for in-site content editing. The `<cms:editable>` tag is used for this and utilizes what is called a direct edit provider. This is a Java class responsible for generating the HTML and JavaScript code required for the edit button to appear in the Offline preview mode. For our page templates however, the default direct edit provider causes alignment problems. OpenCms allows for custom direct edit providers to be registered and created, and also provides alternate direct edit providers that may be used. Fortunately, one of the available alternatives does not cause the problem. The alternate class is specified in our override of the `editable` method:

```
public void editable() throws JspException
{
    CmsJspTagEditable.editableTagAction(getJspContext(),
"org.opencms.workplace.editors.directedit.
CmsDirectEditTextButtonProvider", CmsDirectEditMode.AUTO, null);
}
```

Here, the method simply uses the tag library implementation, passing the name of the alternate direct edit provider class. The alternate provider generates HTML that works better in our template code.

Next in the bean, there is a method used to gather all the blogs together in a folder:

```
public I_CmsXmlContentContainer getBlogsInFolder() {
    try {
        String strPath = null;
        String URI = getRequest().getParameter("uri");
        if (null == URI) {
            strPath = getMostRecentBlogFolder();
        }
        else {
            strPath = URI;
        }
        // we retrieve everything in the folder with
        // the resource id of the BlogEntry type
          m_iContent = contentloadManualEdit(
             "allInFolderDateReleasedDesc",
              strPath.concat("|").
              concat(Integer.toString(BLOG_RESOURCE_TYPEID)));
        } catch (JspException e) {
           e.printStackTrace();
        }
    return m_iContent;
}
```

Aside from returning the list of current blogs, the method also supports the requirement for browsing past blog archives. As discussed in the last chapter, to make this easier to implement, the content has been arranged date wise into folders. This is leveraged by the method. When the `getBlogsInFolder` method is called, it looks for a parameter named `uri`. If the parameter is present, then a list of blogs from the folder that `uri` refers to, is used. Otherwise, the list is obtained from the current blog folder, which is the folder having the most recent date. Recall that in the common template code, the `uri` parameter is generated in the **archives** section.

The method makes use of two utility methods. The first one determines the most current blog folder:

```
public String getMostRecentBlogFolder() {
    String strLatestPath = CONTENT_PATH;
    // get the list of blog folders
    List collectorResult = getBlogFolders();
    if (null != collectorResult &&
       collectorResult.iterator().hasNext()) {
       // the first one in the list is the most recent
       CmsResource res = (CmsResource)
          collectorResult.iterator().next();
       strLatestPath = CONTENT_PATH + res.getName() + "/";
     }
    return strLatestPath;
}
```

The utility method in turn relies on another method to get a list of all the blog folders in the descending date order. It takes advantage of the list order to return only the first item, which is always the most recent and hence, the current folder.

The second utility method is a JSP analogue to the `<cms:contentload>` tag:

```
protected I_CmsXmlContentContainer contentloadManualEdit(
    String collectorName,
    String collectorParam)
    throws JspException {
    return new CmsJspTagContentLoad(null,
        getJspContext(), collectorName, collectorParam,
        null, null, getRequestContext().getLocale(),
        CmsDirectEditMode.MANUAL);
  }
```

Developing Templates

We override this method in order to set the editing mode to MANUAL. This is necessary to ensure that the default direct edit buttons are overridden with our own. The method utilizes the tag constructor directly. This utility method is also used by the `getBlog` method:

```
public boolean getBlog(String URI){
try {
        m_iContent = contentloadManualEdit("singleFile", URI);
        return true;
    } catch (JspException e)  {
      e.printStackTrace();
}
return false;
}
```

This provides support for the **BlogEntry.jsp** template to retrieve the blog that was clicked on from the home page.

Moving on, the `getBlogFolders` method provides a list of blog archive folders:

```
public List getBlogFolders() {
    // Use the collector to obtain a list of resources
    String collectorName = "allInFolderDateReleasedDesc";
    try {
      // now collect the resources
      I_CmsResourceCollector collector =
          OpenCms.getResourceManager().
          getContentCollector(collectorName);
      if (null == collector) {
       throw new CmsException(Messages.get().container(
       Messages.ERR_COLLECTOR_NOT_FOUND_1, collectorName));
      }
      // get list of folders underneath the '/Blogs' folder
      List collectorResult = collector.getResults(
         getCmsObject(), collectorName,
         CONTENT_PATH + "|" + Integer.toString(
         CmsResourceTypeFolder.RESOURCE_TYPE_ID));
      return collectorResult;
    } catch (CmsException e) {
         e.printStackTrace();
    }
    return null;
}
```

To build the folder list, a resource collector is used. This is an OpenCms class that returns a list of resources, given a filter pattern. Use of the class is well documented, and more details can be found in the tag library online documentation. To get the list of blog folders, the parameters specify that only folder resources located in the **/Blogs** path should be returned. The parameters also specify that the returned list is to be ordered by date.

On both the homepage and the blog pages, optional support is available for displaying an image. To simplify template coding , the Java class provides the `getBlogImage` method for retrieving the image:

```
public String getBlogImage(int Height) {
if (fieldExists(FIELD_IMAGE)) {
      CmsImageScaler scaler = new CmsImageScaler();
      scaler.setHeight(Height);
      HashMap<String, String> attributes = new HashMap<String,
            String>();
      String strAlign = getField(FIELD_ALIGNMENT);
      attributes.put("align", strAlign);
      attributes.put("height", Integer.toString(Height));
      return img(getField(FIELD_IMAGE), scaler, attributes);
}
Return NULLSTR;
}
```

As blog images are optional, it first checks to see if the image exists in the data field. If an image is available, the `CmsImageScaler` class is utilized to size it properly. Only the height parameter is used, as the scaler will automatically compute the width and maintains the aspect ratio.

Finally in the Java class, there is a method that returns the list of topics assigned to each blog:

```
public String showTopics() {
// StringBuffer to hold the response
StringBuffer sbCategories = new StringBuffer(NULLSTR);
// get list of categories
I_CmsXmlContentContainer iCategories = contentloop(m_iContent,
FIELD_TOPIC);
boolean bFirst = true;
try {
      while (iCategories.hasMoreContent()) {
         if (false == bFirst) {
            // after first on we can append a comma
            sbCategories.append(", ");
```

```
            } else {
                // no longer the first one
                bFirst = false;
            }
            // add the category
            sbCategories.append(this.contentshow(iCategories));
          }
        } catch (JspException e) {
          e.printStackTrace();
        }
        return sbCategories.toString();
    }
```

The method calls `contentloop` to get a list of field values from the content item. The `contentloop` method is implemented in the base class and is documented in the tag library. The method loops over the content values and returns a `String` for display.

The Blog Template

The second code template we need to write is for the `BlogEntry.jsp` file. This template supports the display of individual blog entries. The template starts out with declarations and imports, and looks a lot like the home page template:

```
<%@page session="true"
        import="com.deepthoughts.templates.*"%>
<%@taglib prefix="cms"
        uri="http://www.opencms.org/taglib/cms"%>
<%
    // create the bean
    BlogJspTemplate blog=new BlogJspTemplate(
        pageContext, request, response);
    // get the blog entry that was clicked on
    blog.getBlog(blog.getCmsObject().
        getRequestContext().getUri());
    // allow edit mode for offline previewing
    blog.editable();
t%>
```

The difference is that instead of getting a list of blogs, it gets just one blog by calling `getBlog`. As we have already seen in the Java code, the `getBlog` method uses a collector to locate a single file with a given URI. The remainder of the template code is similar to the homepage template, including the calls to the common code elements.

That completes the code for the two content templates. We can now use them to view the blog content. To do this, we will need to first understand how templates are applied and loaded for content items. The next section discusses how this is done.

The Content and Template Loading Process

OpenCms uses Java classes called resource loaders for handling the delivery of resources from the VFS. When a request is made for a resource, the OpenCms servlet first locates it in the VFS. After ensuring that the user has access permissions, the servlet determines the type of the requested resource. It then locates a suitable resource loader for that type and passes control to the loader. The resource loader is responsible for handling the details of how a resource is rendered and returned. The following diagram illustrates this process:

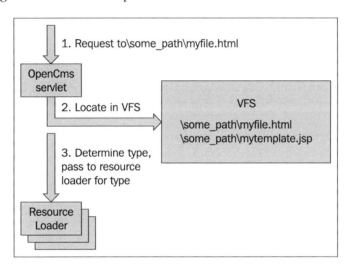

Resource loaders are associated with resource types through unique resource ids, and are registered with OpenCms in the `opencms-vfs.xml` configuration file. Inside the configuration file, we can find the following resource loaders:

- `CmsDumpLoader`: Loads plain text files.
- `CmsImageLoader`: Loads image resources.
- `CmsPointerLoader`: Loads pointers to other content or links.
- `CmsJspLoader`: Loads JSP files.
- `CmsXmlPageLoader`: Loads the xmlpage resource type.
- `CmsXmlContentLoader`: Loads XML structured resource types.

Developing Templates

The last two loaders are responsible for loading XML content types. When they are called, rather than rendering the requested content themselves, they utilize a template to do this. A property value on the original resource identifies the location of the template. When control is passed to the template it uses the original URI to load and render the originating resource, as illustrated here:

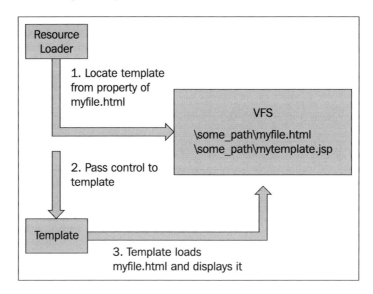

Although both XML loaders use templates to display their content, each loader uses a different property value. The CmsXmlPageLoader uses the **template** property, while the CmsXmlContentLoader uses the **template-elements** property. As for all properties, the value may be set on a parent folder instead of each resource. This allows a default template property to be set for a group of content, and to be individually overridden, if so desired.

The only thing left to do is to set the appropriate property so the loader will invoke our template. For the `index.html` file, we need to set the **template** value to point to the full path of the template. As the template is in the module, the value should be set to:

/system/modules/com.deepthoughts.templates/templates/BlogHomepage.jsp

For the blogs we need to set the **template-elements** property instead of the **template** property. As just mentioned, instead of setting this property on each individual blog entry we can just set it on the **Blogs** parent folder. Any time later a special blog template can be set to an individual blog by setting the value for that blog entry. On the **Blogs** parent folder, the property should be set to:

/system/modules/com.deepthoughts.templates/templates/BlogEntry.jsp

After setting the property values, we can view the content through the templates by clicking on the `index.html` file in the Explorer View. Remember to switch back to the default site in the Workplace Explorer before doing this.

Expressions in JSP Templates

The code we've covered shows how to use custom beans in templates. For many sites however, this is not necessary, as the base tag library can be combined with expressions to achieve many things that don't require custom beans. Support for the use of expressions has been present in OpenCms for a while. However, since the release of 7.0.2, it has become possible to combine these with the JSP tag library. This is a powerful feature that provides access to the XML tag libraries and is an alternative to sub classing.

Using the Tag Library from JSP

Support for using expressions to access the tag library has been added via the `org.opencms.jsp.CmsJspVfsAccessBean` class. This class provides expression access to the tag library from JSP code. To use it, the JSP may just access the methods using expression syntax:

```
<%@page session="false" import="org.opencms.util.*" %>
<%@taglib prefix="cms"
    uri="http://www.opencms.org/taglib/cms" %>
    Context Path: ${pageContext.request.contextPath}<br/>
    URI: ${cms:vfs(pageContext).requestContext.uri}<br/>
    <h1>
 ${cms:vfs(pageContext).property[cms:vfs(pageContext).
    requestContext.uri]["Title"]}
    </h1><br/>
<cms:editable/>
<cms:contentload collector="allInFolderDateReleasedDesc"
    param="/Blogs/2007-07/*.html|blogentry|3" editable="true">
    <cms:contentaccess var="blog" />
    <p>
       <a href="${cms:vfs(pageContext).link[blog.filename]}">
```

[115]

Developing Templates

```
        ${cms:vfs(pageContext).property[blog.filename]["Title"]}
        </a>
    </p>
    <p>
        ${cms:vfs(pageContext).readXml[blog.filename].
        value['BlogText']}<br/>
    </p>
</cms:contentload>
```

Note the inclusion of the tag library using the `cms` prefix. The same namespace prefix is used in the expressions to access the API. Here are some examples that we see in the previous code:

- `${cms:vfs(pagecontext).requestContext.uri}`: Returns the URI of the item that was clicked on, causing control to pass to the template.
- `${cms:vfs(pageContext).property[filename][propertyname]`: Returns the given property on the given filename. In the previous code, it is combined with the requested URI to obtain the `Title` property.
- `${cms:vfs(pageContext).readXml[filename].value[element]`: Returns the value of the element within the XML content of the specified filename. In the example, it is used to obtain the BlogText field of the currently iterated blog.

Documentation for all the methods that are available can be found by looking at the `org.opencms.jsp.CmsJspVfsAccessBean` class.

Combining Expressions with JSTL

It is easy to add JSTL support to JSP by including the necessary tag libraries. Of course, the relevant .jar files will need to be added to the web project as well. It then becomes easy to add the tag library code to do things like date formatting:

```
<%@page session="false" import="org.opencms.util.*" %>
<%@taglib prefix="cms"
    uri="http://www.opencms.org/taglib/cms" %>
<%@ taglib prefix="fmt"
    uri="http://java.sun.com/jsp/jstl/fmt" %>
<%@ taglib prefix="c"
    uri="http://java.sun.com/jsp/jstl/core" %>
        Context Path: <c:out
                value="${pageContext.request.contextPath}" /><br/>
    URI: ${cms:vfs(pageContext).requestContext.uri}<br/>
    <h1>
        ${cms:vfs(pageContext).property[cms:vfs(pageContext).
```

```
            requestContext.uri]["Title"]}
        </h1><br/>
<cms:editable/>
<cms:contentload collector="allInFolderDateReleasedDesc"
    param="/Blogs/2007-07/*.html|blogentry|3" editable="true">
    <cms:contentaccess var="blog" />
    <p>
        <a href="${cms:vfs(pageContext).link[blog.filename]}">
        ${cms:vfs(pageContext).property[blog.filename]["Title"]}
        </a>
    </p>
    <p>
        <fmt:formatDate
            value="${cms:convertDate(blog.file.dateCreated)}"
            type="date" dateStyle="LONG"/>
    </p>
    <p>
        ${cms:vfs(pageContext).readXml[blog.filename].
            value['BlogText']}<br/>
    </p>
</cms:contentload>
```

In the previous example the `<fmt:formatData>` tag is used to convert the blog created date to a human readable format. The Date object required by the tag is obtained using the `blog.file.dateCreated` expression.

> The template example uses the 1.2 version of the JSTL tag library, rather than the 1.1 version. This is because the 1.2 version accepts the use of expressions while version 1.1 does not.

Accelerating Template Development Using WebDAV

We've previously gone over how to setup a development environment for building OpenCms. With the introduction of WebDAV support in Version 7, an IDE such as Eclipse can be used to create and edit templates and other module resources. Let's go over the steps necessary to do this.

Developing Templates

Install the Eclipse WebDAV Plug-in

The WebDAV plug-in must first be installed into Eclipse. This is done through the Eclipse update manager by selecting **Help -> Software Updates -> Find and Install...**. When the dialog appears, select the option, **Search for new features to install**:

After pressing **Next,** check off the site named **The Eclipse Project Updates** and press **Finish**:

Next, select a nearby mirror site and press **OK**. In the next dialog box, the feature for **FTP and WebDAV support** will appear in the list, and should be checked. Pressing the **Next** button and agreeing to the terms will install the feature.

If the feature does not appear, then it probably means that a newer version of Eclipse is being used. Since the WebDAV plug-in is no longer in active development, it is not included in the feature update list, and will thus have to be added manually. In this case, click the **Cancel** button and repeat the process. But at the **Update sites to visit** dialog box, select the **New Remote Site…** button, and enter the following:

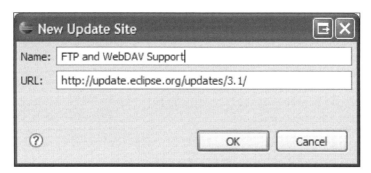

The URL contains the update site for the location of the feature we need. After adding the site, selecting it, and choosing another mirror location, several items will appear in the list. Only the FTP and WebDAV items are needed.

After installing the feature, Eclipse will need to be restarted.

Developing Templates

Create a Site Within Eclipse for the Server

The next step is to add the WebDAV location representing the OpenCms site into Eclipse. The location is added through the Site Explorer view, which can be added to the default Java perspective. Select **Window -> Show View -> Other** to locate the view, and expand the **Target Management** node:

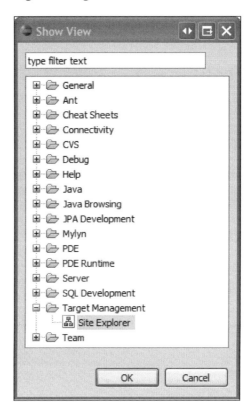

Selecting the **Site Explorer** item will add the view to Eclipse:

[120]

Chapter 4

Right-click in the previous window and select **New -> Target Site** to add the location. Since we want to access the repository via WebDav, select that option and click **Next**. In the next dialog box, the URL and credentials for the site can be entered.

 The server must first be running before we can enter the URL and the credentials information.

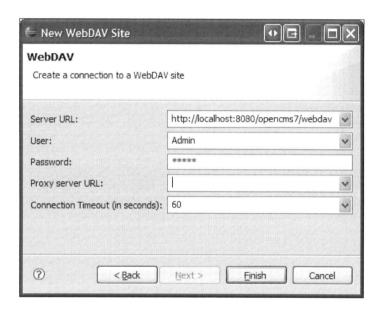

 The Server URL uses the **webdav** servlet rather than the **opencms** servlet. The user credentials can be of any user for whom an OpenCms login account has been created.

[121]

Import Content into the Project

Once the plug-in has been installed and the site has been added, the last thing to do is to import the content from the VFS into our project. This is done by selecting the folder in the project where the content should go, and right-clicking on it. Select the **Import** option and in the dialog box expand the **Other** node. Select the **WebDAV** option and press **Next** to specify where the files should be imported into the project. After pressing **Next** again, the site we have just added will appear:

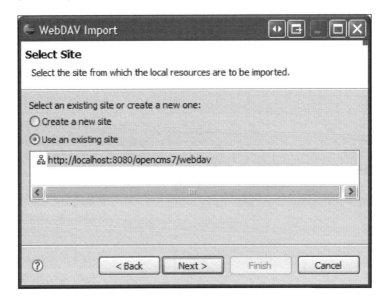

Press **Next** again, and a list of resources at that location will appear. The list can be navigated to locate the resources we want to mirror into our project. For templates, we may want to locate the resources located in our module:

```
/system/modules/com.deepthoughts.templates
```

Select that node, and press **Next**. We can then select the resources to be imported into our project:

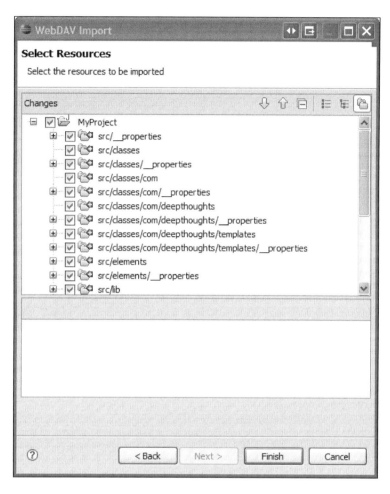

The selected files will then be copied into the local project directory for editing. We then will be able to edit the JSP files in Eclipse. Any local changes made can be synchronized with the VFS repository at any time, using the **Synchronize** view. This view can be added the same way the **Site Explorer** view was added, but appears under the **Team** node. After adding this view, it will track any changes made to the files that were imported.

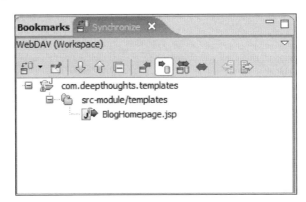

The view contains buttons for uploading any changes to the VFS and for downloading any VFS changes to the local project. Using this feature can speeden up the development time for a JSP template, as the IDE can be used to make changes which are then quickly synchronized with the VFS for viewing.

Summary

In this chapter, we started with a review of the template code for the Deep Thoughts site. We then showed how to create templates that utilize a custom Java class, which subclasses a base OpenCms class. The custom class we created shows how to change some of the default template behavior. It also shows how to provide added features or logic, which is specific to the template requirements. We also discussed resource loaders and the template loading mechanism. The chapter also included a section on using expressions in JSP and how they can be utilized in many cases to avoid custom bean development. We finished up by showing how to utilize the WebDAV feature in OpenCms to accelerate template development.

5
Adding Site Search

In this chapter, we will add search capabilities to our site. We will start with a discussion of the Lucene search engine, and will then discuss how to create a search index for our blog content. After that, we will go over some advanced search engine configurations and introduce a useful Lucene development tool. We will then discuss the code to use the index and provide site search support. Let's first take a look at Lucene.

A Quick Overview of Lucene

Included with OpenCms is a distribution of the Lucene search engine. Lucene is an open source, high-performance text search engine that is both easy to use and full-featured. Lucene is not a product. It is a Java library providing data indexing, and search and retrieval support. OpenCms integrates with Lucene to provide these features for its VFS content.

Though Lucene is simple to use, it is highly flexible and has many options. We will not go into the full details of all the options here, but will provide a basic overview, which will help us in developing our search code. A full understanding of Lucene is not required for completing this chapter, but interested readers can find more information at the Lucene website: `http://jakarta.apache.org/lucene`. There are also several excellent books available, which can easily be found with a web search.

Search Indexes

For any data to be searched, it must first be indexed. Lucene supports both disk and memory based indexes, but OpenCms uses the more suitable disk based indexes. There are three basic concepts to understand regarding Lucene search indexes: Documents, Analyzers, and Fields.

- **Document:** A document is a collection of Lucene fields. A search index is made up of documents. Although each document is built from some actual source content, there is no need for the document to exactly resemble it. The fields stored in the document are indexed and stored and used to locate the document.

- **Analyzer:** An analyzer is responsible for breaking down source content into words (or terms) for indexing. An analyzer may take a very simple approach of only parsing content at whitespace breaks or a more complex approach by removing common words, identifying email and web addresses, and understanding abbreviations or other languages. Though Lucene provides many optional analyzers, the default one used by OpenCms is usually the best choice. For more advanced search applications, the other analyzers should be looked at in more depth.

- **Field:** A field consists of data that can be stored, indexed, or queried. Field values are searched when a query is made to the index. There are two characteristics of a field that determine how it gets treated when indexed:

    - **Field Storage:** The storage characteristic of a field determines whether or not the field data value gets stored into the index. It is not necessary to store field data if the value is unimportant and is used only to help locate a document. On the other hand, field data should be stored if the value needs to be returned with the search result.

    - **Field Indexing:** This characteristic determines whether a field will get indexed, and if so, how. There is no need to index fields that will not be used as search terms, and the value should not be indexed. This is useful if we need to return a field value but will never search for the document using that field in a search term. However, for fields that are searchable, the field may be indexed in either a tokenized or an un-tokenized fashion. If a field is tokenized, then it will first be run through an analyzer. Each term generated by the analyzer will be indexed for the field. If it is un-tokenized, then the field's value is indexed, verbatim. In this case, the term must be searched for using an exact match of its value, including the case.

        The two field types may be combined to form four combinations. While choosing a field type, consideration should thus be given to how the item will need to be located, as well as what data will need to be returned from the index.

Lucene also provides the ability to define a boost value for a field. This affects the relevance of the field when it is used in a search. A value other than the default value of 1.0 may be used to raise or lower the relevance.

These are the important concepts to be understood while creating a Lucene search index. After an index has been created, documents may be searched through queries.

Search Queries

Querying Lucene search indexes is supported through a Java API and a search querying language. Search queries are made up of terms and operators. A term can be a simple word such as "hello" or a phrase such as "hello world". Operators are used to form logical expressions with terms, such as AND or NOT. With the Java API, terms can be built and aggregated together along with operators to form a query. When using the query language, a Java class is provided to parse the query and convert it into a format suitable for passing to the engine. In addition to these search features, there are more advanced operations that may be performed such as fuzzy searches, range searches, and proximity searches.

All these options and flexibility allow Lucene to be used in an application in many ways. OpenCms does a good job of using these options to provide search capabilities for a wide range of content types. Next, we will look at how OpenCms interfaces with Lucene to provide this support.

Configuring OpenCms Search

OpenCms maintains search settings in the `opencms-search.xml` configuration file located in the `WEB-INF/config` directory. Prior to OpenCms 7, most of the settings in this configuration file needed to be made by hand. With OpenCms 7, the Search Management tool in the Administration View has been improved to cover most of the settings. We will first go over the settings that are controlled through the **Search Management** view, and will then visit the settings that must still be changed by hand. The first thing we'll do is define our own search index for the blog content.

Adding Site Search

Creating a new search index is simple with the Administration tool. We access it by clicking on the **Search Management** icon of the **Administrative View**, and then clicking on the **New Index** icon:

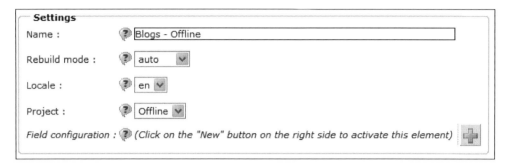

The **Name** field contains the name of the index file. This is the actual name that will be passed along to the Java API, as we will see later on. As the content differs between the online and offline areas, we will create an index for each one. For now, we will start with the offline index. We'll name it: **Blogs – Offline**. The other fields are:

- **Rebuild mode**: This determines if the index is to be built manually or automatically as content changes. We want automatic updating and will hence choose **auto**.
- **Locale**: We must select a locale for the content. OpenCms will extract the content for the given locale when it builds our index. If we were supporting more than one locale, then it would be a good idea to include the locale in the index name.
- **Project**: This selects content from either the Online or Offline project.
- **Field configuration**: This selects a field configuration to be used for the index.

We do not have our own field configuration yet; so for now press **OK** to save the index. Next, we will define a field configuration for the blog content.

Field Configurations

Once the index has been created, we may define the fields we want it to contain by creating a field configuration. The **View field configuration** icon shows existing field configurations and allows creation of new ones. The fields in the configuration relate to the fields that will get created in the search index. Each field has the following settings:

- **Name**: The name of the field.
- **Index**: **True** to index the field, **untokenized** to index the field without running it through an analyzer, and **false** to not index the field.
- **Store**: Checked to have the value of the field stored.
- **Excerpt**: This is an OpenCms setting, which will truncate the field value before storing it. This allows a search to present a synopsis view of the results, without having to actually retrieve the content from the original resource. While the UI allows this option to be selected and disallows the **Store** option, this combination does not make much sense.
- **Display**: This is the display name used for the field.
- **Boost**: This is an optional value that can be provided to adjust the boost.
- **Default**: This is a default value that may be provided for a field value, in case the source field value does not exist.

In addition to these settings, each field also contains one or more mapping definitions which map the data value to a content field in a VFS resource. The mapping definition includes a mapping type, an optional parameter, and an optional default value. There are four types of mappings to choose from:

- **content**: This maps the field data value to the value of the VFS resource content. The value that is retrieved is based upon the resource type. Each resource type has a content extractor responsible for converting the resource content into a string value. For XML resource types, the content extractor concatenates all the data fields of the resource into a single string value. For this mapping, the **Parameter** field is not used.
- **property**: This maps the field data value to a VFS resource property value. If the property value is not found, then the value will be empty. The **Parameter** field must contain the name of the property value to be used.
- **property-search**: This is the same as the property mapping except when the property value is missing on the original resource. It then searches for the value on all the parent folders of the resource. The **Parameter** field must contain the name of the property value to be used.
- **item**: This selection is useful only for XML content. It maps the value to an individual field in the XML content. The XML field is specified in the **Parameter** field using the XPath notation format. For example, for an XML field element with the name of Abstract, the notation used would be **Abstract[1]**. For a repeating element, multiple mappings may be added per field. For example, for the blog comments, we could map the first three comments using three mappings entries with the values: **Comment[1]**, **Comment[2]**, and **Comment[3]**.

Adding Site Search

OpenCms provides a general purpose default field configuration named **standard**. It defines fields that are generally suitable for indexing any OpenCms VFS resource. The **standard** configuration is defined as follows:

- **Content**: This field is both indexed and stored and contains the extracted text of a VFS resource. The actual extracted text contained in this field depends upon the resource type. For a Word or text document for example, the **Content** field will contain all the text contained within the resource. For OpenCms XML content, all the data fields in the resource are concatenated into this field as a single value. This has a nice effect of allowing all data fields of the XML content to be searched, using just this field, such as "content: 90124". However, querying XML content fields using operators, such as "address:main street" NOT "zip: 90124", is not possible.
- **Description**: This field is stored and indexed and contains the description of the resource obtained via the **description** property.
- **Keywords**: This field is stored and indexed, and contains the keywords of the resource obtained via the **keywords** property.
- **Meta**: This field is not stored, but is indexed. It indexes the value of the three content properties: Title, Keywords, and Description.
- **Title**: This field contains the title field value, and is indexed but not stored.
- **Title-key**: This contains the title field value, and is stored as it is, or untokenized by an analyzer.

We could use the standard field configuration for our search index. But we will design our own instead. This is simple to do and will provide us with more flexibility in the future, if necessary.

Creating a Field Configuration

Field configurations are created from within the **Search Management** view by first clicking on the **View field configurations** icon, and then clicking on the **New field configuration** icon:

Chapter 5

After saving the entry and returning to the list of field configurations, click on the field configuration to get to the overview screen:

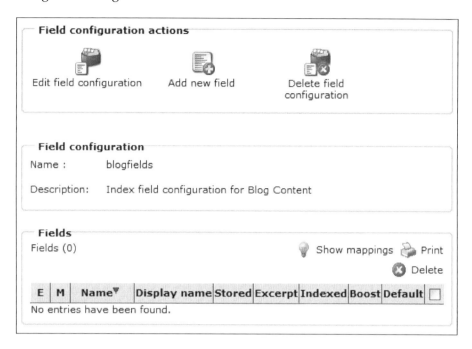

From here fields may be added. Our search index will contain four fields:

- **blogtext**: This field contains our blog text. Unlike the content field in the standard mapping, this field contains only the blog text, and none of the other XML field data. The field is indexed so that we can search for text in it. We will also store the field value, but in an excerpted format, so that we can quickly display a synopsis of the blog in the search result.
- **category**: This field contains the data from the category fields of our content. We create a separate search field so that we can provide the ability to search on category alone. If the category value were to be included within the content field as is the case with the standard field mapping, then we would have no assurance that a search for a category term would find matching text in the blog text.
- **title**: This field contains the indexed value of the title field. The field is indexed to allow it to be searched on. As indexed fields are analyzed, we can choose not to store the resulting value in the data field.
- **title-key**: This field is the inverse of the title field. It is not indexed, but is instead stored verbatim in the field to allow the field to be sorted properly in the search result.

After adding these fields the display should look like this:

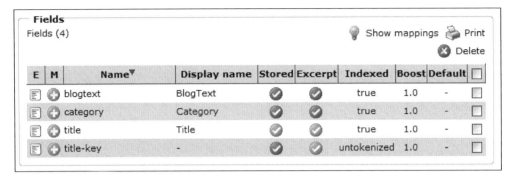

Now we'll add the field mappings by clicking on the name column of the field, and using the **Add new mapping** action. Add the following mappings:

- **blogtext**: This field is mapped to the BlogText field and the type is **item**. The parameter field contains the XML field name for the blog content, which is **BlogText[1]**.
- **category**: This field maps to the blog Category field and the type is **item**. The category field of our Blog XML content can have more than one value. We will therefore need to have multiple mappings for this field. Unfortunately, this is a problem because we don't know how many category fields there are going to be. For now, we will support searching for only the first five category field values. For this, we add five mappings of the type **item**. The parameter values of each item should reflect the corresponding XML field names. For example: **Category[1]**, **Category[2]**, **Category[3]**, **Category[4]**, and **Category[5]**.
- **title**: This field is mapped to a content property and is of the type **property**. The parameter field contains the name of the property, which is **Title**.
- **title-key**: This field is the same as the **title** field and should match its settings.

We can now go back to our index and apply this field configuration to it. Before we do that however, we will do one more thing, create an index source.

Creating an Index Source

An index source defines the locations of content within the VFS that are to be indexed. The first step in doing this is to click on the **View index sources** icon:

From here, we see that OpenCms has provided two search indexes already:

- **source1**: This source includes all document types contained in the default site, which is located under **/sites/default**.
- **source2**: This source includes only the content located under **/system/workplace/locales/**, which is used to build the online help system.

Neither of these is suitable for our use as it includes content outside of the Blog content repository. Let's add a new source for the blog content, by clicking on the **New index source** icon and naming it **BlogContent**:

The indexer field contains the name of a Java class file that implements the
I_CmsIndexer interface. This class interfaces with Lucene and is responsible for
managing the search index. For most cases, the default provided class is sufficient.
However, if more complex content indexing requirements are needed, the flexibility
of OpenCms allows a custom indexing interface to be used. We can use the default
provided class for the blog content. Click **OK** to save the index, and then use the
Assign resources action to assign the blog repository path:

```
Index source
Name :      BlogContent
Indexer:    org.opencms.search.CmsVfsIndexer

Resources
resourcesNames:    /sites/default/Blogs/
```

We've now defined the new source only to contain the resources within the Blog
repository. Next, we need to define the types of documents that we want to include
in the index source.

When the content is indexed, OpenCms iterates over the resources it finds in the
given VFS path. Each resource type has a corresponding document type class
responsible for converting the given resource into a Lucene document for indexing.
OpenCms provides document type classes for all the default resource types. Since
Blog content is XML, we will use the document type already available for XML
content types. The document type class is org.opencms.search.documents.
CmsDocumentXmlContent. No other document types are needed for the blog content
source. To add the document type class, click on the plus icon of the **Document types
available** in the **Assign document types** area:

Chapter 5

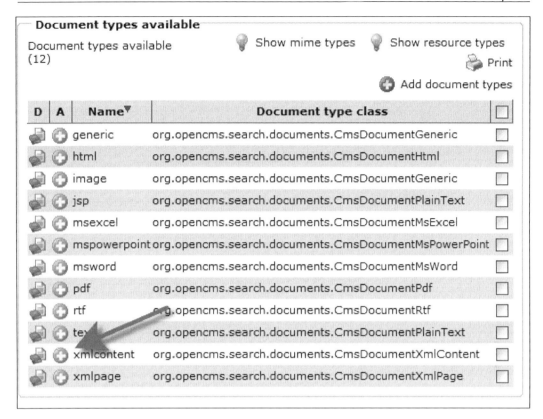

After adding the document type, return to the **Search Management** screen where we will continue with the final step.

Now we can finally complete the search index. Go back to the **Search Management** screen and click on the **Edit** icon to set the field configuration. Select **blogcontent** for the **Field configuration** setting and save it. Then use the **Assign index sources** icon to remove the **source1** source from the list and add the **BlogContent** source to complete the index definition.

That completes the creation of the Offline index, and we can build the index by clicking on the **rebuild** icon. We will also want to create an index for the Online project. The index should be named **Blogs – Online** and will be left as a reader exercise.

Additional Search Settings

There are a few additional search index settings which are not accessible via the **Search Management** interface. In most cases, it is not necessary to change these settings. But it is still useful to understand them. The additional settings may only be changed by editing the `opencms-search.xml` configuration file manually. Within this file are the following settings:

- `directory`: This setting controls the directory location of the index files. It is relative to the `WEB-INF` path of the OpenCms application. Each defined search index will have a subdirectory appearing under this location which matches the index name.
- `timeout`: During indexing, a thread is created for each resource to convert it into a Lucene document. This value specifies the amount of time, in milliseconds, that the indexer will wait for the thread to complete its task.
- `forceunlock`: This setting controls how indexing threads access the search index. The possible values are:
    - `always`: Always attempts to unlock the index.
    - `never`: Never unlocks the index; instead, waits for it to become unlocked.
    - `onlyfull` (default): This setting behaves the same as always, and attempts to unlock the index, if it is locked.
- `excerpt`: This setting controls the size that the value of a field will be truncated to, if the excerpt setting in the field configuration is set to true.
- `extractCacheMaxAge`: When a resource is indexed, the document class responsible for converting it into a Lucene document must convert the content into plain text. As this is often time consuming, OpenCms caches the resulting extracted text on disk. This setting controls the lifetime of the extraction cache. For development purposes, if rebuilding indexes is done frequently, then it may be helpful to set this to a low value, so that the index is rebuilt with recent document content.
- `highlighter`: This specifies a class file that is used to provide support for highlighting the search terms found in the search result.
- `documenttype`: This is where the various Document type classes are configured. Each document type must specify a single resource type and can have one or more mime-types associated with it.
- `analyzer`: This setting defines the analyzer that is used when the text is indexed. The setting allows specification of a single analyzer per locale.

As with all OpenCms configuration file settings, making a change will require a server restart. It should also be noted that even though settings changed via the **Search Administration** view will appear immediately, they also will often require a server restart before taking effect.

Introducing Luke – a Visual Index Tool

We finally have a search index suitable for searching the Blog content. Before we write any search code, we can use a developer tool to browse the index and perform queries. This will let us test some queries before writing any code. There is a great open-source developer tool for Lucene called Luke. Unfortunately, there is not much documentation on how to use it. But for simple tasks, it is straightforward to use. Luke is available for downloading at `http://www.getopt.org/luke`. After downloading and extracting the jar file, it can be started using:

```
> java -jar lukeall-0.7.1.jar
```

After starting up Luke, the first thing to do is to open the search index. It is located in the following location:

`<OPENCMS_INSTALL>\WEB-INF\index\Blogs - Offline`

After opening the index it should look something like this:

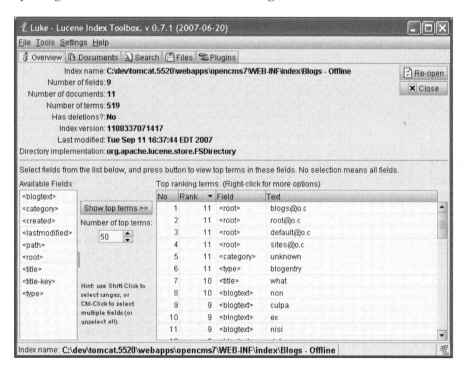

Adding Site Search

The **Overview** tab is opened by default and shows the available fields in the index on the left side. Notice that the field list includes the fields defined in the field configuration as well as a few others, such as created, lastmodified, and type. The additional fields are added by OpenCms to help locate the resource. On the right hand side is a list of top ranking terms that have been indexed from the content.

Clicking on the **Documents** tab will show a list of the documents that are contained in the index. Recall that each document corresponds to an instance of a resource in the VFS. The arrow keys in the upper left are used to browse through the documents in the index. We can see the fields of each document, along with some flags indicating field status, and the field values:

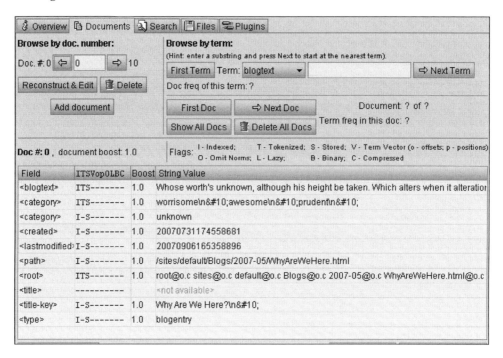

The relevant field status flags are:

- **I**: This field is indexed
- **T**: This field has been tokenized (run through an analyzer)
- **S**: The field value is stored

The additional flags are for more advanced Lucene features not utilized by OpenCms.

Notice that there are two **category** fields in the document. The first one corresponds to the category field we defined in the **blogfields** field configuration. It contains the collated values from the Category field within the content. But where did the second one come from? As mentioned earlier, OpenCms adds additional index fields to support locating the resource, and category is one of the fields added. OpenCms attempts to obtain the value of this field from the **category** property. However, this field appears to be a relic, as the **category** field is not a default content property. Furthermore, OpenCms 7 provides a new Category management feature for resources. For now, we will ignore the extra field but will keep it in mind, in case additional support is provided in the future.

Now let's try a sample query by clicking on the Search tab:

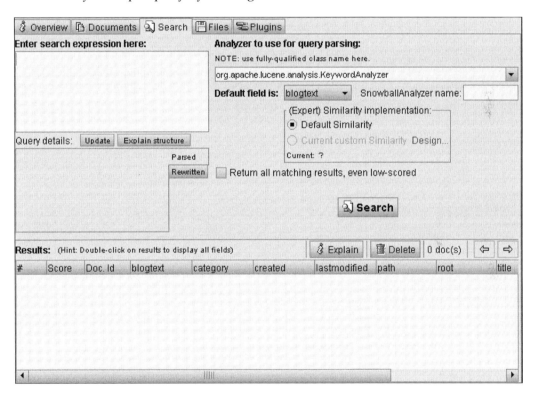

Adding Site Search

On the left side, a search expression can be entered. Before we do this, we want to make sure that we have selected the correct analyzer for parsing our query. Recall that when field values are indexed, they get analyzed first. Any queries made in Luke will get parsed with the same analyzer. We can observe the difference that analyzers make with the following experiment.

1. Enter the query: **It rains in Paris in the spring**
2. Select the Whitespace analyzer: **org.apache.lucene.analysis.WhitespaceAnalyzer**
3. Press the **Update** button
4. Note the parsed result: **blogtext:It blogtext:rains blogtext:in blogtext:Paris blogtext:in blogtext:the blogtext:spring**
5. Now repeat these steps using the standard analyzer: **org.apache.lucene.analysis.StandardAnalyzer**
6. Note the parsed result: **blogtext:rains blogtext:paris blogtext:spring**

Notice how the first analyzer simply parses the terms on whitespace boundaries while the second one filters out common terms like 'it', 'in', and 'the'. This is the effect that the analyzer has on indexed text. It is worth spending some additional time looking at the Lucene documentation to understand the query syntax and performing some additional search queries. Also note that Luke can be used to open any Lucene search index. If there is not a lot of content in the Blog repository then the Offline index can always be used for experimentation.

Writing the Search Code

Now that we understand Lucene, have created a search index, and have tested a few queries, we are ready to write the search code. As always when writing our code, we want to leverage the existing OpenCms code as much as possible. OpenCms provides the **CmsSearch** Java class to provide searching support. It is suitable for use as a Bean on a JSP page, and can be driven off the parameters passed to it via an HTML form. We'll start out with a simple example showing how to use the search bean directly, and then we'll progress to subclassing the bean for our own needs.

A Simple Search Example

To implement a search, we only need to create two JSP files: `SearchForm.html` and `Results.html`. These files could be combined together into one, and often are. But to make the example easy to follow, we will use two separate files. The two files should be of JSP type, and should be placed into the site root. Let's take a look at the `SearchForm.html` JSP:

```
<table border="0">
    <tr>
    <td width="200">
       <form action="Results.html" method="post">
          <fieldset>
             <legend title="Search Form">Search Form</legend>
             <input name="query" type="text" value="Search..."
                  onfocus="this.value=''" title="Search" />
             <input class="searchsubmit" type="submit" value="Go"
                  title="Go" />
             <input type="hidden" name="index" value="Offline project
                  (VFS)"/>
          </fieldset>
       </form>
    </td>
    </tr>
</table>
```

The JSP file contains a simple FORM containing field values used for the search. The action will be posted to the Results.html file. Note that the form contains the following fields:

- query: This contains the search query.
- index: This contains the name of the search index to be used.

These field values will be passed to the second JSP file, which uses the CmsSearch bean to do the bulk of the work. The search bean is easy to use and has the following general usage pattern:

1. Instantiate the bean
2. Set the bean's field values with the search parameters
3. Call the init method
4. Call the getSearchResult method to obtain the search results

Let's take a look at how the bean is used in the Results.html file. The first step is the usual imports and the creation of the familiar JSP action element object:

```
<%@ page import="org.opencms.main.*" %>
<%@ page import="org.opencms.search.*" %>
<%@ page import="org.opencms.jsp.*" %>
<%@ page import="java.util.*" %>
<%@ page import="java.io.*" %>
<%
    //Create a JSP action element
    CmsJspActionElement cms = new CmsJspActionElement(pageContext,
                                                    request, response);
%>
```

Adding Site Search

The next step is the declaration of the search bean. This is declared using the standard `jsp:useBean` tag:

```
<jsp:useBean id="search" scope="request"
           class="org.opencms.search.CmsSearch">
  <jsp:setProperty name="search" property="*"/>
  <% search.init(cms.getCmsObject()); %>
</jsp:useBean>
```

There are two things to notice in the bean declaration. First, the `jsp:setProperty` tag is used to ensure that all available properties of the bean are set. Since this file is accessed from an HTTP POST, any existing variable that matches a field in the `CmsSearch` bean fields will be set. This means the bean fields may be set by just declaring the fields in the form. In our minimal example, we have set only two fields, which are sufficient for obtaining simple search results. The additional fields that may be used can be found by examining the source code comments in the `CmsSearch` bean.

The second thing to note is the call to the `init` method, which must be done before the bean can be used. The next step in the file is the display of the search results:

```
<h3><a href="SearchForm.html">Search Again</a></h3>
<br/><br/>
<h1>Search Results</h1>
<%
    List result = search.getSearchResult();
    if (result == null)
    {
      if (search.getLastException() != null)
      {
      %><h3>Error:</h3> <%= search.getLastException().toString() %><%
      }
```

Calling the `getSearchResult` method returns the search results as a list in `CmsSearchResultList` type. If an error has occurred, then the exception is reported using the `getLastException` method. Otherwise, the search results are displayed by iterating over the list and displaying the returned results:

```
    }else
    {
      %>
      <h2><%= result.size() %> Results found for query &lt;<%=
        search.getQuery() %>&gt; in fields: <%= search.getFields() %>
      </h2>
      <%
          ListIterator iterator = result.listIterator();
```

```
                int i = 0;
                while (iterator.hasNext()) {
                    i++;
                    CmsSearchResult entry =
                            (CmsSearchResult)iterator.next();
    %>
     <h3><%= i %>. <a href="<%= entry.getPath() %>"><%=
         entry.getTitle() %></a> (<%= entry.getScore() %>)
     </h3>
            <h6>Keywords: <%= entry.getKeywords() %></h6>
            <h6>Excerpt: <%= entry.getExcerpt() %></h6>
            <h6>Description: <%= entry.getDescription() %></h6>
            <h6>Last modified: <%= entry.getDateLastModified() %>
            </h6>
    <% } %>
<% } %>
```

This search code can be used in many cases for simple search operations and illustrates how easy it is to support content searching.

Subclassing the CmsSearch Bean

Next, we will make a more complex use of the search bean to support blog searching. We could use form variables to drive the behavior of the base `CmsSearch` bean class. Instead, we will show how to subclass the `CmsSearch` bean to perform more custom search operations. We will do this by creating a class file named `BlogSearch`. It starts out with the usual imports and some constant declarations:

```
package com.deepthoughts.search;
import java.util.Arrays;
import org.opencms.file.CmsObject;
import org.opencms.search.CmsSearch;
import org.opencms.search.CmsSearchParameters;
/**
 * This bean overrides the base CmsSearch implementation to provide
search support for
 * Blog Content.
 */
public class BlogSearch extends CmsSearch {
    /** Constant for the fields we will search */
    static final String[] DOC_QRY_FIELDS = new String[] {"blogtext",
                                            "category", "title"};
    /** The names of our search index files */
    static final String OFFLINE_INDEX = "Blogs - Offline";
    static final String ONLINE_INDEX = "Blogs - Online";
```

Adding Site Search

Recall that the blog search form is very simple, and provides only a single field for searching. As users should not need to know how to form a search query, we will build it for them. In the query, we need to specify which fields we want to search the given term for. For the blog site, we support searching the title, blogtext, and category fields. Our class file has a constant for this list of fields. We also define a set of constants that contain the names of the two search indexes that are used.

```
Next in the class is the constructor:
    /**
     * Empty constructor for bean usage. We override the base class
       and initialize with parameters
     * needed for Blog searching.
     */
    public BlogSearch() {
        super();
        m_parameters.setSort(CmsSearchParameters.SORT_DEFAULT);
        m_parameters.setFields(Arrays.asList
                            (BlogSearch.DOC_QRY_FIELDS));
        m_parameters.setIndex(OFFLINE_INDEX);
        m_parameters.setMatchesPerPage(4);
}
```

Here is where all the parameters necessary for search are provided. The parameters are passed within a `CmsSearchParameters` class. To see how the initial parameter values are set, the base class should be consulted. In our class, we let the base class set its initial parameters and then we add or overwrite our own values. The first parameter specifies how the results will be sorted. We use the default sorting method, which orders by document scoring.

The next field contains the list of fields that we want to search for. Here, we pass our pre-defined array of search fields.

Next, we specify the name of the search index to be used. We use the Offline index by default in the constructor. The index will be changed later, if specified, when the `init` method is called.

Finally, we set the number of results to display per page. For development, we set this to a low number so that we can test without requiring many content results. Later, this value should be changed to a more reasonable number or removed to accept the default.

```
    /**
     * Override the init method in order to set the proper search
     * index. We automatically select
     * the proper index based on the current project in use.
     */
```

```
      public void init(CmsObject cms) {
         super.init(cms);
            // set search index to offline or online based on current
            //user project
            if
            (cms.getRequestContext().currentProject().isOnlineProject())
            {
              m_parameters.setIndex(ONLINE_INDEX);
            } else {
              m_parameters.setIndex(OFFLINE_INDEX);
              }
         }
      }
```

In the `init` method, the only thing needed is to ensure that the correct index is selected. We cannot do this in the constructor because we do not have access to the `CmsObject`, which is used to determine if the Offline or Online project is active.

That does it for our custom search bean! The bean shows how easy it is to create a custom bean that encapsulates special search rules. It is not covered here, but it is suggested that the reader inspect the `CmsSearch` class to understand how it operates. Next, we will take a look at the JSP code that uses the bean.

The Search.jsp Template

The search results are displayed from a JSP file that is specified as the target of the search. Recall from the last chapter that the **common.jsp** file generated a form with an action target of **/system/modules/com.deepthoughts.templates/elements/Search.jsp**. This file will use our bean to perform the search and display the results. It starts out like our other JSP files:

```
    <%@ page session="true" %>
    <%@ page buffer="none" %>
    <%@ taglib prefix="cms" uri="http://www.opencms.org/taglib/cms"%>
    <%@ page import="com.deepthoughts.templates.*" %>
    <%@ page import="org.opencms.main.*" %>
    <%@ page import="org.opencms.search.*" %>
    <%@ page import="org.opencms.file.*" %>
    <%@ page import="org.opencms.jsp.*" %>
    <%@ page import="java.util.*" %>
    <%
        // create the bean
        BlogJspTemplate blog = new BlogJspTemplate(pageContext, request,
                                                             response);
    %>
```

Adding Site Search

```
<jsp:useBean id="search" scope="request"
            class="com.deepthoughts.search.BlogSearch">
    <jsp:setProperty name = "search" property="*"/>
    <%
        search.init(blog.getCmsObject());
    %>
</jsp:useBean>
```

Following the usual JSP declarations and imports, we instantiate an instance of the `BlogJspTemplate` class. This class is used only to access the `CmsObject` needed by the `init` method of the search bean. Next is the instantiation of the search bean. This is similar to the simple example, using the * value to instruct the bean to collect and set all available property values. One of the important field values that the `CmsSearch` bean looks for is the search query value. This value is passed in a variable named `query`, which we have set as the form field name in our search form.

After calling the `init` method with the `CmsObject`, there is some more code for initializing the search result:

```
<%
    int resultno = 1;
    int pageno = 0;
    if (request.getParameter("searchPage")!=null) {
      pageno = Integer.parseInt(request.getParameter("searchPage"))-1;
    }
    int resultno = resultno = (pageno*search.getMatchesPerPage())+1;
    String fields = search.getFields();
    List result = search.getSearchResult();
%>
```

The `pageno` variable contains the current page number in support of pagination. If not on the first page of the result, the `searchPage` query variable will contain the page number that should be shown. Later, in the JSP code, this will be used.

The `resultno` variable contains the index number of each result, as it is iterated. When calculating the value, the current page number is taken into consideration so that the display accurately shows which search hit is shown.

The list of search fields is obtained by using the `getFields` method. This is done to propagate the fields when pagination is supported. We'll discuss more of this later.

Finally a call is made to the `getSearchResult` method to get the results. This method takes into account any other form field variables which were passed. The result is returned in a list of `CmsSearchResult` items. The next part of the template looks a lot like the other templates from Chapter 4 in order to make the search results page look consistent:

```
<!DOCTYPE html PUBLIC "-//W3C//DTD XHTML 1.0 Transitional//EN"
"http://www.w3.org/TR/xhtml1/DTD/xhtml1-transitional.dtd">
<html xmlns="http://www.w3.org/1999/xhtml">
<head>
    <title><cms:property name="Title" /></title>
    <meta http-equiv="Content-Type" content="text/html; charset=utf-
                                                                8" />
   <link rel="stylesheet"
      href="<cms:link>/styles/global.css</cms:link>" type="text/css" />
    <script language="JavaScript"
            src="<cms:link>/script/today.js</cms:link>"></script>
</head>
<body bgcolor="#C0DFFD">
  <%-- Include the header --%>
  <cms:include page="/index.html" element="Header" editable="true" />
  <%-- include the standard header code --%>
  <cms:include file="../elements/common.jsp" element="header" />
      <table border="0" cellspacing="0" cellpadding="0" align="center"
            width="100%">
        <%-- Table, 7 cells across --%>
        <tr align="left" valign="top">
           <%-- Left Rail --%>
           <td class="leftRail" align="left">
              <cms:include file="../elements/common.jsp"
                 element="left_rail" />
           </td>
           <%-- Para spacer left side --%>
           <td class="spacer" align="left"></td>
           <%-- Search Results --%>
           <td colspan="2" valign="top" align="left"><img
              src="<cms:link>/images/spacer.gif</cms:link>"
              alt="" height="1" border="0" /> <br />
              <table border="0" cellspacing="0" cellpadding="0"
                 width="100%">
```

The next interesting code portion is where the results of the search are displayed. Each result is iterated and formatted like the rest of the site. The `getQuery` method is used to indicate what was searched for. Also displayed is the total number of hits, obtained via the `getSearchResultCount` method. After that, we display each search item, with its location in the result list and other details of our search.

```
        <%-- Search Results --%>
        <%
        if (result != null) {
              ListIterator iterator = result.listIterator();
           %>
```

Adding Site Search

```
        <tr>
           <td width="100%" class="blogHeadline">
              Search For: <%=search.getQuery()%> found
              <%= search.getSearchResultCount() %> items
           </td>
        </tr>
        <tr>
           <td class="postDivider"> </td>
        </tr>
        <%
           while (iterator.hasNext()) {
               CmsSearchResult entry =
                 (CmsSearchResult)iterator.next();
        %>
                <TR>
                   <TD class="blogSearchResult" width="100%">
                      <%= resultno %>-
                       <a href="<%=
                          blog.link(blog.getRequestContext().
                            removeSiteRoot(entry.getPath())) %>">
                           <%= entry.getTitle() %> (<%=
                             entry.getScore() %> %)
                       </a>
                   </TD>
                </TR>
                <TR>
                   <TD><p><%= entry.getExcerpt() %></p></TD>
                </TR>
                <TR><TD><BR/></TD></TR>
            <%
              resultno++;
           }
            %>
        <tr>
           <td colspan="2" valign="top" align="left">
             <img src="<cms:link>/images/spacer.gif</cms:link>"
                alt="" width="680" height="1" border="0" />
           </td>
<%
    } else {
        if (search.getLastException() != null) {
%>
        <TR>
           <TD>
```

```
            <h3>Error</h3>
            <%= search.getLastException().toString() %>
        </TD>
    </TR>
<%
    }
}
%>
```

After the code displaying the results comes the code supporting result pagination. The `CmsSearch` class nicely encapsulates this feature by generating the URLs necessary to page through the results. The URLs contain all the parameters necessary to maintain the state of the search result window, and are obtained by calling the `getPreviousUrl` and the `getNextUrl` methods. The only other thing needed is to propagate the fields to include in the search. The fields are obtained earlier and saved into the `fields` variable, so this just needs to be appended to the URL.

```
<TR>
    <TD class="blogCategories"><BR>
        <SPAN class="label">
        <%
        if (search.getPreviousUrl() != null) {
        %>
            <a href="javascript:void(0);"
              onclick="location.href='
                <%= blog.link(search.getPreviousUrl()) %>
                &fields=<%= fields %>';"><< Previous
            </a>
        <%
        }
        Map pageLinks = search.getPageLinks();
        Iterator iter = pageLinks.keySet().iterator();
        while (iter.hasNext()) {
            int pageNumber = ((Integer)iter.next()).intValue();
            String pageLink = blog.link((String)
                pageLinks.get(new Integer(pageNumber)));
            out.print("   ");
            if (pageNumber != search.getSearchPage()) {
        %>
            <a href="<%= pageLink %>
                &fields=<%= fields %>"><%= pageNumber %>
            </a>
        <%
        } else {
        %>
```

Adding Site Search

```
            <span class="currentpage"><%= pageNumber %></span>
            <%
              }
            }
              if (search.getNextUrl() != null) {
            %>
           
        <a href="javascript:void(0);"
          onclick="location.href='
            <%= blog.link(search.getNextUrl()) %>
            &fields=<%= fields %>';">Next >>
        </a>
    <%
      }
    %>
    </SPAN>
  </TD>
 </TR>
</table>
<br />
</td>
```

The result page also indicates each result page numerically, allowing the user to navigate directly to a page by clicking on the number. To support this, the `getPageLinks` method returns a list of the other result pages. The list is iterated to generate each link with its corresponding page index.

The remainder of the search template looks very similar to the other templates that we had developed in Chapter 4.

```
<td width="10">
<img src="<cms:link>/images/mm_spacer.gif</cms:link>"
    alt="" width="10" height="1" border="0" />
</td>
    <%-- Sidebar --%>
<td valign="top">
    <div id="sidebar">
    <ul>
    <%-- Search Form --%>
        <cms:include file="../elements/common.jsp"
            element="search_form" />
    <%-- Ads --%>
        <cms:include file="../elements/common.jsp"
            element="ads"/>
    <%-- Archives --%>
```

```
        <cms:include file="../elements/common.jsp"
            element="archives" />
    <%-- RSS Client --%>
        <cms:include file="../elements/common.jsp"
            element="rss_client" />
    <%-- RSS Feed --%>
        <cms:include file="../elements/common.jsp"
            element="rss_feed" />
        </ul>
        </div>
</td>
<td> </td>
</tr>
    <%-- Footer --%>
        <tr bgcolor="#CCFF99">
<td> </td>
<td colspan="5" class="pageFooter">
        <cms:include file="../elements/common.jsp"
            element="footer" />
        </td>
        <td> </td>
</tr>
</table>
</body>
</html>
```

Summary

In this chapter, we discussed some concepts on how search indexes are structured and queried in Lucene. We also discussed how to configure and create an OpenCms search index, including some settings that are made by hand. We introduced a useful developer tool for looking at search indexes and finally we went over the code for supporting the search feature of our blog site.

6
Adding User Registration and Comment Support

The next step in developing our site is to provide readers with the ability to submit comments. Recall that our site design requires readers to create a user account in order to post comments. We will leverage OpenCms to manage the user accounts and will discuss the OpenCms security model along the way. We will then go over the code for registering users and adding the comments to our XML documents. Also in our code discussions, we will go over how to manipulate and publish content programmatically.

Understanding OpenCms Security

OpenCms has a security model built around Users, Groups, and Roles. It is essential to understand this security model in order to create an effective management environment as well as to support registered web users. The content management environment often needs to restrict content editing or access to certain groups. This is also true for web users where it may be desirable to provide premium content or features to different user tiers. In this section, we will provide an overview of the OpenCms security model.

OpenCms has a rich and mature security model that can sometimes be confusing to understand and configure. In this section, we will describe the various facets of the security system in order to configure our site the way we want. We will start by describing Users, Groups, and Roles, and will then discuss Organizational Units, which have been introduced with OpenCms Version 7.

User, Groups, Roles, and Permissions

An OpenCms user account or **User** contains logon credentials and roles required to access VFS resources and functions in OpenCms. A User is always required to access content in OpenCms. By default, OpenCms provides three user accounts: Admin, Guest, and Export. The Admin account is a special account that has access to all resources and functions in OpenCms. The Guest account is provided as a default account. It is automatically assigned to users who have not logged in, or do not have an account. The Guest account cannot access the Workplace or Offline content. It does however have read access to online content that has been given public access. Finally, there is the Export account which is a special account used by OpenCms when content is exported from the VFS to the real file system. This account has the same access as the Guest account. It exists so that it is possible for exported content to be treated differently as compared with dynamic content, if necessary.

Roles are used in OpenCms to govern access to certain functions or features. When a protected function is accessed, OpenCms checks the roles of the accessing user to ensure that they match those needed to execute the function. The function will be allowed to be executed only if the user has the required roles. OpenCms uses the following role definitions:

Role	Parent Role	Description
Root Administrator	None	Users with this role have access to the entire system.
Workplace Manager	Root Administrator	Users with this role may access Workplace functions, including the following: • Cache management • Workplace Tools features • Resource history access • Job scheduling • Property definition management • Search index management • Downloading of files via the log file viewer
Database Manager	Root Administrator	This role allows the user to be able to add, delete, import, export and edit modules. It also allows the user to import and export data from the VFS.

Role	Parent Role	Description
Administrator	Root Administrator	Users with this role have access to the entire organization unit they are assigned to.
Project Manager	Administrator	This role allows a user to manage projects.
Account Manager	Administrator	This role allows a user to manage users and groups.
VFS manager	Administrator	This role allows a user to manage any resource within the assigned organizational unit, superseding any other permission applied to a resource.
Developer	VFS Manager	This role provides the ability to manage JSP files.
Workplace User	Administrator	Users with this role have the ability to login to the workplace.

Roles may be applied to users, either through the Workplace Explorer or programmatically. Role management can be confusing at first, because OpenCms creates some default Groups that implicitly contain Roles, possibly for compatibility with previous versions. Upon installation, the following default Groups are available:

- **Administrators**: This group is for users who will have the Root Administrator role.
- **Guests:** This group is for users who have no special roles.
- **Projectmanagers**: This group is for users who may manage Projects, including publishing actions on those projects. By default, this group contains the Roles of the Workplace User and the Project Manager.
- **Users**: This group is for users who will have access to the Workplace. By default, this group contains the Role of the Workplace User.

The default Groups are special in that they implicitly contain Roles. It is not possible to remove the Roles from the default Groups, nor is it possible to add Roles to other Groups. If a User is added to one of these Groups, the User will be granted the Roles. However, it is important to understand that Group membership does not imply Role permissions, as the added Roles can be removed independent of the Group membership. In previous OpenCms versions, Group membership may have had implied Role permissions, but this is no longer true.

Adding User Registration and Comment Support

Role definitions are hierarchical such that adding membership to a parent Role always adds membership to any child Roles of the parent. Graphically, the Role hierarchy looks like this:

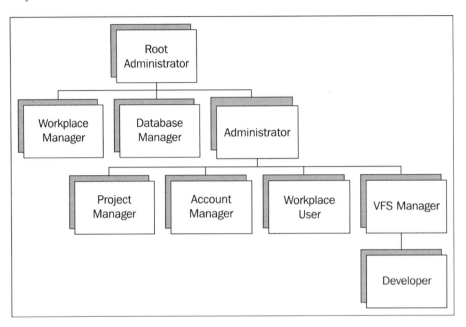

So, for example, if a user account is granted the VFS Manager Role, it will also be granted the Developer Role. Also, although the Workplace User Role is not a child of the Project Manager, Account Manager, or VFS Manager Roles, it will automatically be added, if any of those Roles are added. This is because the Workplace User role is implicitly required to be present to use any of those other Roles.

Finally, it is important to understand that it is not possible to assign Roles to a Group. This is despite the fact that OpenCms implicitly attaches Roles to the default Groups, and that Roles are actually internally maintained using Groups. Instead, Roles are applied directly to Users. The fact that Roles are internally maintained as Groups is an implementation detail which can be confusing. Conceptually, it should be understood that Roles are only applicable to Users. In general, Group membership does not denote Role privileges.

While Roles are used to govern function access, resources in the VFS are protected by permissions. Permissions in OpenCms can be likened to those found in a typical UNIX file system. The available file permissions are:

Permission	Description
Read	Controls the ability of a user to read the content.
Write	Controls the ability of a user to write the content.
Control	Controls the ability of a user to be able to set the permissions of the content.
View	Controls the visibility of the content to the user in the Workplace Explorer.
Direct Publish	Controls the ability to publish the content without requiring 'publish project' permissions.

In OpenCms, permissions are placed on resources according to both Users and Groups. Thus, to perform an action on a resource in the VFS, a User must have both the proper permissions to access the resource, and the proper role to perform the action. We will apply permissions to our Blog content later on, so that our registered web users will be able to add their comments.

Organizational Units

Anyone familiar with LDAP will understand the concept of an Organizational Unit or **OrgUnit**. This is simply a container that is used to collect Users, Groups, or other OrgUnits together for organization. OpenCms ships with the Root Organization Unit enabled at the top of the hierarchy. All other OrgUnits that get created will exist underneath the root.

User, Groups, and Roles are all defined in the context of an OrgUnit. A User account logging into OpenCms may provide an OrgUnit along with it. The OrgUnit is used in conjunction with the user name to provide the complete user account name. This makes it possible to have multiple user accounts with the same login name, residing in different OrgUnits.

There are many ways that OrgUnits may be used to organize users. Typically an OrgUnit is created to segment groups of users who have similar site access or responsibility. For example, an OrgUnit named **ContentEditors** may be used to contain all users who have content editing privileges. In this case, the ContentEditors OrgUnit would appear directly underneath the root:

Root Organizational Unit

    ContentEditors

However, consider the situation where multiple sites are to be managed in OpenCms and each site is to have its own distinct editors. In this case, it might be more desirable to create an OrgUnit for each site, and then to create a **ContentEditors** OrgUnit under each site:

> **Root Organizational Unit**
>
>> Site A
>>
>>> **ContentEditors**
>>
>> Site B
>>
>>> **ContentEditors**

In this way, each site can have its own group of Editors. In fact, with OpenCms, it is possible to maintain both structures. This might be done for a situation where we want to have editors who have access to all sites as well as editors that only have individual access.

As we can see, a properly designed Organizational Unit structure is an essential consideration in configuring accounts. In the case of our blog site, we will create an OrgUnit for our site content managers, and will create a sub-OrgUnit for our registered web users:

> **Root Organizational Unit**
>
>> **DeepThoughts**
>>
>> **SubscribedUser**

With this strategy, any account that is used to manage site content will appear under the OrgUnit: **OU=\DeepThoughts**. These accounts will include content editors who are responsible for writing the blogs. Users who register online and want to add comments will be placed into the sub-OrgUnit: **OU=\DeepThoughts\ SubscribedUser**. This will allow us to segregate reader accounts from management accounts. In addition to this, we will create a Group named **WebUsers** which will contain all users who register online. We can apply resource permissions using this group so that we can ensure that it has access only to Blog Repository content.

Setting up Security for Our Site

We are now ready to setup security settings for our Deep Thoughts site. This will involve creating the necessary Organizational Units, Groups, and file permissions. We want our site users to have read-only content access, but for the things we need to do such as adding accounts and blog comments, those permissions will not be sufficient. To handle this, we will create two accounts that have the necessary permissions and then temporarily switch to those accounts while performing the privileged operations. The two accounts we create are:

- **BlogAdmin**: This account will reside in the DeepThoughts OrgUnit and will have Administrator privileges. The account will be used by an administrator to manage user accounts in our site. We will also use this account programmatically to add new user accounts.
- **CommentPublisher**: This account will reside in the DeepThoughts/SubscribeUser OrgUnit. It will be used programmatically to publish content.

Before creating the account, we must create the necessary Organizational Units, which we will discuss next.

Organization Unit and Group Setup

We can setup our OrgUnits and Groups using the **Account Management** tools in the **Workplace Administrator**. We start with creating the Organization Units by clicking on the **Organizational Unit Management** link, and clicking on the **New sub organizational unit** link:

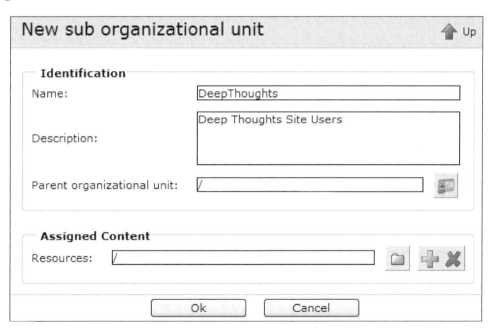

Adding User Registration and Comment Support

Our Organizational Unit for DeepThoughts will be created underneath the root, and we will assign all the resources in our site to it. After clicking **Ok**, will see the new OrgUnit:

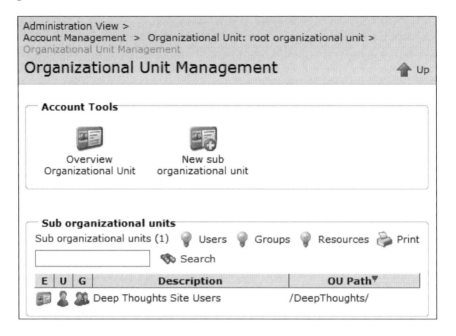

We then add the **SubscribedUsers** sub organizational unit by clicking on the DeepThoughts OrgUnit, then on the **Organizational Unit Management**, and finally on **the New sub organizational unit**:

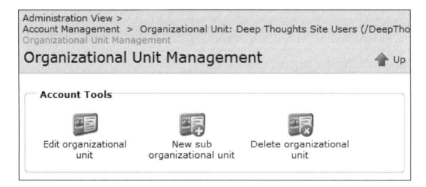

This OrgUnit is slightly different. Here, we want to make sure that the parent OrgUnit is **DeepThoughts**, and that the resources are constrained to the Blog Repository, located at **/Blogs/**:

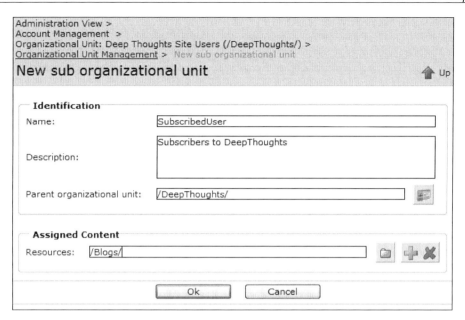

Next, we create the **WebUsers** group in our **SubscribedUsers** OrgUnit by clicking on the **Group Management** and the **New Group** icons:

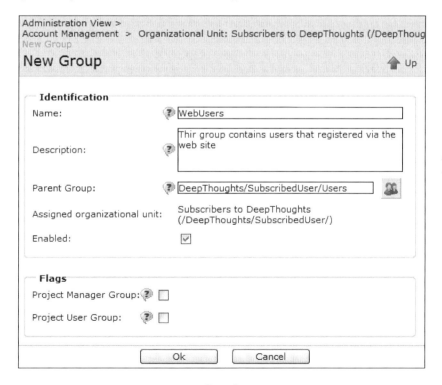

Adding User Registration and Comment Support

We will set the Parent Group to **DeepThoughts/SubscribedUsers/Users**. This group was created for us by OpenCms when the OrgUnit was created. It is based on the default Users group mentioned previously and contains the Workplace User roles which are necessary for our users to access Blog content.

When we are finished, we can see the following structure by clicking on the **Account Management** icon and enabling the **Groups** option:

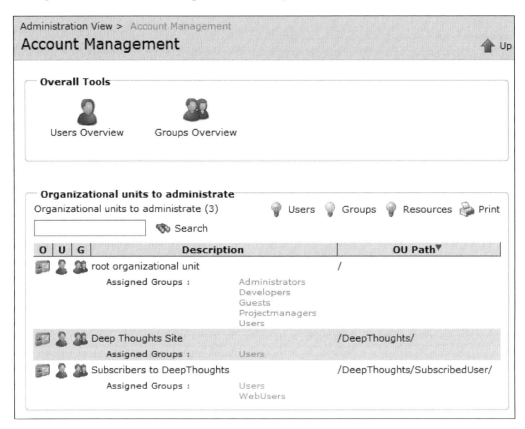

Chapter 6

The next step is to add the users that we mentioned at the beginning of this section.

Adding the Users

The users are added into the groups that were just created. First, we will add the **BlogAdmin** user. From the **Account Management** screen, select the **DeepThoughts Site Users** org unit:

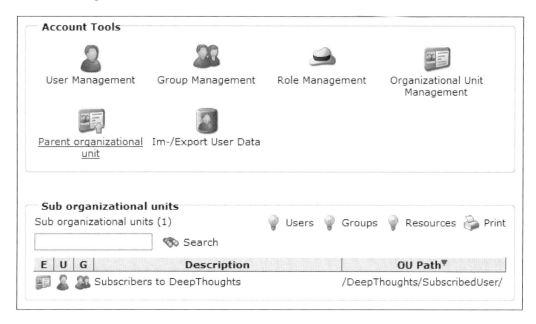

Adding User Registration and Comment Support

Use the **User Management** icon, and click on **New User** to get to the **New User** screen:

Ensure that **/sites/default** is selected as the site and that the Group is set to **DeepThoughts/Users**. Next, we want to ensure that the user is part of the Administrator group. This is done by selecting the **Edit Groups of the User** icon and adding the **Administrators** group:

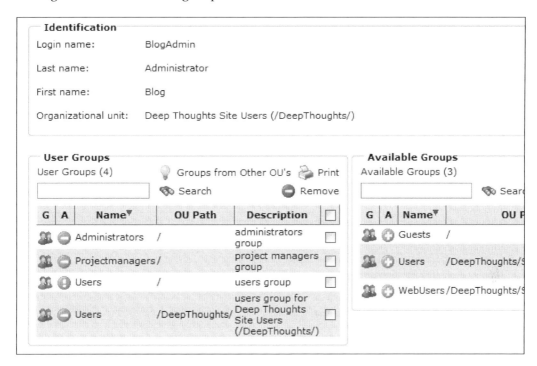

 Adding the **Administrators** group will automatically add the **Projectmanagers** group, and will also add all roles to the user. This follows the the earlier discussion on how roles are transferred from group membership.

Next, we need to add the second user account.

The second user account is created in the **DeepThoughts/SubscribedUser** org unit. This can be selected by going back to the top of the **Account Management** screen and clicking on that org unit. The user should be added in the same manner, ensuring again that the Site is set to **/sites/default**. However, the group for this user is different and should be set to: **Deepthoughts/SubscribedUser/Users**.

As we will cover a little later on, the code will need to switch to this user to publish comments. The code uses the password **blogadmin**, which is set into a constant. In a live environment the password would be stored some place where it can be easily configured, such as a property file. This is an exercise left to the reader.

The **CommentPublisher** requires slightly different privileges as compared to the BlogAdmin user. These are set using the **Edit User Roles** icon:

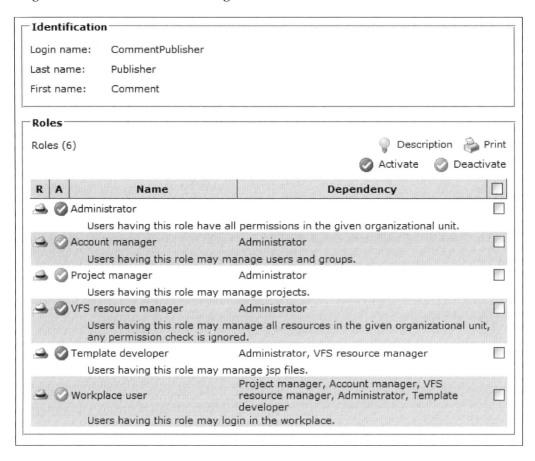

Ensure that the user has the **Account Manager**, **Project Manager**, and **Workplace user** roles.

Now that we've got our Groups and Users setup, we can setup file permissions using the Groups.

Resource Permissions

We've created the **DeepThoughts/SubscribedUser** Organizational Unit to contain all our new web users. We only want to provide web users with the ability to modify the content in the Blog repository, located at the **/Blogs/** path in the VFS. To enforce this, we need to apply resource permissions to the folder.

Chapter 6

OpenCms resource permissions work slightly differently from those applied to a typical file system. In order to restrict access to only a single Group, file permissions first need to be removed (denied) for all groups, and then added (allowed) for the desired Group. In our case, we want to allow the Users and WebUsers Groups access to the **/Blogs/** path. We want to include the Users group, as it contains all our Web Management users who are maintaining our Blogs. The Users group has access by default. So we only have to add access for our WebUsers group. Permissions are set by clicking on the /Blogs/ path and selecting the **permissions** option:

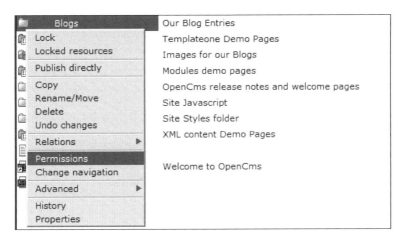

This brings us to the Change permissions dialog box:

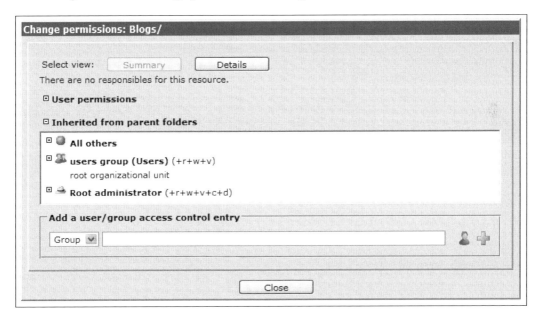

[167]

Adding User Registration and Comment Support

In the Group selector, type in the group name **DeepThoughts/SubscribedUser/WebUsers** group or enter it directly and then click on the green plus sign:

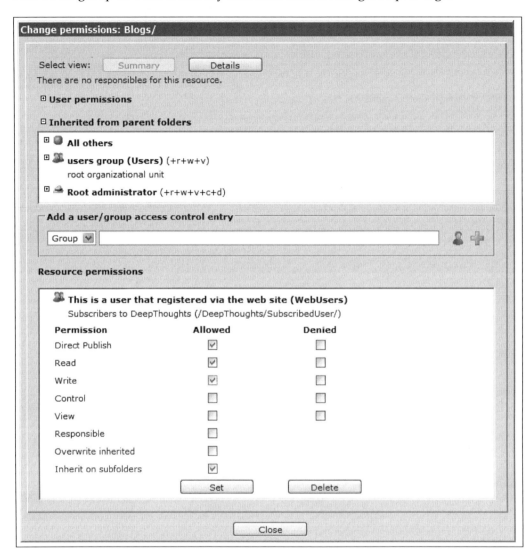

Enable the **Direct Publish**, **Read,** and **Write** permissions and use the **Set** button to add the privileges. This will provide the permissions needed for our web users to interact with the content in the folder.

We now can move onto the coding, registration, and commenting features of our site.

User Login and Registration Code

Our site requires users to register before they can add comments. This will be supported via an 'Add a Comment' link at the end of each blog. Logged-in users will be able to add their comments immediately. All others will be taken to a registration signup page. Registered users may be able to log on at any time through a login button available at the top of the screen.

To enable this feature, we need to add a new JSP for the user registration page. The JSP will reside in the **elements** folder of our module and will be named `Register.jsp`. The JSP page looks similar to our other JSP templates. At the top, we include the imports and tag libraries, and then declare and instantiate the bean class:

```
<%@ taglib prefix="cms" uri="http://www.opencms.org/taglib/cms"%>
<%@ page import="com.deepthoughts.templates.*" %>
<%
    // create the bean
    BlogJspTemplate blog = new BlogJspTemplate(pageContext,
                                           request, response);
%>
```

The rest of the JSP is like the others, except for the center portion of the page, which contains the registration form and logic:

```
<%-- Register --%>
<td colspan="2" valign="top" align="left">
    <img src="<cms:link>/images/spacer.gif</cms:link>" alt=""
        height="40" border="0" />
    <%
        int nAction = blog.registerUserAction();
        if (nAction == BlogJspTemplate.FORMACTION_SHOWFORM ) {
            // display the registration and login forms
            blog.include("common.jsp", "register_form");
        } else {
            // make the appropriate response
            switch(nAction) {
                case BlogJspTemplate.FORMACTION_OK:
                    // output a nice message
                    out.write(" Thank you for registering!<br>");
                    String strBlog =
                            blog.getRequest().getParameter("blog");
                    if (null != strBlog && strBlog.length() > 0) {
                        // allow the user to add the comment now
                        blog.include("common.jsp", "comment_form");
                        out.write("<br>blog: " +
                        blog.getRequest().getParameter("blog") + "<br>");
```

Adding User Registration and Comment Support

```
                } else {
                    // redirect to the home page
blog.getResponse().sendRedirect(blog.link("/index.html"));
                }
                break;
            case BlogJspTemplate.FORMACTION_ERROR:
                %>
                Registration Error:
                        <%=blog.getRegisterActionMessage()%>
                <br/>
                <br/>
                Please try again<br/>
                <%
                break;
        }
    }
    %>
    <br />
</td>
```

The logic starts out by calling a new method in the bean called `registerUserAction`. This method performs the registration action and returns an action code. We will look at that method in a moment. But when the registration page is shown the first time, it returns the `FORMACTION_SHOWFORM` code. This causes the JSP to display the registration form, which is a new template element we've added to the `common.jsp` file:

```
<%-- Register form --%>
<cms:template element="register_form">
    <%
        String strBlog = blog.getRequest().getParameter("blog");
        if (null == strBlog) {
            strBlog = "";
        }
    %>
    <form name="register" method="post"
action="<cms:link>/system/modules/com.deepthoughts.templates/
                            elements/Register.jsp</cms:link>">
        <input type="hidden" name="action" value="register" />
        <input type="hidden" name="blog" value="<%= strBlog %>" />
        <table border="0" cellspacing="0" cellpadding="2" width="100%">
            <tr>
                <th colspan="2">Please Register or Login to add a comment
                </th>
            </tr>
```

```
            <tr>
                <td>Username:</td>
                <td class="bodyText"><input name-"username" type="text"
                                        size="20"/>
                </td>
            </tr>
            <tr>
                <td>Password:</td>
                <td class="bodyText"><input name="password" type="password"
                                        size="15" />
                </td>
            </tr>
            <tr>
                <td>Re-type password:</td>
                <td class="bodyText"><input name="passconfirm"
                                        type="password" size="15" />
                </td>
            </tr>
            <tr>
                <td>First Name:</td>
                <td class="bodyText"><input name="firstname" type="text"
                                        size="15" />
                </td>
            </tr>
            <tr>
                <td>Last Name:</td>
                <td class="bodyText"><input name="lastname" type="text"
                                        size="15" />
                </td>
            </tr>
            <tr>
                <td>eMail:</td>
                <td class="bodyText"><input name="email" type="text"
                                        size="15" />
                </td>
            </tr>
            <tr>
                <td colspan="2" class="bodyText">
                    <img src="<cms:link>/images/spacer.gif</cms:link>"
                        alt="" height="1" width="80" border="0" />
                    <input type="reset" value="Clear"/> 
                    <input type="submit" value="Register"/>
                </td>
            </tr>
        </table>
        </form>
</cms:template>
```

Adding User Registration and Comment Support

We can see that the element has a form code that contains the user input fields necessary for registration and posting the action back to the `Register.jsp` file. When the action is posted back to the JSP, the `registerUserAction` method will perform the registration action. If successful, the method returns the `FORMACTION_OK` code and the JSP file displays a success message. As it is possible to reach the registration page from different areas, the code may behave differently. If the registration page was reached from the context of viewing a blog, then a user will be able to add a comment directly. However, if the page was reached from the homepage link where there was no blog clicked upon, the user will be returned back to homepage.

Now let's take a look at the underlying Java method that performs the actual registration:

```
public int registerUserAction() {
// get the requested action
String strAction = getRequest().getParameter("action");
if (null != strAction) {
    String strUser = getRequest().getParameter("username");
    String strPass = getRequest().getParameter("password");
       // attempt to register the user
       try {
       // see if the username already exists
      CmsPrincipal.readPrincipal(getCmsObject(),
                        CmsPrincipal.PRINCIPAL_USER, strUser);
       setRegisterActionMessage("The user '" + strUser + "' already
                    exists. Please select a different username.");
          return FORMACTION_ERROR;
       } catch (CmsException e1) {
          // this is good, it means the username is available
       }
       // get the rest of the account parameters
    String strPass2 = getRequest().getParameter("passconfirm");
    if (false == strPass2.equals(strPass)) {
       setRegisterActionMessage("Password mis-match, please re-enter
                                           the password.<br>");
          return FORMACTION_ERROR;
    }
    String strFirst = getRequest().getParameter("firstname");
    String strLast = getRequest().getParameter("lastname");
    String strEMail = getRequest().getParameter("email");
    try {
       //to add the user we must first login using the
       // administrative user we created
       getCmsObject().loginUser(USR_DEEPTHOUGHTS_BLOG_ADMIN,
```

```
                            USR_DEEPTHOUGHTS_BLOG_ADMIN_PW);
    // make sure we have a new session after login for security
        reasons
    HttpSession session = getRequest().getSession(false);
        if (session != null) {
            session.invalidate();
}
     session = getRequest().getSession(true);
    // switch to the offline project
    getCmsObject().getRequestContext().setCurrentProject
                    (getCmsObject().readProject("Offline"));
    // add additional user information
CmsUser newUser =
        getCmsObject().createUser(OU_DEEPTHOUGHTS_REGUSERS
        + strUser, strPass, "Web User", new Hashtable());
    newUser.setEmail(strEMail);
    newUser.setFirstname(strFirst);
    newUser.setLastname(strLast);
    // add the user to the WebUsers group
    getCmsObject().addUserToGroup(newUser.getName(),
        OU_DEEPTHOUGHTS_REGUSERS + GRP_DEEPTHOUGHTS_WEBUSERS);
    // add the role to the user
    OpenCms.getRoleManager().addUserToRole(getCmsObject(),
        CmsRole.WORKPLACE_USER, newUser.getName());
    // save changes
    getCmsObject().writeUser(newUser);
    // switch back to online project
    getCmsObject().getRequestContext().
    setCurrentProject(getCmsObject().readProject
                            (CmsProject.ONLINE_PROJECT_ID));
    // now login the newly added user
    return loginUser(strUser, strPass);
} catch (CmsException e) {
    e.printStackTrace();
    setRegisterActionMessage(e.getLocalizedMessage());
    // make sure to logout the admin user, and revert to Guest
    logout();
    return FORMACTION_ERROR;
    }
}
    // no registration action to take
return FORMACTION_SHOWFORM;
}
```

As mentioned previously, this method returns an action code to the caller. We see that the code starts out by looking for a CGI variable named `action`. This variable is present when the user provides registration information and presses the **Submit** button. If the variable is not present, then the method returns the code instructing the JSP to display the registration form.

When the form is posted, the method retrieves the variables and then does some basic checking. First, it verifies whether the username is available by using the `CmsPrincipal.readPrincipal` method. If the method returns an exception, then it means the username does not exist and can be used. Otherwise, an error message is set and an error action code is returned.

After performing another basic check to ensure that both passwords match, we are ready to create the new user account. Creating new accounts requires the Account Manager's privilege. So we must first switch to an account that has this privilege. Rather than use the Admin account which has access to the entire VFS, we use the **BlogAdmin** account mentioned earlier. This account resides within the **DeepThoughts** Organizational Unit and has Administrator privilege only to that OrgUnit. The code temporarily logs in to this user account in order to obtain the access needed to add the new account. To ensure that we remove any session information, the session is also invalidated.

The new user account may now be added. But, we are currently in the Online project. It is not possible to create a user account in the Online project. So we switch to the Offline project, and then call `createUser` to add the account. After creating the account, the user's name and email are added to the `CmsUser` object.

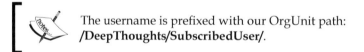
The username is prefixed with our OrgUnit path: **/DeepThoughts/SubscribedUser/**.

Next, we add the user to the **WebUsers** group of our OrgUnit. As the registered user will be allowed to add comments, we have to grant the Workplace User role, which is done by calling the `addUserToRole` method.

To preserve the changes made to the `CmsUser` object, we must save the object, which is done by calling `writeUser`. Finally, we switch back to the Online project, and then log in the user.

Any errors at the end of the method are handled by setting an error return message and printing a diagnostic stack trace. We can also ensure that the user is logged out, in case an error occurs while using the **BlogAdmin** account. This ensures that the user session is lowered back to Guest privilege. A more sophisticated error handling mechanism should be used for a production level application.

That takes care of the registration process. Next we will look at the code that handles the login. At the end of the `registerUserAction` method, a call is made to the `loginUser` method, which handles the login action:

```
protected int loginUser(String User, String Password) {
    // now login as the newly added user
    CmsProject curProj = getRequestContext().currentProject();
    try {
       // attempt to login the user
       String OU = OU_DEEPTHOUGHTS_REGUSERS + User;
       getCmsObject().loginUser(OU, Password);
       // make sure we have a new session after login for security
           reasons
       HttpSession session = getRequest().getSession(false);
    if (session != null) {
       session.invalidate();
    }
    session = getRequest().getSession(true);
    } catch (CmsException e) {
       // return error code
       setRegisterActionMessage(e.getLocalizedMessage());
       return FORMACTION_ERROR;
    } finally {
       // switch back to original project
       getRequestContext().setCurrentProject(curProj);
    }

    return FORMACTION_OK;
}
```

The method starts out by retrieving the project context so that we may restore it after login. It then logs in the user again, first prefixing the OrgUnit name to the username. We once again ensure that any session information is destroyed. Finally, before returning, we ensure that the original project is restored. This login method has been separated from the `registerUserAction` code so that it may be re-used. After a user has registered, he or she may log in by filling in the username and password in the upper righthand side of the site where we have modified the template code to present a login form. We've done this by making some slight changes to the **header** element in the `common.jsp` file:

```
<cms:template element="header">
    <%-- Header Divider --%>
    <table cellspacing="0" cellpadding="0" width="100%"
           align="center" border="0">
       <tbody>
```

Adding User Registration and Comment Support

```
        <%-- Date Bar --%>
        <tr bgcolor="#ccff99">
           <td id="dateformat" colspan="6" height="25">
                
<script language="JavaScript"
        type="text/javascript">document.write(TODAY);
</script> 
<%= blog.getCurrentFolderName() %>
           </td>
  <td align="right">
        <%
           if (blog.getRequestContext().currentUser().
                                        isGuestUser()) {
         %>
     <form class="login" action="
                       <cms:link>/index.html</cms:link>">
     <input name="action" value="login" type="hidden">
     <input name="blog"
            value="<%=request.getParameter("blog")%>"
            type="hidden">
     Username: <input class="input" name="username" value=""
                      type="text" size="10">
     Password: <input class="input" name="password" value=""
                      type="password" size="10">
                <input class="submit" type="submit"
                       name="Submit" value="Login" />
        </form>
 <a href="<cms:link>/system/modules/com.deepthoughts.templates
             /elements/Register.jsp</cms:link>">Register
 </a>
   <%
        } else {
   %>
     Welcome: <%= blog.getCurrentUser() %> 
     <form class="login" name="login"
           action="<cms:link>/index.html</cms:link>">
       <input type="hidden" name="action" value="logout" />
       <input class="submit" type="submit" name="Submit"
              value="Logout" />
        </form>
  <% } %>
  </td>
</tr>
   <%-- Thin spacer --%>
<tr>
```

[176]

```
            <td bgcolor="#003366" colspan="7"><img height="1"
                alt="spacer.gif" width="1" border="0"
                src="<cms:link>/images/spacer.gif</cms:link>" />
            </td>
        </tr>
     </tbody>
   </table>
</cms:template>
```

The new code checks if the current user is a Guest user and if so, displays a login form. If the user is not a Guest user, then it displays the user name and a logout button instead. Note that the login form is submitted back to the index.html file. In order to handle the login request, we need to place our action code somewhere. An easy way to handle this is to place the login handler right inside the constructor of the BlogJspTemplate bean:

```
public BlogJspTemplate(PageContext context, HttpServletRequest req,
                                            HttpServletResponse res) {
    super(context, req, res);
    String strAction = req.getParameter("action");
    if (null != strAction) {
        if (strAction.equals("logout")) {
            logout();
        } else if (strAction.equals("login")) {
            loginUser(req.getParameter("username"),
                    req.getParameter("password"));
        }
    }
}
```

The changes to the constructor causes it to look for the action parameter. If present, it indicates that a submit action was performed. Both the login and logout actions are handled. If the user logs in, it fields the username and password and calls the loginUser method. Otherwise, while logging out, the logout method is called:

```
public void logout() {
    HttpSession session = getRequest().getSession(false);
    if (session != null) {
        session.invalidate();
    }
    // logout was successful
    try {
        getResponse().sendRedirect(link("/index.html"));
    } catch (IOException e) {
        // TODO Auto-generated catch block
        e.printStackTrace();
    }
}
```

The method simply invalidates the session and then redirects the user to the index page.

Adding Comment Support

Now that we've provided a way for users to register and login, we can add code for them to add comments. Although there are many ways to support this feature, we will take an approach that serves to illustrate the capability of programmatically editing content and publishing it. Recall that our Blog content type structure contains nested comment content types. As users post comments, we will append them to the parent Blog content item using nested comments. Readers view content from the online project where it is not possible to make content changes. Our approach then will be to switch the user temporarily to the Offline project, add the comment, publish the blog, and then revert to the Online project.

Before doing this, lets modify the template to display the blog comment information. First, we must add some comments, which can be done easily through the Workplace Explorer. Go ahead and add some comments so that we have some testing data. To display the comment information, we add some code to the `BlogHomepage.jsp` template:

```jsp
<%-- Comments --%>
<tr>
    <td>
        <div id="blogComments">
        <h3 class="blogCommentsTitle">Comments</h3>
          <ul class="blogCommentList">
           <%
             blog.getBlogComments();
             while (blog.hasMoreComments()) { %>
             <li>
             <div class="commentMeta">
             <b>
               <%= blog.getBlogCommentUser() %>
             </b><br/>
             <fmt:formatDate value="<%= blog.getBlogCommentDate() %>"
                 type="date" dateStyle="LONG"
                 pattern="MM/dd/yyyy hh:mm a"/>
             </div>
             <div class="commentText"><%=
                             blog.getCommentField("Comment") %>
             </div>
             <div class="commentSpacer"> </div>
             </li>
```

```
            <% } %>
          </ul>
        </div>
      </td>
    </tr>
    <tr>
      <td class="blogCategories">
        <a href="<%=blog.getAddCommentUrl()%>">Add your
                                              comment
        </a><br/>
      </td>
    </tr>
```

The new JSP code starts by calling the `getBlogComments` method. This method gathers all the comments for the current Blog so that we can iterate over and display them. This method simply uses the inherited `contentloop` method for collecting the comments for later iterations:

```
public void getBlogComments() {
    m_iComments = contentloop(m_iContent, FIELD_COMMENT);
}
```

Next, we use a loop to iterate over each comment, and call some methods to display the comment data, including some meta-information such as who submitted it and when it was submitted.

Outside the loop at the end of the comments, we provide an **Add Comment** link. We use the `getAddCommentUrl` method to retrieve the proper link destination. If the current user is logged in, then the link will go to a JSP for adding a comment, otherwise, the user will be directed to the `Register.jsp` page:

```
public String getAddCommentUrl() {
    CmsUser user = getRequestContext().currentUser();
    String OU = getRequestContext().getOuFqn();
    if (user.isGuestUser()) {
       return link(URL_REGISTER + "?blog=" +
                  m_iContent.getResourceName());
    } else {
       return link(URL_ADD_COMMENT + "?blog=" +
                  m_iContent.getResourceName());
    }
}
```

The method appends the **blog** parameter to the end of the URL so that we may propagate that value through.

Adding User Registration and Comment Support

Now let's take a look at the JSP for adding the comments. We create a new JSP file named `AddComment.jsp` located in our module **elements** directory. This template is also similar to the others except for the middle portion, where we add a form and logic for posting the comment. The JSP is similar to the registration JSP, except that it calls the `addCommentAction` method:

```
<TR>
    <TD class="blogCategories"><BR>
        <%
        int nAction = blog.addCommentAction();
        if (nAction == BlogJspTemplate.FORMACTION_SHOWFORM) {
            // display user form for adding a comment
            blog.include("common.jsp", "comment_form");
        } else {
                blog.getResponse().sendRedirect(blog.link
                        (blog.getRequest().getParameter("blog")));
        }
        %>
    </TD>
</TR>
```

Here, the first time the JSP is called, it displays the comment form, which is another new element added to the `common.jsp` file. Otherwise, the JSP will redirect back to the blog contained in the `blog` parameter. This happens after a comment has been added to re-display the blog with the newly added comment at the end. The `addCommentAction` method does all the work:

```
public int addCommentAction() {
// was anything posted?
    String strComment = getRequest().getParameter("comment");
    if (null != strComment) {
        // yes, now load the blog and add the comment
        try {
            m_iContent.hasMoreContent();
            // add the comment
            addCommentToBlog(m_iContent.getResourceName(), strComment);
            // publish the blog
            publishBlog(m_iContent.getResourceName());
            return FORMACTION_OK;
        } catch (JspException e) {
            e.printStackTrace();
        }
    }
// show the action form
return FORMACTION_SHOWFORM;
}
```

The method first looks for the comment parameter to indicate that a comment is being added. If not, it returns FORMACTION_SHOWFORM code to cause the JSP to display the comment form. If a comment is being added, it makes a call to the hasMoreContent method. This is necessary because of the way the collection mechanism, inherited from the CmsJspCmlContentBean, works. The usage model for this bean is to first call the contentload method to collect the content to the m_iContent collection, and then to display it. However, the implementation is such that content is loaded when the hasMoreContent method is called. After calling this method, the remaining method is split into two parts, one for adding the comment and another for publishing it online.

Adding the Comments to the XML Content

To add a new comment, we must locate the Blog XML content and add a new XML comment element to it. The addCommentToBlog method does this:

```
protected void addCommentToBlog(String Blog, String strComment) {
    try {
       // adding content must be done in the Offline project
          getCmsObject().getRequestContext().setCurrentProject
                            (getCmsObject().readProject("Offline"));
// first we read the blog to count the number of existing comments in
// it. We need to know in order to be able to add another comment to
// the end
          CmsFile docFile = m_iContent.getXmlDocument().getFile();
          CmsXmlContent content =
              CmsXmlContentFactory.unmarshal(getCmsObject(), docFile);
          int nComments = 1;
          List l = content.getValues("Comment",
                                    getRequestContext().getLocale());
       nComments = l.size();
// Now we can add the nested Comment at the end of the list
       I_CmsXmlContentValue val = content.addValue(getCmsObject(),
                   FIELD_COMMENT,getRequestContext().getLocale(),
                                                         nComments);
       // once the comment is added we can set the individual fields
       //into it
       nComments++;
       String strCommentNdx = "[" + Integer.toString(nComments) + "]";
       val = content.getValue(FIELD_COMMENT + strCommentNdx +
                   "/User[1]", getRequestContext().getLocale());
       val.setStringValue(getCmsObject(),
                   getRequestContext().currentUser().getName());
        // set date/time
          val = content.getValue(FIELD_COMMENT + strCommentNdx +
```

```
                        "/Date[1]", getRequestContext().getLocale());
            val.setStringValue(getCmsObject(),
                        Long.toString(System.currentTimeMillis()));
        // set comment
            val = content.getValue(FIELD_COMMENT + strCommentNdx +
                        "/Comment[1]", getRequestContext().getLocale());
            val.setStringValue(getCmsObject(), strComment);
        // now we save the changes to the VFS
            String decodedContent = content.toString();
              try {
                        docFile.setContents(decodedContent.getBytes
                            (CmsEncoder.lookupEncoding("UTF-8", "UTF-8")));
            } catch (UnsupportedEncodingException e) {
            e.printStackTrace();
            }
            String strFile = m_iContent.getResourceName();
            getCmsObject().lockResource(strFile);
            getCmsObject().writeFile(docFile);
            getCmsObject().unlockResource(strFile);
        } catch (CmsXmlException e) {
            // TODO Auto-generated catch block
            e.printStackTrace();
        } catch (CmsException e) {
            // TODO Auto-generated catch block
            e.printStackTrace();
        }
        // switch back to online project
    try {
            getCmsObject().getRequestContext().
        setCurrentProject(getCmsObject().readProject
                                    (CmsProject.ONLINE_PROJECT_ID));
            } catch (CmsException e) {
            // TODO Auto-generated catch block
            e.printStackTrace();
        }
    }
}
```

As content cannot be modified in the Online project, the routine starts out by switching to the Offline project. To work with the content, a `CmsXmlContent` object is obtained by unmarshalling, or parsing the XML. Next, a count of the current number of comments is obtained, as the new comment needs to be added to the end using its new index number.

The new comment is easily added by using the `addValue` method with the name of the field being added. This call adds an empty nested Comment content type at the desired index. The fields in the Comment need to be filled in with the submitted values. The fields are addressed using the XPath syntax, which requires the Comment index number. The resulting field paths look something like:

```
Comment[3]/User[1]
Comment[3]/Date[1]
Comment[3]/Comment[1]
```

We calculate the date and username values and the Comment field comes from the user submission. The new comment is then put back into the document using the `setContents` method.

The last thing left to do is write the changes back to the VFS. We first need to lock the resource so that it can be written to. After doing this, the resource is written and then unlocked. Note that this routine is only illustrative and it is not suggested that this routine be used in production environments. This is because it does not account for scenarios such as the file already being locked by an editor. For production level code, considerations such as this would need to be handled.

Before returning, the routine switches the user back to the online project so that they have read-only content access once again.

Publishing the Comments

Once the comment has been added to the Offline blog, it must be published for viewers to see the new comment. This is implemented in the `publishBlog` method:

```
protected void publishBlog(String Blog) {
    // remember the current user
    CmsUser user = getRequestContext().currentUser();
    try {
        // login publish user we created for publishing comments
        getCmsObject.loginUser(
          USR_DEEPTHOUGHTS_COMMENT_PUBLISHER,
          USR_DEEPTHOUGHTS_COMMENT_PUBLISHER_PW);
        // switch to the offline project
    getCmsObject().getRequestContext().
            setCurrentProject(getCmsObject().
              readProject("Offline"));
        // publish the Blog resource
        CmsPublishManager pm = OpenCms.getPublishManager();
        pm.publishResource(getCmsObject(), Blog);
    } catch (CmsException e) {
        // print out stack trace in case of error
```

```
          e.printStackTrace();
    } catch (Exception e) {
      // print out stack trace in case of error
      e.printStackTrace();
    } finally {
      try {
      // restore original user and switch to online
        OpenCms.getSessionManager().
            switchUser(getCmsObject(),getRequest(), user);
        getCmsObject().getRequestContext().setCurrentProject
                      (getCmsObject().readProject
                      (CmsProject.ONLINE_PROJECT_ID));
      } catch (CmsException e) {
        // something went wrong
        e.printStackTrace();
        // if this fails fall back to logging out
        // and reverting to guest
        logout();
      }
    }
  }
}
```

Online readers do not have any ability to publish content, content may only be published from the Offline project. The publish method uses another account for performing this action, just like the `registerUser` method. The **CommentPublisher** user is used for this purpose.

First, the logged in user is saved into a local variable so it may be restored afterwards. After logging in as the privileged user, the Offline project is switched to. Publishing the content is simple by using the `CmsPublishManager` class. The `publishResource` method required only the resource being published as a parameter. The entire operation is contained within a `try` block so that cleanup can be performed in case any errors occur. The cleanup handler reverses the action by restoring the original user. If a failure occurs during cleanup, then the guest user is fallen back to by logging out.

Summary

That wraps up the addition of comment support. In this chapter, we learned about user accounts, OpenCms security, and the purpose of Organizational Units. We discussed how to set up groups and file permissions. We also discussed the code necessary to manipulate structured content programmatically. Finally, we illustrated the code for publishing content.

7
Providing Site Customization Features

In this chapter, we will add basic customization capabilities to our site, giving registered users the ability to specify a custom RSS feed to be displayed in the righthand side column. During the course of the chapter, we will show how simple it can be to allow for user customizations. We also will show how to integrate third-party features such as RSS support into OpenCms. In a later chapter, we will extend the RSS support to provide an outgoing RSS feed from our blog content.

What is RSS?

RSS is generally known as a content syndication format, but the actual definition of the RSS acronym and its corresponding format has evolved over the years. Its most current definition refers to the following formats:

- RSS 2.0: Really Simple Syndication
- RSS 1.0/RSS 0.90: RDF Site Summary
- RSS 0.91: Rich Site Summary

All these formats specify different XML schemas that are used for content syndication. While the idea of RSS has been around for a while, each format is different and incompatible and there is currently no de-facto standard RSS format. With all these differences, it would be risky to support only a single format as an RSS client. Fortunately, there is a third-party Java library available that attempts to address this problem. The ROME Project is an Open Source Java library that provides a universal programmatic interface to these all popular RSS formats. Documentation and downloads for ROME can be found at: `http://rome.dev.java.net`. We will integrate the ROME library into our site to provide RSS client support for a wide variety of formats.

Creating the Module

Rather than placing the RSS support into the template module, we will create a new module for it. This will allow us to later provide RSS support to other sites we may develop. Let's create the new module and name it: **com.deepthoughts.rss**.

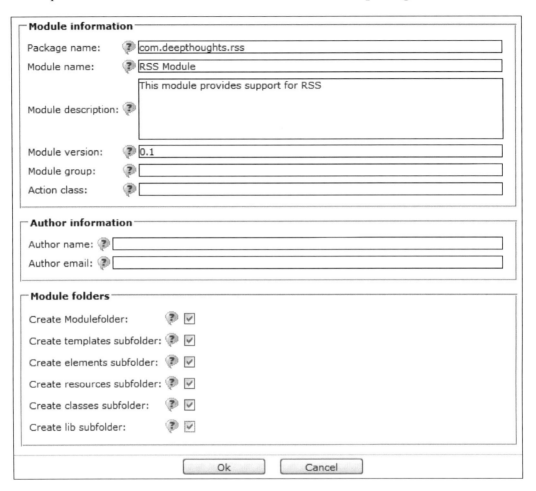

When you create the module, remember to check all the subfolder options as we will use these later on.

When the **Create lib subfolder** option is checked, the **lib** folder will automatically be defined as an export point to the **WEB-INF/lib** folder. This means that to include the required ROME jar files we only need to upload them into the **lib** folder. After uploading the jar files, the **lib** folder should look like this:

		jdom-1.0.jar	jdom-1.0	binary	153253	10/30/07 3:10 PM	Admin
		purl-org-content-0.3.jar	purl-org-content-0.3	binary	22436	10/30/07 3:10 PM	Admin
		rome-0.9.jar	rome-0.9	binary	208025	10/30/07 3:10 PM	Admin

Now, when we publish the module, or if it is exported and imported into another site, the necessary jar files will get deployed for us.

Integrating Jar Files into OpenCms

While integrating jar files from third party libraries, each new jar file must be checked against an existing OpenCms jar file. If a version already exists, then the latest version should always be used. This may require a procedure which involves removing older jar files manually. Also, OpenCms jar file names include version numbers, while third party applications or libraries using the same jar files often do not. For example, a third party library may utilize Apache Commons Logging by including **commons-logging.jar**, which is from the 1.0.2 release. OpenCms also uses this library, named **commons-logging-1.1.jar**. In this case, it is not obvious which version is the most recent. So some work will need to be done to determine this. Failure to resolve conflicts of this type may often cause random errors, so care should be taken to ensure that only one version exists and that it is the latest version.

Next, we will create a bean class and a jar file that our template may use to easily read and display an RSS feed.

The RSS Client Code

The ROME library makes it extremely simple to parse and read RSS feeds. Thorough documentation on the ROME library can be found at its website. So we will only cover its usage briefly. Rather than use ROME directly in our JSP, we wrap up access to the RSS feed through a Java bean. The Java bean code is very straightforward:

```
public class RSSReader {
    /** The URL of the RSS Feed */
    protected String m_strFeed;
    /** SyndFeedInput instance */
    protected SyndFeedInput m_input;
    /** SyndFeed instance */
    protected SyndFeed m_feed;
    /** This contains the list of RSS Items */
    protected List m_lstItems;
    /** This is an iterator for the items */
    protected Iterator m_iItems;
    /** Error message */
    protected String m_strError = "";
```

Providing Site Customization Features

The **RSSReader** class starts out with some instance variable declarations. In the constructor, the variables are initialized and the RSS feed URL is captured:

```
public RSSReader(String Feed) {
    m_strFeed = Feed;
    m_input = new SyndFeedInput();
    m_feed = null;
    m_lstItems = null;
    m_iItems = null;
}
```

An instance of the ROME `SyndFeedInput` class, which will do most of the RSS work, is also created. The `readAll` method is where the actual RSS feed is parsed and read:

```
public boolean readAll() {
    try {
        // Create the URL connection
        URLConnection conn = new URL(m_strFeed).openConnection();
        // some feeds require User-Agent identification
        conn.setRequestProperty("User-Agent", "DeepThoughts RSS
                                                          Reader");
        // build the feed and read all the entries
        m_feed = m_input.build(new XmlReader(conn));
        m_lstItems = m_feed.getEntries();
        return true;
    } catch (IllegalArgumentException e) {
        m_strError = e.getMessage();
    } catch (MalformedURLException e) {
        m_strError = e.getMessage();
    } catch (FeedException e) {
        m_strError = e.getMessage();
    } catch (IOException e) {
        m_strError = e.getMessage();
    }
    return false;
}
```

One important thing to note about this method is that it sets the `User-Agent` request property, which is required by some RSS feeds to work properly. In the event of an error, the simple bean class sets an error string to the returned exception message. A Boolean is returned to indicate success or failure.

The bean has been designed to be used in a loop by the caller and provides the `hasMore` and `getNext` methods to support this pattern:

```
public boolean hasMore() {
    if (null != m_lstItems) {
        if (null == m_iItems) {
            m_iItems = m_lstItems.iterator();
        }
        return m_iItems.hasNext();
    }
    return false;
}
```

The `hasMore` method will seed the iterator the first time it is called and will check it to see if there are any items left to iterate. Finally, the `getNext` method just returns the next item from the iterator:

```
public SyndEntry getNext() {
    if (hasMore()) {
        return (SyndEntry) m_iItems.next();
    }
    return null;
}
```

The `RSSReader` bean class will be put into a jar file and placed into the module lib directory, where it will get deployed along with the rest of the module.

Displaying the RSS Feed in the Template

Now that there is a bean to access an RSS feed, it may be used directly in the template code. For the blog site it will be displayed in the righthand column for all pages. Recall that a placeholder exists for the RSS feeds in the `common.jsp` template file. We just need to fill in the code now to use the `RSSReader` bean:

```
<%-- RSS Client --%>
<cms:template element="rss_client">
    <li class="widget widget_archives" id="archives">
        <h2 class="widgettitle">Feeds</h2>
        <ul>
        <%
            // get feed from user preference
            String feedURL = "http://news.google.com/?output=rss";
            RSSReader r = new RSSReader(feedURL);
            if (r.readAll()) {
                for (SyndEntry e = r.getNext(); e != null; e =
```

Providing Site Customization Features

```
                                         r.getNext()) {
            %>
            <li><a title=""
                   href="<%=e.getLink()%>"><%=e.getTitle()%>
                </a>
        (<%=blog.formatDate(e.getPublishedDate(),"HH:mm")%>)
    </li>
                <%
            }
        } else {
            %><li><%= r.getError()%><%
        }
        %>
        </ul>
    </li>
</cms:template>
```

Notice that a hard-coded RSS feed URL is used as the feed source. Later on, we will retrieve the URL from a user account settings field. Next, an instance of the bean is created with the feed URL and the `readAll` method is called to read the entries. After we read in all the RSS entries they are displayed in a loop and formatted using a List Item tag. The feed data fields are then displayed in the template. If an error occurs while reading the feed, then its corresponding error message will be displayed in place of the feed item list.

Caching RSS Feed Content

Since RSS feeds can take time to parse and may change infrequently, they are good candidates for caching. In fact, all page templates should be considered for caching. OpenCms provides page caching through a feature called **Flexcache**. Examples and use of this feature can be found in the OpenCms documentation set.

As we can see, the use of the ROME library makes it simple to read RSS feeds. The last task is to change the hard-coded feed URL to one that users may change in their account settings.

Adding User Preferences to Accounts

We would like to give registered users the ability to specify a custom RSS feed in their account settings. OpenCms makes this trivial by providing a generic means of setting additional attributes on account information. Account settings may be added in the Workplace Administration user interface via the **User | Edit Additional Info** icon:

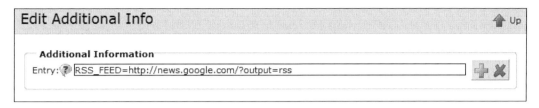

Additional user account information can be added using simple name-value pairs. To allow for custom feeds, we will use a key of RSS_FEED and set its value to the feed URL. Programmatically, the value is accessed by calling the getAdditionalInfo method of the CmsUser object:

```
CmsUser user = (obtain user object);
String strFeed = user.getAdditionalInfo("RSS_FEED");
```

Setting account information is just as easy by first placing name-value pairs into a Map object and then using the setAdditionalInfo method:

```
String strFeed = "http://news.google.com/?output=rss";
Map additionalInfo = new HashMap(1);
additionalInfo.put("RSS_FEED", strFeed);
newUser.setAdditionalInfo(additionalInfo);
```

This provides the framework necessary to allow users to customize their accounts. All this gets tied together with account management code and the JSP template.

Updating the Java Code

Let's start with looking at the changes to the registerUserAction method of the BlogJsptemplate class. We'll alter this method so that it can manage updates to the account information. First, there is some additional code to tie the RSS feed to the user account settings. The RSS feed will be provided by a new form field, which will be added to the registration form:

```
CmsUser newUser = getCmsObject().createUser(OU_DEEPTHOUGHTS_REGUSERS
                + strUser, strPass, "Web User", new Hashtable());
    newUser.setEmail(strEMail);
    newUser.setFirstname(strFirst);
    newUser.setLastname(strLast);
    // add the RSS Feed
    String strFeed = getRequest().getParameter(RSS_FEED_URL);
    Map additionalInfo = new HashMap(1);
    additionalInfo.put("RSS_FEED", strFeed);
    newUser.setAdditionalInfo(additionalInfo);
// add the user to the WebUsers group
```

Providing Site Customization Features

```
    getCmsObject().addUserToGroup(newUser.getName(),
        OU_DEEPTHOUGHTS_REGUSERS + GRP_DEEPTHOUGHTS_WEBUSERS);
// add the role to the user
    OpenCms.getRoleManager().addUserToRole
        (getCmsObject(), CmsRole.WORKPLACE_USER, newUser.getName());
```

The `RSS_FEED_URL` value is a string constant with a value of 'RSS_FEED'. It is used both as a key value for the users' additional info, and for the name of the form field to be filled in by the user.

That takes care of new registrations. For updating account information, a new condition is added to handle the update action. The end of the method checks for the action and handles it by updating the account information:

```
        } else if (strAction.equals("update")) {
          // update the user
          CmsUser user =
              getCmsObject().getRequestContext().currentUser();
          // get the account parameters
          String strPass = getRequest().getParameter("password");
          String strPass2 =
              getRequest().getParameter("passconfirm");
          if (false == strPass2.equals(strPass)) {
            setRegisterActionMessage("Password mis-match, please
                            re-enter the password.<br>");
            return FORMACTION_ERROR;
          }
          // update the settings
          if (strPass.length()> 0) {
          user.setPassword(strPass);
          }
          user.setFirstname(getRequest().getParameter("firstname"));
          user.setLastname(getRequest().getParameter("lastname"));
          user.setEmail(getRequest().getParameter("email"));
          String strFeed = getRequest().getParameter("rss");
          Map additionalInfo = new HashMap(1);
          additionalInfo.put(RSS_FEED_URL, strFeed);
          user.setAdditionalInfo(additionalInfo);
          // save the user object
          try {
            getCmsObject().writeUser(user);
          } catch (CmsException e) {
            e.printStackTrace();
            setRegisterActionMessage(e.getLocalizedMessage());
            return FORMACTION_ERROR;
          }
```

```
            }
        }
        // no registration action to take
        return FORMACTION_SHOWFORM;
}
```

 It is not necessary to switch to the Admin user, as was done for registration, because the user has the necessary privileges for updating his account. This is unlike the registration case, where a new account was being added, requiring a higher privilege.

Now let's move on to the JSP template.

Updating the JSP Templates

To tie all the pieces together, the JSP pages need to be updated to use the new classes just created. First, we add the form field for the users' RSS feed URL. Since this form is also used to update existing accounts, it will be changed to display any existing field values. The registration code is in the `common.jsp` template element. The code updates are highlighted below:

```
<%-- Register form --%>
<cms:template element="register_form">
    <%
        String strBlog = blog.getRequest().getParameter("blog");
        if (null == strBlog) {
           strBlog = "";
        }
        // this form is used for both a new registration and for
           updating
        // user account settings. When updating, the 'forupdate'
           variable
        // will be present
        String strUpdate =
                   blog.getRequest().getParameter("forupdate");
        boolean bUpdate = strUpdate!=null && strUpdate.equals("true");
        String strMsg = bUpdate?
           "Update Account Settings" : "Please Register or Login to
             add comments";
        // get the user
        CmsUser user =
             blog.getCmsObject().getRequestContext().currentUser();
        String strUsername = user.getSimpleName();
```

```jsp
      if (user.isGuestUser())
         strUsername = "";
      // get any RSS feed
      String strFeed = (String) user.getAdditionalInfo().get
                  (BlogJspTemplate.RSS_FEED_PARAM);
      if (null == strFeed)
         strFeed = "";
%>
<form name="register" method="post"
action="<cms:link>/system/modules
  /com.deepthoughts.templates/elements/Register.jsp</cms:link>">
<input type="hidden" name="action"
               value="<%=bUpdate?"update":"register" %>" />
<input type="hidden" name="blog" value="<%= strBlog %>" />
<table border="0" cellspacing="0" cellpadding="2" width="100%">
   <tr>
      <th colspan="2"><%=strMsg%></th>
   </tr>
   <tr>
      <td>Username:</td>
      <td class="bodyText"><input name="username" type="text"
                        <%=bUpdate?"disabled":""%> size="20"
                        value="<%=strUsername%>"/>
      </td>
   </tr>
   <tr>
      <td>Password:</td>
      <td class="bodyText"><input name="password" type="password"
         size="20" />
      </td>
   </tr>
   <tr>
      <td>Re-type password:</td>
      <td class="bodyText"><input name="passconfirm"
                                 type="password" size="20" />
      </td>
   </tr>
   <tr>
      <td>First Name:</td>
      <td class="bodyText"><input name="firstname" type="text"
               size="20" value="<%=user.getFirstname()%>"/>
      </td>
   </tr>
   <tr>
```

```
            <td>Last Name:</td>
            <td class="bodyText"><input name="lastname" type="text"
                        size="20" value="<%=user.getLastname()%>"/>
            </td>
        </tr>
        <tr>
            <td>eMail:</td>
            <td class="bodyText"><input name="email" type="text"
                        size="20" value="<%=user.getEmail()%>"/>
            </td>
        </tr>
        <tr>
            <td>RSS Feed:</td>
            <td class="bodyText"><input name="rss" type="text"
                        size="20" value="<%=strFeed%>"/>
            </td>
        </tr>
        <tr>
            <td colspan="2" class="bodyText">
                <img src="<cms:link>/images/spacer.gif</cms:link>"
                    alt="" height="1" width="80" border="0" />
                <input type="reset" value="Clear"/> 
                <input type="submit"
                        value="<%=bUpdate?"Update":"Register"%>"/>
            </td>
        </tr>
    </table>
    </form>
</cms:template>
```

In order to handle changes made from both the Registration and Account Update actions, the `forupdate` parameter is used. This parameter is passed by the Account Update page only. While updating, the current user account information is retrieved and the existing values are displayed. The form is submitted back to the Registration page with the action code, `update`, to ensure that the update action occurs.

Next, the common template element needs to be updated to display the users' custom RSS feed. To facilitate this, a new method is added to the `BlogJspTemplate` class to retrieve the feed URL:

```
public String getUserRSSFeedURL() {
    // get feed from user preference
    String feedURL = (String)
            getRequestContext().currentUser().getAdditionalInfo
            (RSS_FEED_PARAM);
    // if nothing is set and its not the guest user, then try to
```

```
              read the value
    // from the guest user account
    if (null == feedURL && false ==
             getRequestContext().currentUser().isGuestUser()) {
        try {
           return (String) getCmsObject().readUser
                    (OpenCms.getDefaultUsers().getUserGuest()).
                    getAdditionalInfo(RSS_FEED_PARAM);
        } catch (CmsException e) {
           e.printStackTrace();
        }
    }
    return DEFAULT_RSS_URL;
}
```

The method first attempts to retrieve the settings from the account of the currently logged in user. If no value is found, it then checks to see if the current user is the Guest user. If the user is a Guest user, but no feed is found, then it falls back to a default feed URL. Otherwise, the method uses the Guest account to obtain the RSS_FEED value. This logic allows the Guest account to contain the default RSS fallback URL, rather than having to update any code. The resulting changes are highlighted next:

```
<li class="widget widget_archives" id="archives">
    <h2 class="widgettitle">Feeds</h2>
    <ul>
    <%
        // get the feed from the user account
        RSSReader r = new RSSReader(blog.getUserRSSFeedURL());
        if (r.readAll()) {
           for (SyndEntry e = r.getNext(); e != null; e =
                                        r.getNext()) {
```

Hooking up the Account Management Page

The existing registration page allows new accounts to be created, but a page is also needed to allow existing users to manage their account information. For this, a new JSP page named `Manage.jsp` will be added. This page looks just like the `Register.jsp` page except that it passes some parameters to control the `common.jsp` form element:

```
<td colspan="2" valign="top" align="left">
    <img src="<cms:link>/images/spacer.gif</cms:link>" alt=""
         height="40" border="0" />
    <%
```

```
            int nAction = blog.registerUserAction();
            if (nAction == BlogJspTemplate.FORMACTION_SHOWFORM ){
               // pass some parameters to the form
               // display element
              Map params = new HashMap(1);
              params.put("forupdate", "true");
              params.put("action", "manage");
               blog.include("common.jsp","register_form", params);
            } else {
               // make the appropriate response
               switch(nAction) {
                  case BlogJspTemplate.FORMACTION_OK:
                  // output a nice message
                  out.write("Account Settings Updated.<br>");
               break;
```

Notice that the only difference is that the forupdate parameter is passed to the common.jsp element. This allows the element to set the action and output for updating an account, rather than creating one. With a little more work, the Manage.jsp and Register.jsp files can be merged together, but that exercise will be left to the reader.

Lastly, there needs to be a way for logged in users to get to the Account Management page. This is managed by updating the header element in the common.jsp template:

```
      } else {
         %>
         Welcome: <%= blog.getCurrentUser() %> 
           <form class="login" name="login"
                action="<cms:link>/index.html</cms:link>">
             <input type="hidden" name="action" value="logout" />
             <input class="submit" type="submit"
                 name="Submit" value="Logout" />
         </form>
         <a href="<cms:link>/system/modules/
             com.deepthoughts.templates/elements/
             Manage.jsp</cms:link>">My Account</a>
   <% } %>
```

The additional link to the Account Management page will be displayed for logged in users.

Summary

That wraps up the support for reading custom RSS feeds. In this chapter, we learned how to tie custom settings to user accounts, how to integrate a third party library into OpenCms, and how to use ROME to read RSS feeds. We built upon our existing registration page to allow for account management and updated our common template file to display the Feeds.

We also created a new module to contain our support classes and the ROME library. Placing the libraries into a module allows OpenCms to manage the deployment of the necessary jar files into the OpenCms installation when the module is imported into a new system. In a later chapter, we will expand on this module to also provide support for outgoing RSS Feeds from the blog content.

8
Extending OpenCms: Developing a Custom Widget

As we saw in Chapter 4, when designing a structured content type, there are a variety of user interface widgets available. The default widgets cover most user interface needs. But sometimes, a data field may need to be populated in some other way. OpenCms allows for custom widgets to be created and plugged into its architecture. In this chapter, we will design and create our own widget to illustrate this.

Designing a Custom Widget

Going back to the blog content type created in Chapter 3, we see that the category field is populated from a drop-down list provided by a `SelectorWidget`. The `SelectorWidget` obtains its values from the static configuration string defined within the blog schema file. This design is problematic as we would like category values to be easily changed or added. Ideally, the list of category values should be able to be updated by site content editors. Fortunately, we can create our own custom widget to handle this requirement.

An OpenCms widget is a Java class that implements the `I_CmsWidget` interface, located in the `org.opencms.widgets` package. The interface contains a number of methods that must be implemented. First there are some methods dealing with instantiation and configuration of the widget:

- `newInstance`: This returns a new instance of the widget.
- `setConfiguration`: This method is called after the widget has been initialized to configure it. The configuration information is passed as a string value coming from the declaration of the widget within the schema file of the content type using it.

- `getConfiguration`: This is called to retrieve the configuration information for the widget.

Next, there are some methods used to handle the rendering. These methods are called by widget enabled dialogs that might be used in a structured content editor or an administration screen. The methods provide any Javascript, CSS, or HTML needed by the widget dialogs:

- `getDialogIncludes`: This method is called to retrieve any Javascript or CSS includes that may be used by the widget.
- `getDialogInitCall`: This method may return Javascript code that performs initialization or makes calls to other Javascript initialization methods needed by the widget.
- `getDialogInitMethod`: This method may return Javascript code containing any functions needed by the widget.
- `getDialogHtmlEnd`: This method is called at the end of the dialog and may be used to return an HTML or Javascript needed by the widget.
- `getDialogWidget`: This method returns the actual HTML and Javascript used to render the widget along with its values.
- `getHelpBubble`: This method returns the HTML for displaying the help icon relating to this widget.
- `getHelpText`: This method returns the HTML for displaying the help text relating to this widget.

Lastly, there are some methods used to get and set the widget value:

- `getWidgetStringValue`: This method returns the value selected from the widget.
- `setEditorValue`: This method sets the value into the widget.

All these methods have base implementations in the `A_CmsWidget` class. In most cases, the base methods do not need to be overridden. As such, we will not cover all the methods in detail. If it is necessary to override the methods, the best way to get an idea of how to implement them is to look at the code using them.

All widgets are used in dialog boxes which have been enabled for widgets, by implementing the `I_CmsWidgetDialog` interface. There are two general instances of these dialogs, one is used for editing structured XML content, the other is found in any dialog appearing in the Administration View. The two classes implementing this interface are:

```
org.opencms.workplace.CmsWidgetDialog
org.opencms.workplace.editors.CmsXmlContentEditor
```

The `CmsWidgetDialog` class is itself a base class, which is used by all dialogs found in the Administrative View.

Before designing a new widget, it is useful to examine the existing widget code. The default OpenCms widgets can be found in the `org.opencms.widgets` package. All the widgets in this package subclass the `A_CmsWidget` class mentioned earlier. Often, a new widget design may be subclassed from an existing widget.

Designing the Widget

As mentioned earlier, we would like to have a widget that obtains its option data values dynamically rather than from a fixed configuration string value. Rather than create a widget very specific to our needs, we will use a flexible design where the data source location can be specified in the configuration parameter. The design will allow for other data sources to be plugged into the widget. This way, we can use a single widget to obtain dynamic data from a variety of sources.

To support this design, we will use the configuration parameter to contain the name of a Java class used as a data source. The design will specify a pluggable data source through a Java interface that a data source must implement. Furthermore, a data source can accept parameters via the widget configuration string.

With this design, an example declaration for a widget named `CustomSourceSelectWidget` would look like this:

```
<layout element="Category"
   widget="CustomSourceSelectWidget"
   configuration="source='com.widgets.sources.MySource'|
      option1='some config param'|
      option2='another param'"
/>
```

This declaration would appear in the schema of a content type, using the widget as covered earlier. The configuration parameter consists of name/value pairs, delimited by the vertical bar character. Each name/value pair is separated by the equal to sign and the value is always enclosed in single quotes. The design requires that at least the `source` parameter be specified. Additional parameters will depend upon the specific data source being used.

The example declaration specifies that the data field named `Category` will use the `CustomSourceSelectWidget` widget for its layout. The configuration parameter contains the name of the Java class to be used to obtain the data source. The data source will receive the two parameters named `option1` and `option2` along with their values. Next, lets move on to the code to see how this all gets implemented.

The Widget Code

By examining the existing OpenCms widget code base, we see that the widget can be based on the SELECT widget, which is implemented by the `CmsSelectWidget` class. Recall that the SELECT widget obtains its option values statically from the configuration parameter. We will subclass the widget to modify its behavior, so that it will get the data using the Java data source instead. This turns out to be quite straightforward, requiring only a few method overrides:

```java
public class CmsCustomSourceSelectWidget extends CmsSelectWidget {
    /** The log object for this class. */
    private static final Log LOG =
                CmsLog.getLog(CmsCustomSourceSelectWidget.class);
    /** The list of select values */
    private List m_selectOptions = null;
    /** The widget data source */
    I_WidgetSelectSource m_iDataSource = null;
    /** The configuration options */
    CustomSourceConfiguration m_config;
    public CmsCustomSourceSelectWidget() {
        super();
    }
    public I_CmsWidget newInstance() {
        // create a new widget using the config parameters
        return new CmsCustomSourceSelectWidget();
    }
```

The class starts with the default constructor and some member variables which we'll discuss later on. The `newInstance` method is overridden to return an instance of the widget. To manage the configuration information, the `setConfiguration` method is overridden. This method gets called right after a widget has been constructed to allow it to initialize. The method uses the data source to read the option data:

```java
public void setConfiguration(String configuration) {
    super.setConfiguration(configuration);
    if (m_iDataSource == null) {
        m_config = new
            CustomSourceConfiguration(configuration);
        String strClassName =
            options.getConfigValue("source");
        // read the class name for the data source
        // and instantiate it
        Class sourceClazz;
        try {
            sourceClazz = Class.forName(strClassName);
```

```
            m_iDataSource =
                (I_WidgetSelectSource)sourceClazz.
                    newInstance();
        } catch (Exception e) {
           // Log the error
           LOG.error(Messages.get().
               getBundle().key(
                   Messages.LOG_DATASOURCE_INIT_ERROR_2,
                   strClassName), e);

           // since it failed use the
           // default source provider to be nice
           m_iDataSource = new DefaultDS();
        }
        // set the configuration
        m_iDataSource.setConfiguration(m_config);
    }
}
```

After calling the base class, an instance of the CustomSourceConfiguration class is created with the configuration data. The class is used to encapsulate the parsing and formatting of configuration options. It also provides an easy way to retrieve the configuration values:

```
public class CustomSourceConfiguration {
    private static final Log LOG =
                CmsLog.getLog(CustomSourceConfiguration.class);
    protected final static String OPTION_DELIMITER = "|";
    protected final static String OPTION_VALUE_BEGIN="='";
    protected final static String OPTION_VALUE_END="'";
    /** List of option values */
    private Hashtable<String, String> m_htOptions;
    public CustomSourceConfiguration(String configuration) {
        parseOptions(configuration);
    }
    private void parseOptions(String config) {
        m_htOptions = new Hashtable<String, String>();
        String [] aParms = CmsStringUtil.splitAsArray(config,
                                            OPTION_DELIMITER);
        for (int i=0; i<aParms.length; i++) {
           boolean bBadParamFormat = false;
           // read the parameter name
           String strParm = aParms[i];
           int nParmNameBegin = 0;
           int nParmNameEnd = strParm.indexOf(OPTION_VALUE_BEGIN);
```

```java
            if (-1 != nParmNameEnd) {
               // parameter name
               String strParmName = strParm.substring(nParmNameBegin,
                                                       nParmNameEnd);
               // parameter value
               int nParmValueStart = nParmNameEnd +
                              OPTION_VALUE_BEGIN.length();
               int nParmValueEnd = strParm.indexOf(OPTION_VALUE_END,
                                                    nParmValueStart);
               if (-1 != nParmValueEnd) {
                  String strParmVal =
                    strParm.substring(nParmValueStart, nParmValueEnd);
                  // add the param name-value pair
                  m_htOptions.put(strParmName, strParmVal);
               } else {
               bBadParamFormat = true;
               }
            } else {
               bBadParamFormat = true;
            }
            if (bBadParamFormat && LOG.isInfoEnabled()) {
               LOG.info(Messages.get().getBundle().key
                  (Messages.ERR_MALFORMED_SELECT_OPTIONS_1, strParm));
            }
         }
      }
   }
   public String getConfigValue(String ConfigName) {
      return (String) m_htOptions.get(ConfigName);
   }
}
```

Back in the `setConfiguration` method, the `source` parameter is obtained from the configuration data. This value is then used to construct an instance of the data source using Java reflection. In case of an error, it is logged to the console and a fallback source is used. The fallback source returns the error message in the option value to indicate that there was a configuration problem. After the data source has been instantiated, the configuration information is passed to it. Note that the data source must adhere to the `I_WidgetSelectSource` interface. We will describe that interface later on.

The next method in the class is the `getDialogWidget` method. This method returns the actual HTML for the widget:

```
public String getDialogWidget(CmsObject cms, I_CmsWidgetDialog
                widgetDialog, I_CmsWidgetParameter param) {
    String id = param.getId();
    // build the SELECT HTML
    StringBuffer result = new StringBuffer(16);
    result.append("<td class=\"xmlTd\" style=\"height:
                        25px;\"><select class=\"xmlInput");
    if (param.hasError()) {
       result.append(" xmlInputError");
    }
    result.append("\" name=\"");
    result.append(id);
    result.append("\" id=\"");
    result.append(id);
    result.append("\">");
    // read the option data values
    getSelectOptionData(cms);
    // finish the HTML
    if (null != m_selectOptions) {
       String selected = getSelectedValue(cms, param);
       Iterator i = m_selectOptions.iterator();
       while (i.hasNext()) {
           SelectOptionValue option = (SelectOptionValue)
                                                    i.next();
           // create the option
           result.append("<option value=\"");
           result.append(option.getValue());
           result.append("\"");
           if ((selected != null) &&
                        selected.equals(option.getValue())) {
              result.append(" selected=\"selected\"");
           }
           result.append(">");
           result.append(option.getName());
           result.append("</option>");
       }
    }
    result.append("</select>");
    result.append("</td>");
    return result.toString();
}
```

Extending OpenCms: Developing a Custom Widget

The code was copied from the base `CmsSelectWidget` implementation as it is very similar. After building the SELECT tag, the option values are read from the data source. This is encapsulated in the `getSelectOptionData` method which places the data list into a member variable. The `option` tags are then built from the data list.

The `getSelectedValue` method is used to retrieve the value of any previously selected option value. This method is implemented by the base class, and does not need to be changed.

While building the `Option` tags, the code looks for a current value and sets the SELECTED attribute, if a match is found. This ensures the state of any previously selected value. At the end of the class is the method used to obtain the option values from the data source:

```
protected List getSelectOptionData(CmsObject cms) {
    // set the configuration in the data source
    m_iDataSource.setConfiguration(m_config);
    // read the option values
    // data values are not cached by default, but can be
    // cached by setting the configuration option
    //   "cacheData='true'"
    String strCache = m_config.getConfigValue("cacheData");
    if (null!=strCache && strCache.equalsIgnoreCase("true")) {
        if (m_selectOptions == null) {
            m_selectOptions = m_iDataSource.getValues(cms);
        }
        return m_selectOptions;
    } else {
        return m_iDataSource.getValues(cms);
    }
}
```

The method first passes the configuration information to the data source to give it a chance to initialize itself. It then reads the data from the data source. By default, the data is read each time the method is called. But in some cases, this may be time consuming. To speed this up, the method supports caching the result if the `cacheData` option parameter is set.

That's it for the widget class. Next we'll go over the data source interface, which is very straightforward.

Custom Source Interface and Implementations

The interface designed for data sources is quite simple, consisting of only two methods:

```
public interface I_WidgetSelectSource {
    /**
     * This method is called after the data source is
     * constructed and before the option values are
     * retrieved. It passes the configuration string to
     * the widget.
     *
     * @param config String value of the configuration string
     */
    public void setConfiguration(CustomSourceConfiguration config);
    /**
     * Returns a List of SelectOptionValue objects to be
     * displayed in the SELECT list.
     */
    public List getValues(CmsObject cms);
}
```

As seen in the widget code, the setConfiguration method is first called to give the data source a chance to initialize and capture any configuration data. The getValues method is then called to retrieve the option data. The option data must be returned in a List of SelectOptionValue objects, which is a simple bean class containing name/value pairs used for the option tag.

Let's have a look at couple of data sources that implement this interface. First, there is the DefaultDS class. This data source is used as a fallback in case the configured one can not be instantiated:

```
public class DefaultDS implements I_WidgetSelectSource {
    public DefaultDS() {
    }
    public List getValues(CmsObject cms) {
       ArrayList<SelectOptionValue> aVals = new
          ArrayList<SelectOptionValue>();
       aVals.add(new SelectOptionValue(
          Messages.get().getBundle().key(
          Messages.DEFAULT_DS_ERROR_MSG_0), "null"));
       return aVals;
    }
    public void setConfiguration(CustomSourceConfiguration config) {
       // don't care
    }
}
```

Extending OpenCms: Developing a Custom Widget

The `getValues` method constructs an `ArrayList` and adds a single value to it. The value is an error string indicating that the configuration has failed. The string is retrieved using the OpenCms `Messages` class, which is discussed later on. The data source doesn't use the configuration data. So, the `setConfiguration` method is empty.

Now let's look at a more interesting data source. Recall that we would like the select widget to retrieve values from some list that content editors can edit. A structured content type is a perfect candidate for such a list. The `valuelist` content type will allow many instances of data lists to be created:

```xml
<!-- ============================================================
    XSD content definition file for the ValueList type
    ============================================================ -->
<xsd:schema xmlns:xsd="http://www.w3.org/2001/XMLSchema"
    elementFormDefault="qualified">
    <xsd:include schemaLocation="opencms://opencms-xmlcontent.xsd" />
    <xsd:element name="ValueLists" type="OpenCmsValueLists"/>
    <xsd:complexType name="OpenCmsValueLists">
        <xsd:sequence>
            <xsd:element name="ValueList" type="OpenCmsValueList"
                    minOccurs="0" maxOccurs="unbounded"/>
        </xsd:sequence>
    </xsd:complexType>
    <xsd:complexType name="OpenCmsValueList">
        <xsd:sequence>
            <xsd:element name="Value" type="OpenCmsString"
                    minOccurs="1" maxOccurs="1000" />
        </xsd:sequence>
        <xsd:attribute name="language" type="OpenCmsLocale"
                    use="optional"/>
    </xsd:complexType>
</xsd:schema>
```

The content type has a single field named `Value`, and has an arbitrary upper limit of 1000 items. Recall from Chapter 3 that to install a content type the `resourcetype` and `explorertype` entries need to be added to the `opencms-modules.xml` configuration file. First is the resource type entry:

```xml
<resourcetypes>
    <type class="org.opencms.file.types.CmsResourceTypeXmlContent"
            name="valuelist" id="3002">
        <param name="schema">
            /system/modules/com.deepthoughts.templates/
            schemas/valuelist.xsd
        </param>
    </type>
</resourcetypes>
```

And then the explorer type entry:

```
<explorertype name="valuelist" key="fileicon.valuelist"
    icon="xmlcontent.gif" reference="xmlcontent">
  <newresource
     uri="newresource_xmlcontent.jsp?
          newresourcetype=valuelist" order="25"
          autosetnavigation="false" autosettitle="false"
          info="desc.valuelist"/>
  <accesscontrol>
  <accessentry principal="ROLE.WORKPLACE_USER"
      permissions="+r+v+w+c"/>
  </accesscontrol>
</explorertype>
```

After adding the new content type, a new list can be created within the Workplace Explorer. The list will maintain the Category values assigned to Blog entries and will be placed somewhere that the content editors can access it.

The last thing needed is a data source that gets its option values from an instance of this content type. Again, we will use a design that is more general in purpose rather than specific. The data source class will be able to read values from any content type that has repeating fields. This way it will not be limited to reading list values from the `ValueList` content type. This will be done by using the configuration parameter to instruct the data source how to get the values. The configuration string will need to have these options:

- source: This parameter is required for the widget. In this case it will contain the name of the generic data source class.
- contenttype: This will contain the type of the structured content that data will be obtained from.
- location: This will specify the location of the resource in the VFS.
- fieldname: This will contain the name of the field within the resource that holds the data values. The data source will read all occurrences of this field and return them as INPUT option values.

Now lets look at the code which implements this. The data source class is named `ContentFieldListDS`:

```
public class ContentFieldListDS implements I_WidgetSelectSource {
    /** The content type containing the list of values */
    String m_strContentType;
    /** VFS path to the instance of the resource */
    String m_strLocation;
```

Extending OpenCms: Developing a Custom Widget

```
    /** Name of the field within the resource */
    String m_strFieldname;
    /**
     * Public constructor needed
     */
    public ContentFieldListDS() {
        m_strContentType = null;
        m_strLocation = null;
        m_strFieldname = null;
    }
```

The member variables will contain the configuration data. They are initialized in the constructor, and then set in the `setConfiguration` method:

```
    public void setConfiguration(CustomSourceConfiguration config)
    {
        // get the configuration options
        m_strContentType = config.getConfigValue("contenttype");
        m_strLocation = config.getConfigValue("location");
        m_strFieldname = config.getConfigValue("fieldname");
    }
    private boolean isConfigValid() {
        return m_strContentType != null &&
            m_strLocation != null &&
            m_strFieldname != null;
    }
```

A utility method is used to check the configuration parameters. Last is the `getValues` method, where the content values are actually read from the data source:

```
    public List getValues(CmsObject cms) {
        ArrayList<SelectOptionValue> lstVals = new
            ArrayList<SelectOptionValue>();
        if (false == isConfigValid()) {
            lstVals.add(new SelectOptionValue("Missing or invalid
    configuration options!", "null"));
        } else {
            // read the resource containing the values, in the specified
                location
            try {
                CmsResource res = cms.readResource(m_strLocation);
                    // check it against the desired type
                    if (m_strContentType.equalsIgnoreCase
                        (OpenCms.getResourceManager().
                         getResourceType(res).getTypeName())) {
                        // retrieve the values
```

```
                CmsXmlContent content =CmsXmlContentFactory.unmarshal
                                    (cms, cms.readFile(res));
                // using the specified fieldname
                List lVals = content.getValues(m_strFieldname,
                        cms.getRequestContext().getLocale());
            Iterator j = lVals.iterator();
            while (j.hasNext()) {
                I_CmsXmlContentValue iVal =
                            (I_CmsXmlContentValue)j.next();
                // add the value
                lstVals.add(new SelectOptionValue
                    (iVal.getStringValue(cms) iVal.getStringValue(cms)));
            }
            } else {
                lstVals.add(new SelectOptionValue("Specified resource
                            (" + m_strLocation + ") is not of type:" +
                            m_strContentType, "null"));
            }
        } catch (CmsException e) {
            // return the error in the list to be nice
            lstVals.add(new SelectOptionValue("Error reading " +
                    m_strLocation + ": " + e.getMessage(), "null"));
        }
    }
    return lstVals;
}
```

The method begins by allocating a list to contain the returned values. If the configuration values cannot be set properly, then an error return message is returned in the list. Otherwise, the routine reads the configured CmsResource. Another validation check is done to insure that the content type of the resource matches the configured one. Again, an error message is returned if this is not the case.

After the validation check, the resource is read and unmarshalled. This converts its XML representation into a CmsXmlContent instance. After this is done, the configured content fields are read into an array and then converted into SelectOptionValue instances. For safety, the entire effort is surrounded with a catch block which returns any caught errors. The error messages have not been externalized as done in the earlier class. This exercise will be left to the reader. But first we will cover the Messages class used for doing this.

Using OpenCms Message Strings for Localization

OpenCms provides full support for localization. In the earlier chapters, we discussed the use of the `messages.properties` file to contain user interface strings. The property values can also be used to localize message strings in Java classes. The `I_CmsMessageBundle` interface provides the support for this. The interface can be a bit confusing at first, but fortunately, most of the methods are already implemented in the `A_CmsMessageBundle` class. To support localized strings in our own classes, we just need to provide a subclass of the `A_CmsMessageBundle` class. Each Java package can have its own `messages.properties` file with a corresponding Java class. The convention is to name the class `Messages`. Let's take a look at the one used by the widgets:

```java
public final class Messages extends A_CmsMessageBundle {
    /** Name of the used resource bundle. */
    private static final String BUNDLE_NAME =
        "com.deepthoughts.widgets.messages";
    /** Static instance member. */
    private static final I_CmsMessageBundle INSTANCE = new
                                                      Messages();
    /**
     * Hides the public constructor for this utility class.<p>
     */
    private Messages() {
        // hide the constructor
    }
    /**
     * Returns an instance of this localized message accessor.<p>
     *
     * @return an instance of this localized message accessor
     */
    public static I_CmsMessageBundle get() {
        return INSTANCE;
    }
    /**
     * Returns the bundle name for this OpenCms package.<p>
     *
     * @return the bundle name for this OpenCms package
     */
    public String getBundleName() {
        return BUNDLE_NAME;
    }
    /** Message constants for key in the resource bundle. */
    public static final String LOG_DATASOURCE_INIT_ERROR_2 =
        "LOG_DATASOURCE_INIT_ERROR_2";
    public static String DEFAULT_DS_ERROR_MSG_0 =
        "DEFAULT_DS_ERROR_MSG_0";
}
```

A static declaration containing the name of the bundle appears first. The name will always match the package that the Java class is in. Next, is the static declaration and instantiation of the class. There needs to be only one instance of the class, as messages are a read-only resource. To further ensure that only one instance of the class is created, the default constructor is declared `private`. The next two methods return the class instance and the name of the bundle respectively.

Last in the class is the list of localized messages. The convention used to format the messages is to declare the message name as a string constant and to have the message value match the constant name. A localized message can then be retrieved through its message constant value, for example:

```
String msg = Messages.get().getBundle().
                   key(Messages.DEFAULT_DS_ERROR_MSG_0)
```

Looking at the variations of the `key` method on the `I_CmsMessageBundle` interface, we see that it supports the ability to parameterize the message string with up to three values. The convention used to format message keys is to append a numeral at the end, indicating the number of parameters in the message. This was done in the error handling of the widget's `setConfiguration` method to return the name of the class and the exception message:

```
Messages.get().getBundle().
key(Messages.LOG_DATASOURCE_INIT_ERROR_2, strClassName), e);
```

Relating message constant values to the message strings in the `messages.properties` file is easy. Each entry in the properties file is named according to the string value of the message constant:

```
# messages.properties for widget
DEFAULT_DS_ERROR_MSG_0           =
   Missing or incorrectly configured option value - please fix
LOG_DATASOURCE_INIT_ERROR_2      =
   Error instantiating DataSource object of class "{0}" - "{1}"
```

Parameterized messages are formatted using numbered macro placeholders, as shown previously.

Registering the Widget with OpenCms

The last step in creating the widget is to register it with OpenCms. Widgets are registered in the XML file located in the configuration directory:

```
<OPENCMS_INSTALL>\WEB-INF\config\opencms-vfs.xml
```

Extending OpenCms: Developing a Custom Widget

To add the widget, locate the `<WIDGETS>` section and add the widget definition:

```
<!-- Custom Widget -->
<widget
  class="com.deepthoughts.widgets.CmsCustomSourceSelectWidget"
  alias="CustomSourceSelectWidget"
/>
```

The class parameter contains the fully qualified class name of the widget. The alias is the name that will be used in the layout declaration of a schema file using the widget. Any changes made to the file will require a restart of OpenCms to take effect.

After compiling the code, deploying the class files and registering the widget it can finally be used. Here is an example of what a schema file using the widget will look like:

```
<layout
   element="Category"
   widget="CustomSourceSelectWidget"
   configuration=
     "source='com.deepthoughts.widgets.sources.ContentListDS'|
      contenttype='ValueList'|
      location='/Blogs/BlogCategories'|
      fieldname='Category'"
/>
```

The layout goes into the `blogentry.xsd` file we had created in Chapter 3. The declaration specifies that the `Category` field uses the `CustomSourceSelectWidget` widget. The `ContentListDS` class is specified as the data source and it uses a content type of `ValueList`. The resource instance of the `ValueList` content type is located at `/Blogs/BlogCategories` and the field within the content type containing the values is named `Category`. After making these changes to the schema file, the content editor will have a pull-down that obtains the values dynamically.

Summary

In this chapter, we talked about how to create a custom widget. We first covered the interfaces necessary to implement a widget and then went through the design of a widget for the blog content. After that, we went over the widget code and how to register a widget with OpenCms. Although the widget we developed is used to retrieve category values from a list, we've designed it to have broader use. It's an easy matter to configure the widget to read from a different resource containing different values or a different resource type altogether. The widget design allows for other data sources to be configured. In the next chapter, we will do this very thing and add another data source for the widget.

9
Extending OpenCms: Adding RSS Feed Support

In Chapter 7, we showed how to support incoming RSS feeds by integrating ROME. In this chapter, we will continue to extend the base OpenCms feature set by adding support for RSS feeds. To accomplish this, we will build upon our previous work, doing the following things:

- Create a new module to contain the RSS feed support.
- Create a new structured content type for feeds.
- Add a new data source for the custom widget built in Chapter 8.
- Create some templates to deliver the RSS content.

At the end of the chapter, we will have a new module that will contain the ability to create an RSS feed from any content type within OpenCms. We will then use the module to deliver the RSS feeds for our blog content.

RSS Feed Design

Let's start out by discussing the approach we will take to support RSS feeds. Although our immediate need is to create RSS feeds for the blog content, there are lots of other content types we may want to create RSS feeds for in the future. Rather than build a one-time solution specific to the blog site, we will take a generic approach to allow feeds to be defined by any structured content type. The new content type will contain metadata that defines the RSS feed. The required fields for an RSS channel can be found by looking at the RSS specification, which is located at: `http://www.rss-specifications.com/`. To support the RSS feeds, we expand upon the use of the ROME library introduced in Chapter 7. After looking at the specification and the ROME library, the design for the RSS Channel Definition content type looks like this:

RSS Channel Definition
Feed Title
Feed Description
Copyright (optional)
Author (optional)
Publication Date (optional)
Image (optional)
Image Title (optional)
Nested RSS Channel Source(s)

It includes the required RSS feed fields and some optional feed fields that we've opted to support. At the end of the content type there is a nested content definition which will define the VFS resources to be used as RSS feed items. The channel definition will allow for multiple VFS sources to be included in the RSS channel. Each nested RSS channel source definition has these fields:

RSS Channel Source
Source Content Type
Source Location
Max Feed Items
RSS Title Field Mapping
RSS Description Field Mapping
RSS Author Field Mapping

The first three fields are straightforward and describe the content type, its location in the VFS, and the maximum number of items to include. The remaining fields map the source content to each RSS field.

To allow any structured content type to be used as a feed source, there needs to be a way to map the source content item to a RSS field. The source content data fields can generally be lumped into three categories: metadata fields, property values, and content fields. Meta fields are accessible through the Java API and are partially exposed in the Workplace Explorer. These fields include:

- **User Created**: Name of the user that created the content item.
- **User Last Modified**: Name of the user who last modified the content item.
- **Date Content**: Contains the last modification date for the content item. This date applies to changes made to the content of the item, rather than its properties. If only properties are modified, then this value is not updated.
- **Date Created**: Contains the creation date for the content item.

- **Date Expired**: Contains the expiration date for the content item.
- **Date Last Modified**: Contains the last modification date for the content item. This value is updated when any change is made to the content, including just property value changes.
- **Date Released**: Contains the release date for the content item.

Property values come directly from global property definitions and are also available for inspection through the Workplace Explorer. The final category is the content fields, which only apply to structured content.

To allow the field values to be mapped, we will use a prefix to define the field source. For example, to map to a metadata field, the `meta` prefix will be used:

```
meta.UserCreated
meta.UserLastModified
meta.DateContent
meta.DateCreated
meta.DateExpired
meta.DateLastModified
meta.DateReleased
```

Likewise, the property value is mapped using the `property` prefix, followed by the name of the property:

```
property.NavText
```

Since properties values may be inherited from a parent folder, the + sign may be added to search for the property value on the parent:

```
Property.NavText+
```

Finally, the content fields are mapped using the `field` prefix. This is also followed by the name of the content field to be retrieved. For example:

```
field.BlogText
```

As RSS items are usually displayed as teasers, we will allow the field length to be limited by adding an additional size qualifier:

```
field.BlogText[200]
```

Additionally, the method used to trim the size may be controlled by adding a + or – to the end of the size qualifier. The indicator is used to prevent trimming in the middle of text by seeking the next logical break, in a forward or backward direction. This example would trim the field to 200 characters moving upward to the next word break:

```
field.BlogText[200+]
```

And this example would trim to 150 characters, trimming downward to the previous word break:

```
field.BlogText[150-]
```

Now that the design is all worked out, lets move on to writing the code.

The RSS Feed Content Type

The `RssChannelDef` structured content type will be used to contain the feed definition. The new type will be added to the `com.deepthoughts.rss` module that we had created in Chapter 7. When creating the file, remember that the XSD schema file for the content type must go into the **schemas** folder:

```
<!--     XSD file to define an RSS channel -->
<xsd:schema xmlns:xsd="http://www.w3.org/2001/XMLSchema"
            elementFormDefault="qualified">
  <xsd:include schemaLocation="opencms://opencms-xmlcontent.xsd"/>
  <xsd:include schemaLocation="opencms://system/modules/
          com.deepthoughts.rss/schemas/rsschannelsrc.xsd"/>
  <xsd:element name="RSSChannelDefs" type="OpenCmsRSSChannelDefs"/>
  <xsd:complexType name="OpenCmsRSSChannelDefs">
    <xsd:sequence>
      <xsd:element name="RSSChannelDef" type="OpenCmsRSSChannelDef"
                   minOccurs="0" maxOccurs="unbounded"/>
    </xsd:sequence>
  </xsd:complexType>
  <!-- Data field definitions -->
  <xsd:complexType name="OpenCmsRSSChannelDef">
    <xsd:sequence>
      <!-- Required Channel Fields -->
      <xsd:element name="Title" type="OpenCmsString"
                   minOccurs="1" maxOccurs="1" />
      <xsd:element name="Description" type="OpenCmsString"
                   minOccurs="1" maxOccurs="1" />
      <!-- Optional -->
      <xsd:element name="Copyright" type="OpenCmsString"
                   minOccurs="0" maxOccurs="1" />
      <xsd:element name="Author" type="OpenCmsString"
                   minOccurs="0" maxOccurs="1" />
      <xsd:element name="PublishDate" type="OpenCmsDateTime"
                   minOccurs="0" maxOccurs="1" />
      <xsd:element name="Image" type="OpenCmsVfsFile"
                   minOccurs="0" maxOccurs="1" />
      <xsd:element name="ImageTitle" type="OpenCmsString"
                   minOccurs="0" maxOccurs="1" />
```

```
            <xsd:element name="divider" type="OpenCmsString"
                        minOccurs="1" maxOccurs="1" />
            <!-- RSS Channel Sources -->
            <xsd:element name="ChannelSource"
                        type="OpenCmsRssChannelSrc".minOccurs="1"
                        maxOccurs="25" />
        </xsd:sequence>
        <xsd:attribute name="language" type="OpenCmsLocale"
                        use="optional"/>
    </xsd:complexType>
```

By now, the XSD schema file should look familiar. So let's skip down to the data fields in the top half of the file, which map directly to the design. The last data field contains the nested `RssChannelSrc` content type. This is used to define the RSS item sources, which we'll go over next. But first, let's look at the annotations section:

```
    <xsd:annotation>
        <xsd:appinfo>
            <!-- Mappings allow data fields to be mapped to content
                properties -->
            <mappings>
                <mapping element="Title" mapto="property:Title" />
                <mapping element="Description" mapto="property:Title" />
                <mapping element="PublishDate"
                        mapto="attribute:datereleased" />
            </mappings>
            <!-- Default values can be set for each field type -->
            <defaults>
                <default element="PublishDate" value="${currenttime}"/>
                <default element="divider" value="&lt;div
                        style='background:#f0f0f0; border:solid 1px
                        grey; border-radius: 1em; padding: 2px; font-
                        family:Segoe UI,trebuchet ms,arial,sans-
                        serif,tahoma,verdana; '&gt;
                &lt;b&gt;For RSS Title and Description Field Mappings,
                use this syntax:&lt;/b&gt;&lt;br&gt;&lt;pre&gt;
            To map to meta-value use:
            &lt;b&gt;meta.metaname&lt;/b&gt;&lt;br&gt;
                where metaname is one of the following: UserCreated,
                UserLastModified,&lt;br&gt;
                DateContent, DateCreated, DateExpired,
                DateLastModified, DateReleased&lt;br&gt;
                To map to a property value use:
                &lt;b&gt;property.propertyname+&lt;/b&gt;&lt;br&gt;
                where propertyname is any valid property&lt;br&gt;
                (adding the optional plus sign at the end will search
                the parent)&lt;br&gt;
```

Extending OpenCms: Adding RSS Feed Support

```
             To map to content field use:
             &lt;b&gt;field.fieldname[size+-]&lt;/b&gt;&lt;br&gt;
               where fieldname is the name of the content
               field&lt;br&gt;
               (adding the optional size will truncate the size in
               the feed listing)&lt;br&gt;
               use + to truncate up to the next period or
               end&lt;br&gt;
               or use - to truncate down&lt;/pre&gt;&lt;/div&gt;"/>
          </defaults>
          <!-- Layouts -->
          <layouts>
            <!-- Horizonal Rule for a divider -->
            <layout element="divider1" widget="DisplayWidget"/>
            <layout element="divider2" widget="DisplayWidget"/>
            <!-- Image picker -->
            <layout element="Image" widget="ImageGalleryWidget"/>
            <!-- List of Content Types -->
            <layout element="SourceContentType"
                    widget="CustomSourceSelectWidget"
              configuration="source='com.deepthoughts.widgets.
                sources.ContentTypesDS'|exclude='rsschanneldef'"/>
            <!-- Author Field Mapping -->
            <layout element="SourceAuthorField"
                    widget="SelectorWidget"
              configuration="meta.UserCreated:Use Created By
                Field|meta.UserLastModified:Use Updated By Field"/>
          </layouts>
          <!-- UI Localization -->
          <resourcebundle name="com.deepthoughts.rss.workplace"/>
          <!-- Previewing URI -->
          <preview uri="${previewtempfile}" />
        </xsd:appinfo>
      </xsd:annotation>
   </xsd:schema>
```

Here we see that the `Title` and the `Description` fields are mapped to their respective resource properties, and the `PublishDate` field is mapped to the `datereleased` attribute.

Next is the `defaults` section, containing initial values for some of the fields. First is the `PublishDate`, which is populated with the current time. Following this is a default value for the `divider` field. In the content editing form, this field can be used as a visual divider between the channel definition and channel source fields. Because the mapping syntax is difficult to remember, we will use a read-only field to contain the instructional text for the mapping fields. It is possible to use HTML in this field as long as valid XML is used. This means that XML entities must be used for any HTML brackets, as shown.

Finally, contained in the `layouts` section are the widgets used for editing the content fields.

 The read-only `DisplayWidget` is used to display the `divider` field.

Now let's return to the nested `RssChannelSrc` content field. The data field definitions for that content type look like:

```
<xsd:complexType name="OpenCmsRssChannelSrc">
    <xsd:sequence>
        <!-- Source specification -->
        <!-- XSD data type of the feed source -->
        <xsd:element name="SourceContentType"
                type="OpenCmsString".minOccurs="1" maxOccurs="1" />
        <!-- VFS file location of the feed source -->
        <xsd:element name="SourceLocation" type="OpenCmsVfsFile"
                minOccurs="1" maxOccurs="1" />
        <!-- Upper size limit -->
        <xsd:element name="FeedLimit".type="OpenCmsString"
                minOccurs="1" maxOccurs="1" />
        <!-- Source Field Mappings -->
        <xsd:element name="SourceTitleField" type="OpenCmsString"
                minOccurs="1" maxOccurs="1" />
        <xsd:element name="SourceDescField" type="OpenCmsString"
                minOccurs="1" maxOccurs="1" />
        <xsd:element name="SourceAuthorField".type="OpenCmsString"
                minOccurs="1" maxOccurs="1" />
    </xsd:sequence>
    <xsd:attribute name="language" type="OpenCmsLocale"
                use="optional"/>
</xsd:complexType>
```

Like its parent type, each field is mapped directly from the design. After creating the schema files and registering the new content type, as we had done in Chapter 3 for the Blog type, we can create new RSS Channel Definitions:

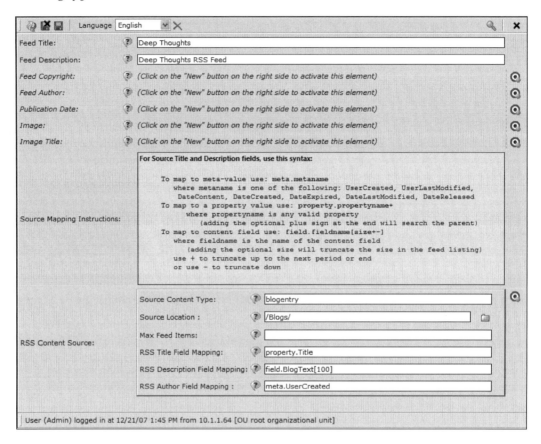

In the middle of the form is the clear instructional text followed by the content source definition instances. However, the form is not so good because the user needs to know the OpenCms name of the content type. We can improve the form by adding a widget which makes the content type selection easier.

One way to do this is to use a vanilla `CmsSelect` widget with a list of content types in the configuration string. The drawback to this approach is that if a new content type is introduced, the configuration string needs to be updated. A better approach is to build the list dynamically, which we can do by leveraging the `CustomSourceSelectWidget` from Chapter 8.

Creating a Supporting Widget

The new widget will use the framework created in Chapter 8 by defining a new data source. The data source will read the content types registered with OpenCms for presentation into a selection box. Recall that the framework allows new data sources to be added through implementing the `I_WidgetSelectSource` interface:

```
public class ContentTypesDS implements I_WidgetSelectSource {
    /** xmlpage content type */
    protected static final String XMLPAGE = "xmlpage";
    /** List of exclusions */
    Hashtable<String, String> m_htExclusions;
    public ContentTypesDS() {
       m_htExclusions = new Hashtable<String, String>();
    }
```

The class constructor allocates a list, which will be used for exclusions. The list of exclusions is obtained from the configuration string in the widget declaration, and contains content types that should not be included. This provides better control over the selection of content types.

The class file also has a constant for the `xmlpage` content type. The constant contains the name of the XML Page resource type and is used to handle a special case when obtaining the list of content types within the `getValues` method:

```
    public List getValues(CmsObject cms) {
        // list of return values
        ArrayList<SelectOptionValue> aVals = new
                                ArrayList<SelectOptionValue>();
        // get the message bundle for the workplace manager
       CmsMessages wpMessages = OpenCms.getWorkplaceManager().getMessages
                                (CmsLocaleManager.getDefaultLocale());
        // The XML Page is structured content, but is not 'derived' from
           xmlcontent, so we special case it
        if (null == m_htExclusions.get(XMLPAGE)) {
        // Only add it if it hasn't been excluded
        aVals.add(new SelectOptionValue(wpMessages.key
                                ("fileicon.xmlpage"), XMLPAGE));
}
        // get a list of all configured resource types from the explorer
           config file
        Iterator i = OpenCms.getWorkplaceManager().
                                getExplorerTypeSettings().iterator();
while (i.hasNext()) {
   CmsExplorerTypeSettings settings =
                                (CmsExplorerTypeSettings)i.next();
```

```
            // look for structured content types
            String strRef = settings.getReference();
            if (CmsStringUtil.isNotEmpty(strRef)) {
                    // we only care about structured content types (types
                    // that have a reference to 'xmlcontent')
                    if (strRef.equals("xmlcontent")) {
                    // and that can be created in the UI
                       if (CmsStringUtil.isEmpty
                                        (settings.getNewResourceUri())) {
                       // no 'new resource' URI specified, don't allow it
                        continue;
                       }
                       // don't add if it is excluded
                       if (null == m_htExclusions.get(settings.getName())) {
                       // add found setting to list
                       aVals.add(new SelectOptionValue(wpMessages.key
                                    (settings.getKey()), settings.getName()));
                       }
                    }
            }
       }
    }
    return aVals;
}
```

The method starts by using the `OpenCmsWorkplaceManager` class to retrieve its message bundle. Recall from Chapter 8 how a message bundle was created for the widget module. In this case, however, a message bundle from another package is being used. The bundle is later used to obtain the human readable names of the structured content types.

Next, the method adds the XML Page type to the return list if it has not been excluded. This type is used to handle a special case and is described in more detail in a bit. The remaining structured content types are obtained by using the `CmsWorkplaceManager` class to retrieve a list of resource types. This class manages the settings pertaining to the OpenCms Workplace Explorer. The settings include the resource type definitions contained in the `opencms-vfs.xml` and `opencms-modules.xml` configuration files.

From here, it is a simple matter of finding all types that reference the `xmlcontent` type. Recall from Chapter 3 that all structured content types are derived from this base type. The one exception to this is the XML Page content type which is a structured type not derived from `xmlcontent`. This type is included as it is very likely that RSS feeds will come from instances of this content type. Finally in the code, we see how the message bundle is used to convert the content type name to its human readable counterpart.

The `setConfiguration` method completes the data source definition:

```
public void setConfiguration(CustomSourceConfiguration config) {
    // read the list of exclusions
    String strExclusions = config.getConfigValue("exclude");
    if (null != strExclusions) {
        String[] parts = CmsStringUtil.splitAsArray(strExclusions,
                                                    ",");
        for (int i = 0; i < parts.length; i++) {
            String part = parts[i].trim();
            if (part.length() == 0) {
                // skip empty parts
                continue;
            }
            // add the type to the list
            m_htExclusions.put(part, part);
        }
    }
}
```

Here, the configuration string is parsed, and any content type that should be excluded is determined.

Going back to the content type definition, we see how the widget is declared in the `layouts` section.

```
<layouts>
    <!-- List of Content Types -->
    <layout element="SourceContentType"
            widget="CustomSourceSelectWidget"
            configuration= "source='com.deepthoughts.widgets.
                sources.ContentTypesDS'|exclude='rsschanneldef'"/>
    <!-- Author Field Mapping -->
    <layout element="SourceAuthorField"
            widget="SelectorWidget"
            configuration="meta.UserCreated:Use Created By
                Field|meta.UserLastModified:Use Updated By Field"/>
</layouts>
```

To make the form friendlier, a layout is also used for the `SourceAuthorfield`. The resulting dialog is now easier to use:

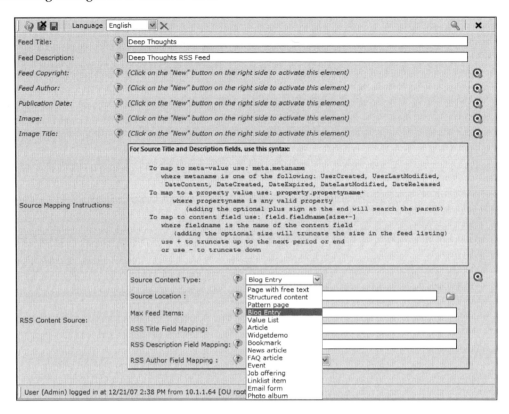

The source content type field automatically contains a list of available structured resource types, and will be updated whenever a new type is added to the system.

The RSS Feed Template and Java Classes

Now that RSS Channel Definitions can be created, the next step is to generate the RSS. A template is used for this, and the `template-elements` property of RSS content instances is used to specify it. As usual, the template goes into the **templates** folder of a module. Here is what the template code looks like:

```
<%@ page import="com.deepthoughts.rss.*" %>
<%
    // instantiate the RSS bean and get the feed
    RssFeedBean rss = new RssFeedBean(pageContext, request,
                                                 response);
    rss.getFeed();
%>
```

There is not much to it as all the work is done in the `RssFeedBean` Java class:

```
public class RssFeedBean extends CmsJspActionElement {
    /** URL parameter to specify the RSS feed format */
    public static final String PARAM_FEED_FORMAT = "fmt";
    /** the VFS path to the RssChannelDef instance */
    protected String m_strChannel;
    /** POJO to represent the channel definition */
    protected RssChannelDef m_rssChannelDef;
    /** Current feed format (defaults to RSS 2.0) */
    protected String m_strFormat = "rss_2.0";
    /**
    * Empty constructor, required for every JavaBean.
    */
    public RssFeedBean() {
       super();
    }
    public RssFeedBean(PageContext context,
         HttpServletRequest req, HttpServletResponse res) {
       super(context, req, res);
       m_strChannel =
              getCmsObject().getRequestContext().getUri();
       String strFormat = req.getParameter(PARAM_FEED_FORMAT);
       if (!StringUtils.isNull(strFormat)) {
         m_strFormat = strFormat;
       }
    }
}
```

The bean subclasses the familiar `CmsJspActionElement` bean used in the template code. After some constants and a default constructor there is a constructor for the servlet parameters. Since the bean is used in a template, the request URI will contain the path to the RSS Channel Definition content item that was clicked on. This path is saved into a class variable in the constructor. Since ROME supports a wide variety of feed formats, each one is supported through the use of a URL parameter. If present, the `fmt` parameter may be used to override the default 2.0 RSS feed format. The formats currently supported by ROME are:

- rss_0.9
- rss_0.92
- rss_0.93
- rss_0.94
- rss_1.0
- rss_2.0
- atom_0.3
- atom_1.0

Changing the feed format is a simple matter of setting the URL parameter. After the bean is constructed, the template calls a single method to return the RSS feed:

```
public void getFeed() throws JspException {
   try {
      m_rssChannelDef = new RssChannelDef(getCmsObject(),
                                          m_strChannel);
      // build the feed header
   SyndFeed rssFeed = new SyndFeedImpl();
   rssFeed.setFeedType(m_strFormat);
   // Title
   rssFeed.setTitle(m_rssChannelDef.getFeedTitle());
   // Link/URL
   String strLink = m_strChannel + "?" + PARAM_FEED_FORMAT + "=" +
                                          m_strFormat;
   rssFeed.setLink(link(strLink));
   // Description
   rssFeed.setDescription(m_rssChannelDef.getFeedDescription());
   // Channel Published Date
   rssFeed.setPublishedDate(new Date
                  (m_rssChannelDef.getPublishedDate()));
   // locale
   rssFeed.setLanguage(getLocale().toString());
   // Handle optional Fields
   // Image
   String strVal = m_rssChannelDef.getFeedImage();
   if (!StringUtils.isNull(strVal)) {
            SyndImage img = new SyndImageImpl();
            img.setUrl(link(strVal));
            img.setLink(link(strLink));
            strVal = m_rssChannelDef.getFeedImageTitle();
            if (!StringUtils.isNull(strVal)) {
               img.setTitle(strVal);
            }
            rssFeed.setImage(img);
      }
      // Copyright
      strVal = m_rssChannelDef.getFeedCopyright();
      if (!StringUtils.isNull(strVal)) {
         rssFeed.setCopyright(strVal);
      }
      // Author
      strVal = m_rssChannelDef.getAuthor();
      if (!StringUtils.isNull(strVal)) {
         rssFeed.setAuthor(strVal);
```

```
        }
        // get the entries for the feed
        rssFeed.setEntries(getFeedEntries());
        // write the output
           try {
                  SyndFeedOutput feedOutput = new SyndFeedOutput();
                  feedOutput.output(rssFeed, getResponse().getWriter());
           } catch (IOException e) {
              throw new JspException(e);
           } catch (FeedException e) {
              throw new JspException(e);
           }
    } catch (CmsException e) {
       throw new JspException(e);
    }
 }
```

The bulk of the method deals with the ROME library, which is well documented, and hence is not covered here. The key components of the class lie in the construction of the `RssChannelDef` object, and the population of the feed entries by using the `getFeedEntries` method. The `RssChannelDef` object is a Java class, which wraps the corresponding structured content instance. Though it is not necessary to create a corresponding Java class for new content types, it can make them easier to work with. We'll see the wrapper class later on, but for now, let's look at the method that retrieves the feed entries:

```
protected List getFeedEntries() throws CmsLoaderException {
// now build the feed items
List<SyndEntry> entries = new ArrayList<SyndEntry>();
// get the list of content sources
RssChannelSrc[] sources = m_rssChannelDef.getFeedSources();
// build items from each source
for (int i=0; i<sources.length; i++) {
    String strType = sources[i].getSourceContentType();
    int nResType = OpenCms.getResourceManager().getResourceType
                                      (strType).getTypeId();
    // this is the filter to use when reading the resource from the
    //specified source
    // a future enhancement would be to allow the filter to be a
    //parameter
    CmsResourceFilter filter = CmsResourceFilter.DEFAULT.
    addRequireType(nResType).addExcludeFlags
                            (CmsResource.FLAG_TEMPFILE);
    String strPath = sources[i].getRssItemSource();
    // in each location, read all the resources of the given type
```

Extending OpenCms: Adding RSS Feed Support

```
            try {
                // see if there is a limit specified for this channel
                //source
                int nLimit = sources[i].getSourceItemLimit();
                // read all the resources on the given path using the
                //filter
                List lstRssItems = getCmsObject().readResources(strPath,
                                                                filter);
                Iterator iterRss = lstRssItems.iterator();
                int nItem = 0;
                while (iterRss.hasNext()) {
                    if (nLimit > 0 && ++nItem > nLimit) {
                    // limit reached
                    break;
                    }
                    CmsResource res = (CmsResource) iterRss.next();
                    // convert the resource to the RSS item entry
                    entries.add(getEntryFromResource(sources[i], res));
                }
            } catch (CmsException e) {
                // TODO Auto-generated catch block
                e.printStackTrace();
            }
        }
        // return the RSS items
        return entries;
    }
```

After allocating an array to contain the returned items, the method gets a list of sources from the `RssChannelDef` object instance. Like the `RssChannelDef`, there is an `RssChannelSrc` wrapper class used to contain the RSS channel sources. The list of sources is then iterated over and converted to an RSS item.

Within the loop, each channel source is used to determine the location and the resource type to read the content from. The `CmsResourceFilter` class is used to specify how resources are read within each location. An improvement on the design would allow for each channel source to specify a filter. This is an exercise left to the reader.

Next, the resources are read and converted to RSS feed items, honoring any size limits that may have been set for the channel source. The last part of converting the resource to an RSS feed item is handled by the `getEntryFromResource` method:

```
    protected SyndEntry getEntryFromResource(RssChannelSrc src,
    CmsResource res) {
        // create the new entry
```

```
        SyndEntry entry = new SyndEntryImpl();
            // Entry Title
            entry.setTitle(src.getRssItemTitle(res));
            // Entry Link
            entry.setLink(link(getCmsObject().getSitePath(res)));
            // Entry Published Date
            entry.setPublishedDate(new Date
                            (m_rssChannelDef.getPublishedDate()));
            // Entry Updated Date
            entry.setUpdatedDate(new Date(res.getDateContent()));
            // Entry Description
        SyndContent description = new SyndContentImpl();
            description.setType("text/plain");
            description.setValue(src.getRssItemDescription(res));
        entry.setDescription(description);
            // Entry Author
            entry.setAuthor(src.getRssItemAuthor(res));
    return entry;
    }
```

The code is very straightforward, again using the ROME library to set the RSS item attributes. We can see how using the RssChannelSrc wrapper object to access content fields has made the method simple. Now, we can take a look at the two content wrapper classes.

Content Wrapper Java Classes

We've already seen how OpenCms makes it easy to create new structured content types and also provides a Java API to access the XML data in those content types. Sometimes, it is easier to create a Java wrapper class for the data types rather than use the XML API everywhere. The RssChannelDef class has been created to make it simpler to access the content within the RSS content type :

```
    public class RssChannelDef {
        /** The resource type id for the RSSChannelDef type */
        public static final int RSSCHANNELDEF_TYPEID = 3001;
        public static final String FIELD_CHANNELSOURCE = "ChannelSource";
        /** CmsObject */
        protected CmsObject m_cms;
        /** The CmsResource containing the rsschanneldef */
        protected CmsResource m_res;
        /** The un-marshalled rsschanneldef instance */
        protected I_CmsXmlDocument m_iDoc;
        /** contains the Rss Channel Sources */
```

```java
        private RssChannelSrc[] m_contentSources;
    /** data fields */
    private String m_title;
    private String m_Description;
    private String m_Copyright;
    private String m_Author;
    private String m_Image;
    private String m_ImageTitle;
    private long m_PublishedDate;
        public RssChannelDef(CmsObject cms) {
            m_cms = cms;
        }
        public RssChannelDef(CmsObject cms, CmsResource res) throws
                                                    CmsException {
            initFromResource(cms, res);
        }
        public RssChannelDef(CmsObject cms, String Path) throws
                                                    CmsException {
            initFromResource(cms, cms.readResource(Path));
        }
        private void initFromResource(CmsObject cms, CmsResource res)
                                                throws CmsException {
            m_cms = cms;
            m_res = res;
            // sanity check - make sure it is an rss channel definition
            if (m_res.getTypeId() != RSSCHANNELDEF_TYPEID) {
                throw new CmsException(Messages.get().container
                    (Messages.ERR_RESOURCE_NOT_RSS_1, res.getName()));
            }
            // populate the fields
            m_title = getField("Title");
            m_Description = getField("Description");
            m_Copyright = getField("Copyright");
            m_Author = getField("Author");
            m_Image = getField("Image");
            m_ImageTitle = getField("ImageTitle");
            m_PublishedDate = m_res.getDateReleased();
            // read the definition and parse it
            CmsFile rssDef = getCmsObject().readFile(m_res);
            m_iDoc = CmsXmlContentFactory.unmarshal
                            (getCmsObject(), rssDef);
            // read the list of sources
            int nSources = m_iDoc.getValues
                    (FIELD_CHANNELSOURCE, getLocale()).size();
            m_contentSources = new RssChannelSrc[nSources];
```

```
        for (int i = 0; i < nSources; i++) {
            String basePath = CmsXmlUtils.createXpath
                            (FIELD_CHANNELSOURCE, i+1);
            m_contentSources[i] = new RssChannelSrc
                        (getCmsObject(), m_iDoc, basePath);
        }
    }
```

The interesting part of the class starts with the `initFromResource` method. The method first ensures that the resource this class is constructed from, is indeed the correct content type. It then un-marshals, or parses, the resource content and saves it to a member variable. Later on, the member variable will be used to retrieve the content data fields. The method ends by creating an array of `RssChannelSrc` objects from the nested content.

The remainder of the class code consists of getter and setter methods, which is typical of a Java bean. The data field values are initially populated using the `getField` method:

```
    private String getField(String FieldName) {
        I_CmsXmlContentValue xml = m_iDoc.getValue(FieldName,
                                            getLocale());
        if (xml != null) {
            return xml.getStringValue(getCmsObject());
        }
        return null;
    }
```

Creating a bean wrapper class for XML content types can be useful in other situations as well. In the next chapter, we'll show how using a wrapper class makes it easier to access XML content types in an administration dialog screen.

The `RssChannelSrc` wrapper class is similar but slightly different because it is a nested content type. The class also provides support for handling the field mapping syntax defined earlier:

```
    public class RssChannelSrc {
        /** Date Format String */
        private static final DateFormat DATE_PARSER = new
                            SimpleDateFormat("yyyy-MM-dd");
        /** CmsObject */
        CmsObject m_cms;
        /** un-marshalled document */
        I_CmsXmlDocument m_iDoc;
        /** XML path to this nested content */
        String m_basePath;
        /** data fields */
```

```
            private String m_sourceContentType;
            private String m_sourceLocation;
            private String m_sourceTitleField;
            private String m_sourceDescField;
            private String m_sourceAuthorField;
            private String m_feedLimit;
            public final static String META_META = "meta.";
            public final static String META_PROPERTY = "property.";
            public final static String META_FIELD = "field.";
            public static final int DEFAULT_FEED_LIMIT = -1;
            public RssChannelSrc(CmsObject cms, I_CmsXmlDocument
                                             Doc, String Path) {
        m_cms = cms;
        m_iDoc = Doc;
        m_basePath = Path;
        m_sourceContentType = getField("SourceContentType");
        m_sourceLocation = getField("SourceLocation");
        m_sourceTitleField = getField("SourceTitleField");
        m_sourceDescField = getField("SourceDescField");
        m_sourceAuthorField = getField("SourceAuthorField");
        m_feedLimit = getField("FeedLimit");
    }
```

The constructor for the wrapper just saves the passed parameters for use later on and then initializes the data fields. The `getField` method implementation for this class differs slightly from the `RssChannelDef` method:

```
    private String getField(String FieldName) {
    try {
            return m_iDoc.getStringValue(m_cms, CmsXmlUtils.concatXpath
                                 (m_basePath, FieldName), getLocale());
        } catch (CmsXmlException e) {
           return StringUtils.NULLSTR;
        }
    }
```

Since this class represents a nested content item, the path to each field must contain the path from the parent content item. The parent name defined on the `RssChannelDef` content type is `ChannelSource`, so the path looks something like this:

```
    ChannelSource[1]/SourceContentType
```

The index value indicates the positional instance of the channel source within the parent. Each instance will have its own index.

Finally, to handle the mapped content fields like the RSS item title, the `getMappedfieldValue` method is used:

```
public String getRssItemTitle(CmsResource res) {
    return getMappedFieldValue(res,
                               getField("SourceTitleField"));
}
protected String getMappedFieldValue(CmsResource res, String
FieldName) {
String strField;
    try {
       if (0 == FieldName.indexOf(META_META)) {
          strField = FieldName.substring(META_META.length());
          return getMetaField(res, strField);
       } else if (0 == FieldName.indexOf(META_PROPERTY)) {
          // mapped to a property, values are read as specified
          strField =
             FieldName.substring(META_PROPERTY.length());
          CmsProperty prop =
             getCmsObject().readPropertyObject(res, strField, false);
          return prop.getValue();
       } else if (0 == FieldName.indexOf(META_FIELD)) {
          // mapped to a field, values are read as specified
          strField = FieldName.substring(META_FIELD.length());
          return getContentField(res, strField);
       }
    } catch (CmsException e) {
       return e.getMessage();
    }
    return StringUtils.NULLSTR;
}
```

This method parses the field specifier according to the input syntax and then retrieves its value accordingly.

The remaining class methods are related to string parsing of meta-field values and are hence not discussed in detail. The source code can be examined to get a better understanding of the remaining methods.

Wrapping It Up

At last we are done! The site blog content can now be easily served up as an RSS feed by creating an instance of an RSS Channel Definition somewhere. The RSS feed support we added is generic, supporting many content types. To create a feed from the blog content, the channel definition entry fields looks like this:

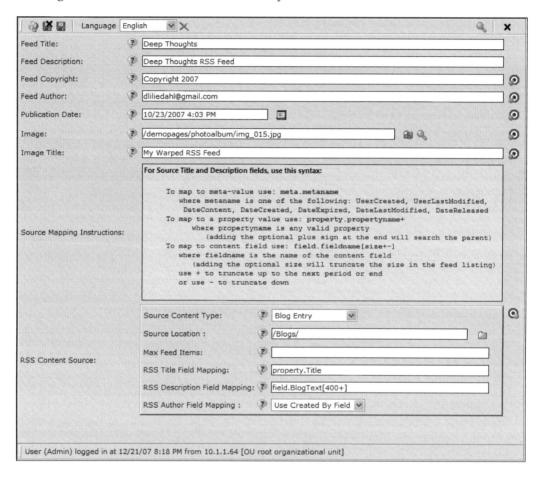

The channel definition can go into the /Blogs/ folder:

	Name	Title	Navigation Text	Type	Size
	2007-05	May 2007		folder	
	2007-06	June 2007		folder	
	2007-07	July 2007		folder	
	BlogCategories	A List containing Categories		valuelist	579
	DeepThoughts.rss	Deep Thoughts		rsschanneldef	2385

Chapter 9

To complete the site template, we just need to add a link to the channel definition file in the template code. For each RSS format we want to support, we just need to add a URL parameter with the format. The `rss_feed` element in the `common.jsp` file is where the change is made:

```
<%-- RSS Feed --%>
<cms:template element="rss_feed">
    <li class="widget widget_text" id="text-6">
        <h2 class="widgettitle">Subscribe</h2>
        <div class="textwidget">
        <br/>
          <ul>
             <a type="application/rss+xml"
                rel="alternate"
                title="Subscribe to my feed"
                href="<cms:link>/Blogs/DeepThoughts.rss?fmt=rss_0.9
                    </cms:link>"><img style="border: 0pt none ;"
                alt="RSS 0.9"
                src="<cms:link>/images/xml.gif</cms:link>">
                 RSS 0.9 Feed</a>
          </ul>
          <ul>
             <a type="application/rss+xml"
                rel="alternate"
                title="Subscribe to my feed"
                href="<cms:link>/Blogs/DeepThoughts.rss?fmt=rss_1.0
                    </cms:link>"><img style="border: 0pt none ;"
                alt="RSS 1.0"
                src="<cms:link>/images/xml.gif</cms:link>">
                 RSS 1.0 Feed</a>
          </ul>
          <ul>
             <a type="application/rss+xml"
                rel="alternate"
                title="Subscribe to my feed"
                href="<cms:link>/Blogs/DeepThoughts.rss</cms:link>">
                    <img style="border: 0pt none ;"
                alt="RSS 2.0"
                src="<cms:link>/images/xml.gif</cms:link>">
                 RSS 2.0 Feed</a>
          </ul>
          <ul>
             <a type="application/rss+xml"
```

```
                    rel="alternate"
                    title="Subscribe to my feed"
                    href="<cms:link>/Blogs/DeepThoughts.rss?fmt=atom_1.0
                        </cms:link>"><img style="border: 0pt none ;"
                    alt="Atom 1.0"
                    src="<cms:link>/images/xml.gif</cms:link>">
                     Atom 1.0. Feed</a>
            </ul>
        </div>
    </li>
</cms:template>
```

After adding the feed links and clicking on a feed, the resulting page looks like this:

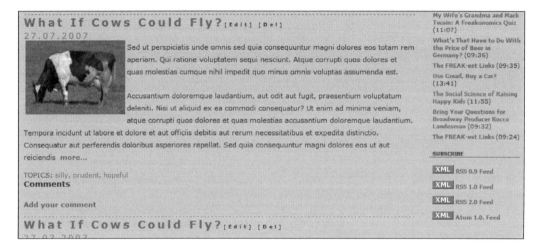

Site visitors can now subscribe to an RSS feed by clicking the RSS link or pasting it into their favorite RSS reader.

Summary

In this chapter, we've now shown how OpenCms can be extended to add new features. We created an example of this with an RSS feed module. The module introduced a new content type and added the capability to build an RSS feed from any OpenCms content type. We also built upon our last chapter by introducing a new widget. The widget leveraged the data source framework from Chapter 7, thereby adding a new data source type. The new data source returns a list of structured content types for use in editing forms. We wrapped up the chapter by showing how the module is used by the site template to support RSS content feeds for our site.

10
Extending OpenCms: Adding an Administration Point

In this final chapter, we will cover adding an Administration Point in the Workplace Explorer Administration View. The Administration Point will provide a way to manage the RSS feeds, for which we provided support in the previous chapter. Rather than create a new module for this, we will add the administration support into the existing RSS module. In this chapter, we will go over the following:

- How to create an Administration Point in OpenCms.
- Using OpenCms Dialogs to achieve a consistent look.
- How to programmatically use OpenCms widgets.

When we are done, the RSS module will have an administrative interface that has a native OpenCms look and feel.

Administrative Points

Administrative Points appear as icons in the Workplace Explorer Administration View. Several of these are provided with the default installation of OpenCms. Adding a new administrative point is a programming task, but is relatively straightforward. All Administration Points are read from folders located in the VFS under the **/system/workplace/admin/** location:

Extending OpenCms: Adding an Administration Point

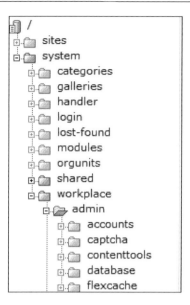

OpenCms constructs an icon in the Administration View for each folder in this location based on the property values present on the folder. It is important to note that the folders and properties are read from the Online project only. This means that any changes made to the Offline project must first be published, before they are visible. Also, the information is read only once and then cached. So, a server restart is also necessary.

The properties are used to control the text, icons, groups, and layout of the icons in the Administration view. The usage of the property values will vary slightly, based on where the administrative item is placed. The following table details the properties and their usage.

Property Name	Usage
Description	This property contains the help text that appears in the upper left of the administration view, when the administrative item is hovered over.
NavImage	This property contains paths to image icons for the administrative item. It may contain two icon paths separated by a colon. The first icon is used in the main view area on the right, and must be a 32x32 PNG or GIF image file. The second icon appears in the column area on the left, for top level administrative items only. Top level items are resources located directly in the **/system/workplace/admin/** folder. The specified icon must be a 20x20 PNG or GIF image. All icon images must reside underneath the **resources** folder in the OpenCms web application directory.

[240]

Property Name	Usage
NavInfo	This property contains the name of the administration icon group that the Administrative item is to be contained within. All items with the same group name will be grouped together according to the position specified in the **NavPos** property. OpenCms items are contained with a group named **Administration.**
NavPos	This property contains a numeric value that is used to order the icon within its group. Lower numbered items appear first, wrapping left to right, top to bottom. Groups of icons will also be ordered according to this numeric value.
NavText	This property contains the text that appears under the icon for the item in the main area. It may also contain text displayed as a subheading within the icons related administrative area. The subheading text within this property must be appended to the icon text and separated with a colon. If no subheading text is present, then the icon text is also used for the subheading.
Title	The title property is not used within the administration area, but it is a good practice to provide a useful title to make it easier to identify.
admintoolhandler-args	This property provides optional arguments that are passed to the admintoolhandler-class (described below).
admintoolhandler-class	This property contains the name of a class used to control the visibility and access of the administration tool. The class must implement the `I_CmsToolHandler` interface. There are several tool handlers located in the `org.opencms.workplace.tools` package, which may be used.
default-file	This property applies to folder items only. It may be used to provide the name of the default file, used for the given administration area. When the icon for the folder item is clicked on, OpenCms will run the specified file in addition to building any navigation groups. The output of the file will be displayed in the administration area, along with any groups that were found. If the property is empty, then the **index.jsp** will be used as the default file.

Since the Workplace interface is meant to support multiple locales, it is a good idea to localize the string values. This is easily done by placing the strings into the **workplace.properties** file within the module.

After creating the folder and applying the properties, the Administration Point can be implemented with a JSP file inside the folder. The simplest way is to write the JSP file to contain any forms or information necessary to administer the item. An example of this can be found by looking at the **index.jsp** in the **flexcache** admin folder.

Within an administration point, it is also possible to create further sub-groups, or administration items. A sub-group is created for each unique instance of the **NavGroup** property, found on all files or folders within the parent administration folder. A good example of this may be found by looking at the **contenttools** administration folder:

	Name	Title	Navigation Text
📁	change	Property Change	${key.GUI_CHANGEELEMENT_CONTE
📁	check	Content Check	${key.GUI_CHECKCONTENT_ADMIN_
📁	delete	Property Delete	${key.GUI_DELETEELEMENT_CONTEN
📁	merge	Merge Pages	${key.GUI_MERGE_CONTENTTOOLS_
📁	renameelement	Rename Element	${key.GUI_RENAMEELEMENT_CONTEN
📁	reports	Reports	
JSP	changeelementlocale.jsp	Change element locale	${key.GUI_CHANGEELEMENTLOCALE_
JSP	tagreplace.jsp	Replace HTML Tags	${key.GUI_TAGREPLACE_ADMIN_TO(
JSP	xmlcontentrepair.jsp	Repair XML contents	${key.GUI_XMLCONTENTREPAIR_ADN

The properties on the resources in this folder are used to form the administration screen for the Content Tools area. Each resource containing the appropriate properties will be represented in a group, with an associated icon. The resulting administration area looks like this:

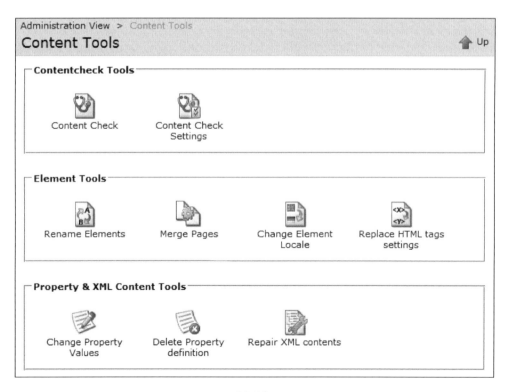

The administration area contains three icon groups. Since the parent **contenttools** folder does not have the **default-file** property set, OpenCms would normally use index.jsp to render the administration area. However, in this case, as the administration point does not contain the file, only the groups appear. If an index.jsp file were present, then its output would appear on the screen and it would be ordered with each group based on the **NavPos** property. Now that we have an understanding of how to structure Administration points, let's create one for the RSS feeds.

The Administration View

To make the RSS Feed Administration point look as if it were a part of OpenCms, it will have to be placed into the Administration icon group. The resulting **Administration View** would appear like this:

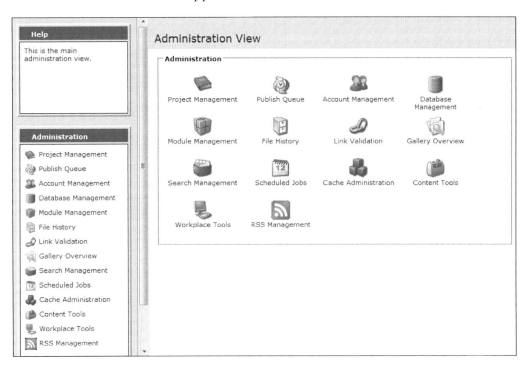

First, using the Workplace Explorer, create a new folder to contain the Administration Point:

/system/workplace/admin/rss

Then, set the following properties on the folder:

Property	Value	
Description	${key.GUI_RSS_ADMIN_TOOL_HELP_0}	☑
Keywords		☐
NavImage	tools/rss/icons/big/rssicon.png:tools/rss/icons/small/rssicon.png	☑
NavInfo	Administration	☑
NavPos	150.0	☑
NavText	${key.GUI_RSS_ADMIN_TOOL_NAVTEXT_0}:${key.GUI_RSS_ADMIN_TOOL_SUBTEXT_0}	☑
Title	RSS Feed Management	☑
admintoolhandler-args		☐
admintoolhandler-class	org.opencms.workplace.tools.CmsOnlyAdminToolHandler	☑

Here are the properties in detail:

- **Description**: This contains the text to appear in the help bubble.
- **NavImage**: This contains the path to two icons that have been created for the Administrative item. The two images are separated with a colon. As mentioned earlier, the images must be located on the physical file system under the resources directory. Later on, we'll go over how to include the images in the module.
- **NavInfo**: This contains the icon group for the administration point. To place the administration point in with the rest of the OpenCms items, the icon group named Administration is used.
- **NavPos**: This specifies the index of the item within the group. To ensure that the RSS item gets placed at the end of the group, we examine the value for the last icon and set a value that is higher. As the **workplace** icon, which is last, has a value **120.0**, we will use a higher value of **150.0**.
- **NavText**: Two text items are entered, again separated by a colon. The first is for the icon text and the second is for the subheading in the actual dialog.
- **admintoolhandler-class**: The specified handler ensures that the administration point is only available to users with the Administrator role.

Some of the properties accept macro notation. This allows the values to be localized in the workplace.properties file. The workplace.properties file should be located under the classes folder of the RSS module:

/system/modules/com.deepthoughts.rss/classes/com/deepthoughts/rss

Chapter 10

The relevant keys appear at the end of the property file:

```
#
# These properties are for the RSS Administration Point
#
GUI_RSS_ADMIN_TOOL_HELP_0 = Manage RSS Feeds
GUI_RSS_ADMIN_TOOL_NAVTEXT_0 = RSS Management
GUI_RSS_ADMIN_TOOL_SUBTEXT_0 = RSS Feed Management
```

Before we create the files needed to implement the administration point, we will create an `index.jsp` file, and put some text into it as a placeholder:

```
This is the JSP for the RSS Administration
```

After saving the JSP and publishing the folder, the server needs to be restarted. The new administration point should appear in the Administration View. As the initial index file is simple, clicking the icon will just display the text we created. Before going on to implementing the Administration point, we'll finish hooking it up to the RSS module.

Hooking the Administration Point Up to the Module

So far, the changes made have been to the VFS in the **/system** folder. To make the administration point portable, it will need to be placed into a module. This way it can be exported and later installed on other systems.

The first thing to take care of is the images used for the icons. This is done by just adding references to the necessary images from within the module. When the module is imported into another system, OpenCms conveniently exports the resources to the real file system.

The images are referenced in the **Module Resources** section of the RSS module. Note that there are also other VFS areas which are referenced:

One of the referenced areas is the administration point folder, added earlier. Also note that there is a reference to the **/system/shared/rssfeeds/** folder. This is the folder where RSS feeds that have to be managed by the RSS Administration point will reside. As the RSS capability has been added as a new system feature, the feeds are placed in a central location, rather than a site-specific location.

After adding the changes, exporting the module will cause the required administration point resources to get included along with it. Conversely, importing the module into another system will create the resources in the proper locations. Now that the basics are done, let's move on to implementing the administration point for the RSS module.

The RSS Administration Module

A quick and dirty administration handler can be easily created by adding a form and a handler to the **index.jsp** created earlier. But instead, we will create something that looks more integrated in order to maintain the OpenCms look and feel. Let's start with reviewing the features, which the administration panel will support.

The RSS administration panel will support the following tasks:

- Create new RSS feed containers (channels must be added manually).
- View details of existing RSS feeds.
- Edit existing RSS feed containers (no channel editing).
- Delete RSS feeds.
- Publish RSS Feeds.

To support these actions, the administration panel has to look like this:

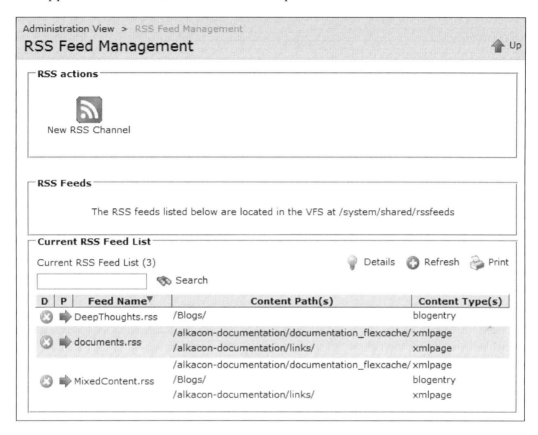

Extending OpenCms: Adding an Administration Point

At the top of the panel is an icon used to create new RSS channels. Underneath that there is a listing of the existing RSS feeds being managed. Each feed appearing in the list may be edited, deleted, or published. The list also supports searching and has the ability to show more details about each entry:

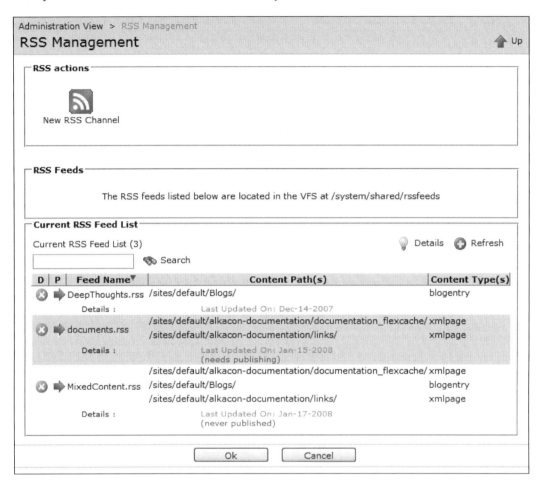

To support the screen layout, the administration point consists of two JSP files: `index.jsp` and `new_rsschannel.jsp`. The top icon group is created by the presence of the `new_rsschannel.jsp` file, as it contains the necessary navigation properties for an icon group. The bottom area of the screen including the **RSS Feeds** outlined area is created from the output of the `index.jsp` file.

The `new_rsschannel.jsp` file contains the following properties:

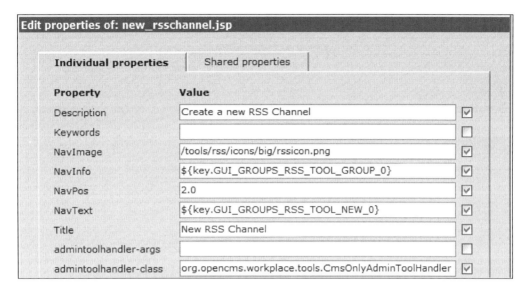

- **Description**: This appears in the navigation help area on the left.
- **NavImage**: This is the icon for the item. Since this item is not in the top level group, a small icon is not necessary.
- **NavInfo**: This contains the group name, 'RSS actions'.
- **NavPos**: If more than one item is present, then this would control the icon order.
- **NavText**: This is the text that appears under the icon.
- **admintoolhandler-class**: The CmsOnlyAdminToolHandler is used to ensure that only Administrators have access to the feature.

Let's look at the contents of each JSP file, starting with **index.jsp**:

```
<%@ page import="com.deepthoughts.rss.admin.* " %>
<%
    RSSFeedsList admin =
            new RSSFeedsList(pageContext, request, response);
    admin.displayDialog();
%>
```

There's not much to it; it is a simple wrapper around the `RSSFeedsList` class. This class is responsible for creating the entire user interface and does all the work. Let's take a closer look at it.

Leveraging the OpenCms Dialog Classes

OpenCms provides a number of dialog classes that are used by the administration screens. These classes provide a consistent look and feel and can be used by other administration points that want to have a more finished look. We'll use these classes in the RSS administration screens to make the screens look like OpenCms.

Declaring the Dialog

All dialog screens in OpenCms are based on the `CmsDialog` base class, which can be found in the `org.opencms.workplace` package. The `A_CmsListDialog` class is a more specific derivation of this class, which is designed to support list-style dialogs. We will subclass it with our own `RSSFeedsList` class to display the list of feeds:

```java
public class RSSFeedsList extends A_CmsListDialog {
    /** list id constant. */
    public static final String LIST_ID = "rssfi";
    /** list column name id constants */
    public static final String LIST_COLUMN_NAME = "cn";
    private static final String LIST_COLUMN_TYPE = "ct";
    private static final String LIST_COLUMN_PATH = "cp";
    public static final String LIST_COLUMN_EDIT = "ce";
    public static final String LIST_COLUMN_DELETE = "cd";
    public static final String LIST_COLUMN_PUBLISH = "cb";
    /** list column action id constants */
    public static final String LIST_ACTION_REFRESH = "rf";
    public static final String LIST_ACTION_DETAILS= "de";
    public static final String LIST_ACTION_EDIT = "ae";
    public static final String LIST_ACTION_DELETE = "ad";
    public static final String LIST_ACTION_PUBLISH = "ap";
    /**
     * Public constructor with JSP variables.<p>
     *
     * @param context the JSP page context
     * @param req the JSP request
     * @param res the JSP response
     */
    public RSSFeedsList(PageContext context, HttpServletRequest req,
                                            HttpServletResponse res) {
        super(new CmsJspActionElement(context, req, res),
           LIST_ID,
           Messages.get().container
                   (Messages.GUI_RSSFEEDS_LIST_DIALOG_GROUP_NAME_0),
           LIST_COLUMN_NAME,
           CmsListOrderEnum.ORDER_ASCENDING, null);
    }
```

Once again, the top of the class contains a few string constants. The first is an identifier for the list dialog. The value of this identifier must be unique across all dialog instances and is used in the constructor. Following the identifier are some more constants used for column names and column action codes. The names and action codes must also be unique, but only within the dialog instance.

After the constant declarations comes the class constructor. This passes along some parameters to the super class constructor. The first parameter contains an instance of a `CmsJspActionElement`, which the dialog will attach to. This is followed by the unique dialog identifier and then the name of the dialog. The dialog name text has been localized and is thus first retrieved from the Message bundle.

The next two parameters are used for sorting. To support sorting, the name of the sort column and the initial support order is specified. The last parameter is null, but may be used to specify a column name for searching. Later in the code, we will do this differently to support searching within all columns.

After the constructor is an override of the `initMessages` method, which is called upon to set any message strings.

```
protected void initMessages() {
   // add specific dialog resource bundle
   addMessages(Messages.get().getBundleName());
   super.initMessages();
}
```

To support localization, all user interface strings have been placed into a `Messages` class file. The messages are registered by calling the `addMessage` method. Subsequent user interface references to message strings will then be resolved from the message bundle.

Defining Dialog Columns

The next method contains a lengthy bit of code that defines the columns for the list dialog:

```
protected void setColumns(CmsListMetadata metadata) {
    // Create a column for deletion action
    CmsListColumnDefinition deleteCol = new CmsListColumnDefinition
                                        (LIST_COLUMN_DELETE);
    deleteCol.setName(Messages.get().container
                 (Messages.GUI_RSSFEEDS_LIST_COL_DELETE_0));
    deleteCol.setHelpText(Messages.get().container
                 (Messages.GUI_LIST_COLS_RSSDELETE_HELP_0));
    deleteCol.setWidth("20");
    deleteCol.setAlign(CmsListColumnAlignEnum.ALIGN_CENTER);
```

Extending OpenCms: Adding an Administration Point

```
            deleteCol.setSorteable(false);
            // add delete action
            CmsListDirectAction deleteAction = new CmsListDirectAction
                                        (LIST_ACTION_DELETE);
            deleteAction.setName(Messages.get().container
                    (Messages.GUI_RSSFEEDS_LIST_ACTION_DELETE_NAME_0));
            deleteAction.setHelpText(Messages.get().container
                    (Messages.GUI_RSSFEEDS_LIST_ACTION_DELETE_HELP_0));
            deleteAction.setConfirmationMessage
                    (new CmsMessageContainer(null, "Are you sure you want
                                to delete the selected RSS Channel?"));
            deleteAction.setIconPath(ICON_DELETE);
            deleteCol.addDirectAction(deleteAction);
            metadata.addColumn(deleteCol);
            // Create a column for publish action
            CmsListColumnDefinition publishCol = new CmsListColumnDefinition
                                        (LIST_COLUMN_PUBLISH);
            publishCol.setName(Messages.get().container
                        (Messages.GUI_RSSFEEDS_LIST_COL_PUBLISH_0));
            publishCol.setHelpText(Messages.get().container
                        (Messages.GUI_LIST_COLS_RSSPUBLISH_HELP_0));
            publishCol.setWidth("20");
            publishCol.setAlign(CmsListColumnAlignEnum.ALIGN_CENTER);
            publishCol.setSorteable(false);
            // add publish action
            CmsListDirectAction publishAction = new CmsListDirectAction
                                        (LIST_ACTION_PUBLISH);
            publishAction.setName(Messages.get().container
                    (Messages.GUI_RSSFEEDS_LIST_ACTION_PUBLISH_NAME_0));
            publishAction.setHelpText(Messages.get().container
                    (Messages.GUI_RSSFEEDS_LIST_ACTION_PUBLISH_HELP_0));
            publishAction.setConfirmationMessage(new CmsMessageContainer
                        (null, "Are you sure you want
                            to publish the selected RSS Channel?"));
            publishAction.setIconPath("list/rightarrow.png");
            publishCol.addDirectAction(publishAction);
            metadata.addColumn(publishCol);
            // add column for name
            CmsListColumnDefinition nameCol = new CmsListColumnDefinition
                                        (LIST_COLUMN_NAME);
            nameCol.setName(Messages.get().container
                        (Messages.GUI_RSSFEEDS_LIST_COL_NAME_0));
            nameCol.setWidth("33%");
            nameCol.setSorteable(true);
            nameCol.setHelpText(Messages.get().container
                            (Messages.GUI_LIST_COL_RSSEDIT_HELP_0));
```

```
        // Add edit action by clicking on it
        CmsListDefaultAction defEditAction = new CmsListDefaultAction
                                                    (LIST_ACTION_EDIT);
        nameCol.addDefaultAction(defEditAction);
        metadata.addColumn(nameCol);
        // add edit action
        CmsListDirectAction editAction = new CmsListDirectAction
                                                    (LIST_ACTION_EDIT);
        editAction.setName(Messages.get().container
                (Messages.GUI_RSSFEEDS_LIST_ACTION_EDIT_NAME_0));
        editAction.setHelpText(Messages.get().container
                    (Messages.GUI_RSSFEEDS_LIST_ACTION_EDIT_HELP_0));
        editAction.setIconPath(ICON_ADD);
        // Add column for content paths
        CmsListColumnDefinition pathCol = new CmsListColumnDefinition
                                                    (LIST_COLUMN_PATH);
        pathCol.setName(Messages.get().container
                            (Messages.GUI_RSSFEEDS_LIST_COL_PATH_0));
        pathCol.setWidth("33%");
        pathCol.setSorteable(true);
        metadata.addColumn(pathCol);
        // Add column for content types
        CmsListColumnDefinition typeCol = new CmsListColumnDefinition
                                                    (LIST_COLUMN_TYPE);
        typeCol.setName(Messages.get().container
                            (Messages.GUI_RSSFEEDS_LIST_COL_TYPE_0));
        typeCol.setWidth("33%");
        typeCol.setSorteable(true);
        metadata.addColumn(typeCol);
    }
```

The method receives a `CmsListMetadata` instance, which is to be populated with the column information. Each column is constructed from a `CmsListColumnDefinition` object, using the unique column id. Desired attributes are then set on the column object, such as a name, help text, alignment, or size.

A column may be set up only for display, or it may also have an action associated with it. An action is associated by constructing a `CmsListDirectAction` object with a column action code. The action is applied to the column by calling the `addDirectAction` method of the column object. The completed column definition is then added to the `CmsListMetadata` instance. When the action is fired, the associated action code can be used to differentiate between columns.

Returning the Column Data

The list dialog class retrieves column information through the `getListItems` method. This method is called whenever the list data needs to be refreshed:

```
    protected List getListItems() throws CmsException {
        List lstItems = new ArrayList();
        // get the list of RSS Feeds
        List lstFeeds = RSSFeedManager.getFeedManager
                                    (getCms()).getChannels();
          if (null != lstFeeds) {
          Iterator iFeeds = lstFeeds.iterator();
             while (iFeeds.hasNext()) {
                CmsResource feed = (CmsResource)iFeeds.next();
                RssChannelDef channel = new RssChannelDef
                                             (getCms(), feed);
               // name
                CmsListItem item = getList().newItem(channel.getName());
                item.set(LIST_COLUMN_NAME, channel.getName());
               // paths
                RssChannelSrc[] aSources = channel.getChannelSources();
                StringBuffer sbPath = new StringBuffer();
                StringBuffer sbType = new StringBuffer();
                for (int i=0; i<aSources.length; i++) {
                   sbPath.append(aSources[i].getSourceLocation());
                   sbPath.append("<p>");
                   item.set(LIST_COLUMN_PATH, sbPath.toString());
                   // type
                   sbType.append(aSources[i].getSourceContentType());
                   sbType.append("<p>");
                   item.set(LIST_COLUMN_TYPE, sbType.toString());
                }
                lstItems.add(item);
             }
          }
          return lstItems;
    }
```

The method must return a `List` of `CmsListItem` instances, each representing a row of data. The data for each column in the returned row is set by calling the `set` method with the column id and value. The RSS dialog uses the `RSSFeedManager` class to retrieve a list of all RSS feeds, which are then populated into the table. We'll go over the `RSSFeedManager` class a little later on.

Adding Column Actions

Dialogs derived from the `A_CmsListDialog` class can support single, multiple and independent actions on their list items.

Single Actions: These are performed on individual list items and are defined when the columns are defined in the `setColumns` method. The `executeListSingleActions` method is called when the action should be executed for the item.

Multiple Actions: These are actions that may be performed on more than one item at a time. Multiple actions may be defined with the `setMultiActions` method. When an action is performed for multiple items, the `executeListMultiactions` method will be called to perform the action.

Independent Actions: These are actions that may be performed without selecting any list items. These types of actions include things such as Refresh and Print and usually appear at the top of the list. Independent actions may be defined by using the `setIndependentActions` method. The `executeListIndepActions` method is called when an independent action needs to be executed.

Now that we know the rules, lets look at the code. We've already seen how to define single actions. So, look at how those actions get implemented:

```
public void executeListSingleActions() throws IOException,
                ServletException, CmsRuntimeException {
    // get the selected item row
    CmsListItem item = getSelectedItem();
    // get the name of the feed (VFS path)
    String strFeed = item.get(LIST_COLUMN_NAME).toString();
    if (getParamListAction().equals(LIST_ACTION_EDIT)) {
        // go to the 'new rss' page
        Map params = new HashMap();
        params.put("feed", strFeed);
        // set action parameter to initial dialog call
        params.put(CmsDialog.PARAM_ACTION, CmsDialog.DIALOG_INITIAL);
        getToolManager().jspForwardTool(this, getCurrentToolPath() +
                                    "/new_rsschannel", params);
    } else if (LIST_ACTION_DELETE.equals(getParamListAction())) {
        // delete the feed
        RSSFeedManager.getFeedManager(getCms()).deleteChannel
                                            (strFeed);
    } else if (LIST_ACTION_PUBLISH.equals(getParamListAction())) {
        // publish the feed
        RSSFeedManager.getFeedManager(getCms()).publishChannel
                                            (strFeed);
```

```
        refreshList();
    } else {
        throwListUnsupportedActionException();
    }
    // save any changes
    listSave();
}
```

This method is called when an action needs to be performed on a single item. Upon being called, the method obtains the item to take action on by calling getSelectedItem, which returns an instance of CmsListItem. The column values may be retrieved from the returned item.

The method determines which action to execute by looking at the return value of the getParamListAction method. The returned value may be compared with the constant action codes to determine the appropriate action. In our case, the actions for delete and publish are passed to the RSSFeedManager class.

The edit action is however different and forwards to the new_rsschannel.jsp item. This is explained later on. But note that a URL parameter, with the path to the item, is passed to the JSP. This will be used to differentiate between editing an existing item as against creating a new one.

For now, let's move on to the method handling the independent actions.

```
    protected void setIndependentActions(CmsListMetadata metadata) {
        // makes the list searchable by several columns
        CmsListSearchAction searchAction = new CmsListSearchAction
                    (metadata.getColumnDefinition(LIST_COLUMN_NAME));
        searchAction.addColumn(metadata.getColumnDefinition
                                            (LIST_COLUMN_PATH));
        searchAction.addColumn(metadata.getColumnDefinition
                                            (LIST_COLUMN_TYPE));
        metadata.setSearchAction(searchAction);
        // add feed details action
        CmsListItemDetails rssItemsDetails = new CmsListItemDetails
                                            (LIST_ACTION_DETAILS);
        rssItemsDetails.setAtColumn(LIST_COLUMN_NAME);
        rssItemsDetails.setVisible(false);
        rssItemsDetails.setShowActionName(Messages.get().container
                    (Messages.GUI_RSSFEEDS_SHOW_DETAIL_NAME_0));
        rssItemsDetails.setShowActionHelpText(Messages.get().container
                    (Messages.GUI_RSSFEEDS_SHOW_DETAIL_HELP_0));
        rssItemsDetails.setHideActionName(Messages.get().container
                    (Messages.GUI_RSSFEEDS_HIDE_DETAIL_NAME_0));
        rssItemsDetails.setHideActionHelpText(Messages.get().container
```

```
                        (Messages.GUI_RSSFEEDS_HIDE_DETAIL_HELP_0));
    rssItemsDetails.setName(Messages.get().container
                        (Messages.GUI_RSSFEEDS_DETAIL_NAME_0));
    rssItemsDetails.setFormatter(new CmsListItemDetailsFormatter
                        (Messages.get().container
                        (Messages.GUI_RSSFEEDS_DETAIL_NAME_0)));
    metadata.addItemDetails(rssItemsDetails);
    // add refresh action
    CmsListIndependentAction refreshAction = new
                        CmsListIndependentAction(LIST_ACTION_REFRESH);
    refreshAction.setName(Messages.get().container
                        (Messages.GUI_RSSFEEDS_REFRESH_NAME_0));
    refreshAction.setHelpText(Messages.get().container
                        (Messages.GUI_RSSFEEDS_REFRESH_HELP_0));
    refreshAction.setIconPath(ICON_MULTI_ADD);
    metadata.addIndependentAction(refreshAction);
}
```

This method is similar to the `setColumns` method, in that the information gets set into the `CmsListMetadata` object. Recall that in the constructor a search column for the list was not used. Doing so would have limited searching to just one column. Instead, multiple columns are supported by instantiating a `CmsListSearchAction` object with an initial column name and then adding the additional columns to it. The metadata is then updated with the definition.

The remaining code in the method adds an action to display a detailed view of the list, and another to perform a list refresh.

The next method handles the execution of the independent actions:

```
public void executeListIndepActions() {
    if (getParamListAction().equals(LIST_ACTION_REFRESH)){
       refreshList();
    }
    super.executeListIndepActions();
}
```

There's not much to it because it is handled elsewhere. Support for searching is handled by the base class, and the detailed view is handled by the `fillDetails` method:

```
protected void fillDetails(String detailId) {
    // get content
    List users = getList().getAllContent();
    Iterator itUsers = users.iterator();
    while (itUsers.hasNext()) {
```

Extending OpenCms: Adding an Administration Point

```
            CmsListItem item = (CmsListItem)itUsers.next();
            String feedName = item.get(LIST_COLUMN_NAME).toString();
            CmsResource feed;
            try {
              feed = getCms().readResource
                  (RSSFeedManager.getFeedRepositoryPath() + feedName);
              StringBuffer html = new StringBuffer(512);
              if (detailId.equals(LIST_ACTION_DETAILS)) {
                 SimpleDateFormat sdf = new SimpleDateFormat
                                                  ("MMM-dd-yyyy");
                 html.append("Last Updated On: ");
                 html.append(sdf.format(feed.getDateLastModified()));
                 html.append("<br>");
                 // has it changed since last publish?
                 if (feed.getState().isChanged() &&
                                          !feed.getState().isNew()) {
                    html.append("<font color='red'>(needs publishing)
                                 </font>");
                 } else if (feed.getState().isNew()) {
                    html.append("<font color='red'>(never published)
                                 </font>");
                 }
              } else {
                 continue;
              }
              item.set(detailId, html.toString());
            } catch (CmsException e1) {
              e1.printStackTrace();
            }
         }
      }
   }
```

This method is called iteratively by the super class for each item in the list. It then provides additional details on the item. The detail information is formatted as desired and appears in the row of the dialog.

Last is the implementation of multiple actions. Since our list dialog does not have any multiple actions, the code is very straightforward:

```
   protected void setMultiActions(CmsListMetadata metadata) {
       // not supported - do nothing
   }
   public void executeListMultiActions() throws IOException,
                                                 ServletException,
         CmsRuntimeException {
         // (we don't support any)
            throwListUnsupportedActionException();
      }
```

There are additional methods in the base class that may be overridden, if necessary. But, for most cases, these are the ones that must be implemented.

We've made the admin dialog a little fancier by including an informational bar at the top. This is supported through some custom HTML, another feature of the dialog classes.

Custom Rendering

To make the layout of the administration dialog a little better, the top of the dialog contains some informational text. This is added through the use of the `customHtmlStart` method. HTML can also be added to the end of the dialog by using the `customHtmlEnd` method. Both methods simply return a string containing the custom HTML:

```
protected String customHtmlStart() {
    StringBuffer result = new StringBuffer(512);
    result.append(dialogBlockStart(this.getMessages().key(
        Messages.GUI_RSSFEEDS_LIST_DIALOG_TITLE_NAME_0)));
    result.append("<br><center>The RSS feeds listed
        below are located in the VFS at /system/shared/rssfeeds
                    </center><br>");
    result.append(dialogBlockEnd());
    return result.toString();
    }
}
```

Although any HTML can be used, a more consistent look is achieved by using the `dialogBlockStart` and `dialogBlockEnd` methods. These cause the output to be framed in a box, consistent with the rest of OpenCms.

This completes the code for the RSS feed listing dialog. Before we move on to the other dialog areas, we'll take a look at the helper class referenced in the code.

The Feed Manager Class

To support the various actions that are performed in the administration screens, the `RSSFeedManager` class is used. The class makes it easier for the RSS administration dialogs to interact with the feeds and also abstracts the location of the feeds:

```
public class RSSFeedManager {
    /** VFS path to the rss feed repository */
    protected static final String FEED_REPOSITORY_PATH =
                                    "/system/shared/rssfeeds/";
    /** Resource type ID for RSS Feeds */
    protected static final int RSS_RESOURCE_TYPE_ID = 3001;
```

```
    /** Schema location */
    protected static final String RSS_SCHEMA =
                "/system/modules/com.deepthoughts.rss/
                            schemas/rsschanneldef.xsd";
    /** Reference to the CmsObject */
    protected CmsObject m_cms;
```

First are a few constants that define the RSS schema file, repository location, and resource type identifier. The RSS channels are managed in a shared folder location specified by the FEED_REPOSITORY_PATH constant.

Next is the constructor, along with some property access methods:

```
    public static RSSFeedManager getFeedManager(CmsObject cms) {
        return new RSSFeedManager(cms);
    }
    public RSSFeedManager(CmsObject cms) {
        m_cms = cms;
    }
    public static String getFeedRepositoryPath() {
        return RSSFeedManager.FEED_REPOSITORY_PATH;
    }

    public static String getFullName(String Feed) {
        return getFeedRepositoryPath() + Feed;
    }
```

The CmsObject passed to the constructor is used to initialize the returned instance. It is required to allow the class to interact with the VFS later on.

Supporting the Feed Operations

The remaining methods of the class support the various actions that may be performed on a feed channel. The first one returns a list of channels in the repository:

```
    public List getChannels () {
        // Use the collector to obtain a list of resources
        String collectorName = "allInFolderDateReleasedDesc";
        try {
           // now collect the resources
           I_CmsResourceCollector collector =
                            OpenCms.getResourceManager().
               getContentCollector(collectorName);
               if (null == collector) {
               throw new CmsException(Messages.get().container
                   (Messages.ERR_COLLECTOR_NOT_FOUND_1,collectorName));
```

```
        }
        // get list of feeds in the repository
        List collectorResult = collector.getResults(m_cms,
            collectorName, FEED_REPOSITORY_PATH + "|" +
            Integer.toString(RSSFeedManager.RSS_RESOURCE_TYPE_ID));
        return collectorResult;
    } catch (CmsException e) {
        e.printStackTrace();
    }
    return null;
}
```

The OpenCms collector interface is used to retrieve the resources, returning them on a list. This interface is used in a fashion similar to that used for retrieving the blog content in the template code.

Next is the support for deleting a channel:

```
public void deleteChannel(String Channel) {
    try {
        String resName = RSSFeedManager.getFullName(Channel);
        getLock(resName);
        // ensure resource is locked
        // delete it
        m_cms.deleteResource(RSSFeedManager.getFullName(Channel),
                             CmsResource.DELETE_PRESERVE_SIBLINGS);
    } catch (CmsException e) {
        e.printStackTrace();
    }
}
```

The code simply uses the `deleteResource` method to remove the specified resource. Note that the code ensures that the resource is first locked by calling the `getLock` method. This method checks to see if the file is locked by someone else, and if so, steals the lock:

```
protected void getLock(String Channel) throws CmsException {
    CmsLock lock = m_cms.getLock(Channel);
    if (!m_cms.getLock(Channel).isUnlocked()) {
        // steal lock
        m_cms.changeLock(Channel);
    } else {
        // lock resource to current user
        m_cms.lockResource(Channel);
    }
}
```

Extending OpenCms: Adding an Administration Point

Ensuring that the resource is locked is required for successful deletion.

Next is a method used to save or update changes made to a channel. This method accepts an instance of the `RssChannelDef` and writes it to the VFS as an XML content item. If the resource exists, then it is updated; otherwise it is created.

```
public void saveOrUpdateChannel(PageContext ctx,
    RssChannelDef Channel) {
try {
    String resName =
        RSSFeedManager.getFullName(Channel.getFilename());
    // if it exists then read the content
    // otherwise create a new one
    CmsXmlContent xmlContent;
    boolean bExists;
    try {
        CmsResource res = m_cms.readFile(resName);
        bExists = true;
        xmlContent = CmsXmlContentFactory.unmarshal(m_cms,
                                        res, ctx.getRequest());
    } catch (CmsException e) {
        bExists = false;
        // get the schema definition
        CmsXmlContentDefinition contentDefinition =
                CmsXmlContentDefinition.unmarshal(m_cms, RSS_SCHEMA);
        // create and instance of the XML content
        xmlContent =
                CmsXmlContentFactory.createDocument(m_cms,
                m_cms.getRequestContext().getLocale(),
                OpenCms.getSystemInfo().getDefaultEncoding(),
                contentDefinition);
    }.
    // set the field values into the content
    addOrUpdateFieldIfNonNull(xmlContent, "Title",
                                    Channel.getTitle());
    addOrUpdateFieldIfNonNull(xmlContent, "Description",
                                    Channel.getDescription());
    addOrUpdateFieldIfNonNull(xmlContent, "Copyright",
                                    Channel.getCopyright());
    addOrUpdateFieldIfNonNull(xmlContent, "Author",
                                    Channel.getAuthor());
    addOrUpdateFieldIfNonNull(xmlContent, "PublishDate",
                Long.toString(Channel.getPublishedDate()));
    addOrUpdateFieldIfNonNull(xmlContent, "Image",
                                    Channel.getImage());
    addOrUpdateFieldIfNonNull(xmlContent, "ImageTitle",
                                    Channel.getImageTitle());
```

```
        // set the title and description properties
        List properties = new ArrayList(2);
        CmsProperty prop = new CmsProperty();
        prop.setName(CmsPropertyDefinition.PROPERTY_TITLE);
        prop.setValue(Channel.getTitle(),
                        CmsProperty.TYPE_INDIVIDUAL);
        properties.add(prop);
        prop = new CmsProperty();
        prop.setName(CmsPropertyDefinition.PROPERTY_DESCRIPTION);
        prop.setValue(Channel.getDescription(),
                        CmsProperty.TYPE_INDIVIDUAL);
        properties.add(prop);
        // now we save the changes to the content
        String decodedContent = xmlContent.toString();
        try {
           if (bExists) {
              CmsFile docFile = xmlContent.getFile();
              docFile.setContents(decodedContent.getBytes(
                   CmsEncoder.lookupEncoding("UTF-8", "UTF-8")));
              getLock(resName);
              m_cms.writeFile(docFile);
              m_cms.unlockResource(resName);
           } else {
              m_cms.createResource(resName,
                   RSS_RESOURCE_TYPE_ID, decodedContent.getBytes(
                   CmsEncoder.lookupEncoding("UTF-8", "UTF-8")),
                                                  properties);
           }.
        } catch (UnsupportedEncodingException e) {
           e.printStackTrace();
        }
    } catch (CmsIllegalArgumentException e) {
      e.printStackTrace();
    } catch (CmsException e) {
      e.printStackTrace();
    }
  }
}
```

The top of the method obtains an instance of a CmsXmlContent item. It first tries to read the existing item based on the resource name. If this fails, then it assumes that the resource does not exist and creates a new instance of the resource. Note that in the case of reading the resource, the CmsXmlContent item is obtained directly from calling the unmarshal method. This differs from the creation case, where the content definition needs to be obtained first before a new instance of the document can be created. In both cases, we end up with the content instance.

Next, the method populates the `CmsXmlContent` item instance with the data from the `RssChannelDef`. To handle the situation where it is overwriting an existing field or adding a new field, it uses the `addOrUpdateFieldIfNonNull` method:

```
protected void addOrUpdateFieldIfNonNull(
    CmsXmlContent iContent, String Fieldname, String newVal) {
    // first try to read back the value
    I_CmsXmlContentValue curVal = iContent.getValue(Fieldname,
    m_cms.getRequestContext().getLocale());
    if (null != curVal) {
        // field is already there so update it
        curVal.setStringValue(m_cms, newVal);
    } else {
        // no existing field, only set one if a value is
        // provided
        if (null != newVal) {
            curVal = iContent.addValue(m_cms, Fieldname,
            m_cms.getRequestContext().getLocale(), 0);
            curVal.setStringValue(m_cms, newVal);
        }
    }
}
```

This is a small but useful method that sets the value into the given field of the XML content, but only if it is not null.

Going back to the method, we see that it sets the property values and ends by saving the resource to the VFS. Note that here it also saves the contents differently, based on whether an existing resource is updated or a new one is created. More robust error handling is left as an exercise for the reader.

The last method in the class supports publishing the channel. This method utilizes the `CmsPublishManager` class to do the work:

```
public void publishChannel(String Channel) {
    try {
        // publish the Channel
        CmsPublishManager pm = OpenCms.getPublishManager();
        pm.publishResource(m_cms,
                    RSSFeedManager.getFullName(Channel));
    } catch (Exception e) {
        // print out stack trace in case of error
        e.printStackTrace();
    }
}
```

In case of an error, a stack trace is printed out. More sophisticated error handling can be added if desired.

The New Channel Action

Now let's move on to the other area of the RSS Administration screen, which handles the creation of new feeds. Invoking this action creates two successive dialog pages. The first page contains a form that looks similar to the RSS Channel editor:

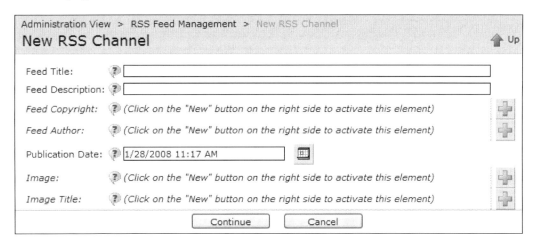

Clicking on the **Continue** button will invoke a second dialog page, which contains a single field for specifying the RSS feed filename:

The **Back** button may be used to return to the previous page to make changes. The code for this dialog is contained in the `new_rsschannel.jsp` file.

```
<%@ page import="com.deepthoughts.rss.admin.*" %>
<%
    RSSNewChannelDialog admin =
        new RSSNewChannelDialog(pageContext, request, response);
    admin.displayDialog();
%>
```

As in the `index.jsp` file seen earlier, this file is also a thin wrapper around a Java class.

Declaring the Dialog

As in the list dialog, the `RSSNewChannelDialog` is derived from the `CmsDialog` base class. The class is a subclass of the `CmsWidgetDialog` class, which gives it the ability to programmatically use widgets. It also has the ability to contain multiple pages. Let's take a look:

```
public class RSSNewChannelDialog extends CmsWidgetDialog {
    public static final String KEY_PREFIX = "rssadmin";
    public static final String[] PAGE_ARRAY =
                        {"channel_info", "channel_name"};
    public static final List PAGE_LIST =
                        Arrays.asList(PAGE_ARRAY);
    RssChannelDef m_channel;
    String infoText;

public String getInfoText() {
    return infoText;
}
public void setInfoText(String infoText) {
    this.infoText = infoText;
}
```

Again, we start with the constants. The first constant is used to define a key prefix for localized messages. This will prevent duplicate keys in other modules from being used, while retrieving strings for this dialog. For this reason, it is important for this key to be unique among all the dialog instances. Following this is an array and a list defining the pages making up the dialog. Each page must have a unique name within this dialog.

Last are some data members, including an instance of the `RSSChannelDef` class, and some informational text. The text has associated getter and setter methods, allowing it to be accessed as a property. The constructor comes next:

```
public RSSNewChannelDialog(PageContext context,
        HttpServletRequest req, HttpServletResponse res) {
    super(new CmsJspActionElement(context, req, res));
}
protected String[] getPageArray() {
    return PAGE_ARRAY;
}
protected void initMessages() {
    // add default resource bundles
    addMessages(Messages.get().getBundleName());
    super.initMessages();
}
```

The required `getPageArray` method must return an array of the dialog pages declared earlier. This is followed by the `initMessages` method, which is the same as the one for the list dialog covered earlier. Remember that messages are contained in the **messages.properties** file, and that message keys are prefixed with the `KEY_PREFIX` value. Here is a sample of what the message file looks like:

```
label.rssadmin.title = Feed Title
label.rssadmin.desription = Feed Description
label.rssadmin.copyright = Feed Copyright
Label.rssadmin.title.help = Enter the title for this RSS feed
Label.rssadmin.desription.help = Enter a description for this RSS
                                                              feed
```

The message strings used are the same as they are for structured content covered earlier. Like a structured content type, widgets can also be used in Java-based dialogs. Let's take a look at how to declare them for use in a Java dialog.

Declaring the Widgets

We've used the the `CmsWidgetDialog` class because it supports the same widgets that are used by the structured content editors. Defining the widgets is straightforward and is done through subclassing the `defineWidgets` method:

```
protected void defineWidgets() {
    getDialogData();
    // Page 1
    addWidget(new CmsWidgetDialogParameter(m_channel,
                "title", PAGE_ARRAY[0], new CmsInputWidget()));
    addWidget(new CmsWidgetDialogParameter(m_channel,
                "description", PAGE_ARRAY[0], new CmsInputWidget()));
    addWidget(new CmsWidgetDialogParameter(m_channel,
                            "copyright", null, PAGE_ARRAY[0],
                               new CmsInputWidget(), 0, 1 ));
    addWidget(new CmsWidgetDialogParameter(m_channel,
                              "author", null, PAGE_ARRAY[0],
                               new CmsInputWidget(), 0, 1 ));
    addWidget(new CmsWidgetDialogParameter(m_channel,
                        "publishedDate", null, PAGE_ARRAY[0],
                           new CmsCalendarWidget(), 0, 1));
    addWidget(new CmsWidgetDialogParameter(m_channel,
                               "image", null, PAGE_ARRAY[0],
                             new CmsVfsFileWidget(), 0, 1));
    addWidget(new CmsWidgetDialogParameter(m_channel,
                          "imageTitle", null, PAGE_ARRAY[0],
                              new CmsInputWidget(), 0, 1));
    // Page 2
    infoText = "Please enter a file name for this channel";
```

```
    addWidget(new CmsWidgetDialogParameter(this,
          "infoText", null, PAGE_ARRAY[1], new CmsDisplayWidget()));
    addWidget(new CmsWidgetDialogParameter(m_channel,
          "filename", null, PAGE_ARRAY[1], new CmsInputWidget()));
}
```

The method starts by making a call to the local `getDialogData` method, which we will skip for the moment. Next, it calls the `addWidget` method for each field being edited. This method utilizes Java reflection to access the data field and accepts a widget class to be used for editing that field. The method also accepts a dialog page name where the widget will appear. Next, we'll take a look at how data is handled within the dialog.

Persisting Data Across Pages

We've seen in the screens and the code that the dialog supports multiple pages. To handle this, the state from a previous screen needs to be saved and then restored when going to the next page.

Fortunately, this is made easy with the `initWorkplaceRequestValues` method. This method is implemented in the base class and is called each time the dialog is instantiated. Each new screen causes a new instantiation of the dialog, and hence a call to this method:

```
protected void initWorkplaceRequestValues(
        CmsWorkplaceSettings settings, HttpServletRequest request) {
    // set the dialog message prefix
    setKeyPrefix(KEY_PREFIX);
    super.initWorkplaceRequestValues(settings, request);
    // save the current state of the job
    setDialogObject(m_channel);
}
```

First, the message key prefix is established to ensure that subsequent widget instantiations get the correct message strings. The base class implementation is then called, as no changes to its behavior are needed. It may be useful to take a look at the code to see the base class implementation. By calling the base class, a call to the `defineWidgets` method, which we looked at in the above section, will get called. This is where the widgets will get added to the screen.

The method ends by calling the `setDialogObject` method. This method is used to save the state of the dialog data between screen changes. `CmsWidgetDialog`-based classes may use the `getDialogObject` and `setDialogObject` methods for managing state information. The methods manage the state information in a `Map` that is stored in the user session. Data placed into the `Map` is keyed and may be retrieved using the class name of the dialog.

In the case of the RSS administration dialog, there are several cases that need to be handled to manage the m_channel data. This is because the dialog supports the creation of new channels, as well as editing existing ones. Recall that the list dialog uses the JSP new_rsschannel.jsp as an action, when a channel is clicked on. In addition to this, the dialog has to handle multiple screens. All these cases are handled by the getDialogData method that was skipped over earlier:

```
private void getDialogData() {
    Object o = getSettings().getDialogObject();
    if (null == o) {
       // first time, handle edit or new
       // either a new channel or invoked from 'edit'
       if (! editChannelClicked()) {
          m_channel = new RssChannelDef(getCms());
       }
    } else {
       // non-null dialog object, retrieve bean from state
       Object existingChannel =
                 ((Hashtable)o).get(this.getClass().getName());
       if (null != existingChannel) {
          m_channel = (RssChannelDef) existingChannel;
       } else {
          if (! editChannelClicked()) {
             m_channel = new RssChannelDef(getCms());
          }
       }
    }
}
```

The method first checks to see if the dialog data has been set. If not present, then another helper method is used to determine if the edit channel action was invoked. If not, then it must mean that a new channel action was invoked, and thus a new data member is instantiated.

If data has been set, then it is returned as an Object instance. The object instance is a Map containing the persisted data for all dialog classes. Each dialog class obtains its persisted data using a key matching the dialog's class name. The returned data is then cast to the proper type, and the data field is updated. The final case handled is when there is a previous state, but the user has clicked on the edit action.

Both cases use a helper method to deal with the edit channel action:

```
private boolean editChannelClicked() {
    String strFeed =
               getJsp().getRequest().getParameter("feed");
    if (null != strFeed) {
       try {
          // load the channel into the bean
```

```
            m_channel = new RssChannelDef(getCms(),
                RSSFeedManager.getFeedRepositoryPath() + strFeed);
            return true;
        } catch (CmsException e) {
            e.printStackTrace();
        }
    }
    return false;
}
```

Recall that each item in the list was constructed with a URL parameter named `feed`. This method simply detects the parameter, and instantiates the data field using the path to the corresponding channel.

Handling the Dialog Actions

The last action to handle is the dialog **OK** action, which is taken care of with the `actionCommit` method:

```
public void actionCommit() throws IOException,
    ServletException {
    // Save the channel
    RSSFeedManager.getFeedManager(getCms()).
            saveOrUpdateChannel(getJsp().getJspContext(),
                                            m_channel);
    // clear the object
    getSettings().setDialogObject(null);
    m_channel = null;
}
```

The `RSSFeedManager` class is used to save or update the changes. Since the action returns to the main RSS administration area, the dialog state and channel data is also cleaned up here.

Summary

We've now seen how to extend OpenCms by adding an administration point. We've shown how to define a new administration point and the various parameters used to control the user interface. We also went over how to tie the administration point to a module, to obtain portability. In implementing the administration point, we've gone over how OpenCms dialog classes can be leveraged to get a more integrated look. The administration dialog we covered also illustrated how to create multiple screens, and how to manage state information across the screens. Finally, we covered how to localize the dialogs, and how widgets can be used.

Index

A

account management page
　about 196, 197
　Manage.jsp, adding 196, 197
additional widgets, schema features
　OrgUnitWidget 80
　PasswordWidget 80
　PrincipalWidget 80
　RadioSelectWidget 79
administration view
　about 243
　properties, setting 244
administration view, properties
　admintoolhandler-class 244
　description 244
　NavImage 244
　NavInfo 244
　NavPos 244
　NavText 244
administrative points
　about 239
　adding 239
　content tools 242, 243
　hooking up to module 245
　module resources 245, 246
　properties 240
　sub-group 242
administrative points, properties
　admintoolhandler-args 241
　admintoolhandler-class 241
　default-file 241
　NavImage 240
　NavInfo 241
　NavPos 241
　NavText 241
　Title 241
Ant
　OpenCms, building 44

C

comments
　AddComment.jsp 180
　addcommentAction 180
　adding 179
　adding, to XML content 181-183
　comment support, adding 178
　publishing 183
comments, publishing
　CommentPublisher 184
common code elements, templates
　about 100, 101
　advertisements 102
　blog archives 103, 104
　footer element 106
　header code 101
　RSS client 105
　RSS feeds 105
　search form code 102
　URL, blog archives 104
configuring, OpenCms search index
　additional settings 136
　analyzer setting 136
　Blogs-Offline 128
　content mapping 129
　dirctory setting 136
　document type setting 136
　excerpt setting 136
　extractCacheMaxAge setting 136
　field, settings 128, 129
　field configuration 128

field configuration, creating 130
field configurations 128
forceunlock setting 136
highlighter setting 136
index source, creating 133-135
item mapping 129
locale 128
Luke 137
mappings, fields 129
project 128
property-search mapping 129
property mapping 129
rebuild mode 128
standard configuration 130
timeout setting 136

content
creating 90-94

custom widget
creating 199
getConfiguration method 200
interface, implementing 200
newInstance method 199
setConfiguration method 199
widget Dialogs methods 200
widget value, getting 200
widget value, setting 200

D

developer skills, site
basic development 12, 13
custom content types 13
custom development 14
custom features 14

directory structure, OpenCms
classes, WEB-INF 16
config, WEB-INF 16
directories, real file system layout 16
export 17
imageCache, WEB-INF 17
index, WEB-INF 17
jsp, WEB-INF 17
META-INF 17
opencms-importexport.xml, config 16
opencms-modules.xml, config 16
opencms-search.xml, config 16

opencms-system.xml, config 16
opencms-vfs.xml, config 16
opencms-workplace.xml, config 16
opencms.properties,config 16
opencms.xml, config 16
packages, WEB-INF 17
real file system layout 15
resources 17
setup 17
setupdata, WEB-INF 17
sites, virtual file system layout 18
system, virtual file system layout 18
virtual file system layout 18
WEB-INF 16

E

Eclipse
environment setup, to build OpenCms 33
environment setup, without building OpenCms 46

Eclipse environment setup, OpenCms
Ant tasks 44
Apache Ant 1.70, tools 33
classpath, setting for compilation 40
distribution package building, ANT used 41-43
Eclipse WTP 1.5.4, tools 34
OpenCms, debugging 45
Oracle JDBC Driver, tools 34
project from CVS, checking 34, 35
Sysdeo Eclipse Tomcat Launcher plug-in, tools 34
tools 33

environment setup, JSP code
about 24
external editor, using 25
files editing, file synchronization used 26
file synchronization, configuring 26-28
Hello.jsp.file, creating 25
JSP code, debugging in OpenCms 30-33
WebDAV, used for editing 28-30

expressions, JSP templates
JSTL, combining with 116, 117
tag library, using 115, 116

F

feed manager class, RSS administration
  about 259, 260
  feed operations, supporting 260
feed operations, feed manager class
  addorupdateFileldIfNonNull method 264
  changes, saving 262, 263
  changes, updating 262, 263
  channel, deleting 261
  channel, publishing 264
  channel, returning 260
field configuration, OpenCms search index
  blogtext 131
  category 131
  creating 130
  new mapping action, adding 132
  tittle 131
  tittle-key 131

G

groups, OpenCms security
  administrators 155
  guests 155
  projectmanagers 155
  users 155

J

Java class 227
Java code
  updating 191-193
Java wrapper class
  creating 231
  getMappedfieldValue method 235
  RssChannelDef class, creating 231-233
  RssChannelSrc class, creating 233, 234
JSP code
  environment set up 24
JSP templates
  expressions 115
  updating 193-196

L

Lucene
  overview 125
  search indexes 125
  search indexes, querying 127
  search queries 127
Luke, OpenCms search index
  about 137
  using 137-140

M

module
  creating 186, 187
modules. *See* **OpenCms module**
module types, OpenCms module
  admin module 50
  content module 50
  content type module 50
  extention module 50
  integration module 50
  template module 50

N

new RSS channel, RSS administration
  data, persisting across pages 268
  dialog, declaring 266
  dialog actions, handling 270
  getdialogData method 269, 270
  initWorkplaceRequestValues method 268
  message file 267
  widgets, declaring 267, 268

O

OpenCms
  about 14
  administrative points, adding 239
  application server 15
  architecture 19, 20
  building, Eclipse environment setup 33
  database server, in back-end 15
  directory structure 15
  JSP from VFS, executing 30
  modules 20, 50
  overview 14
  resource loaders 21
  sample blog site, features 21
  structured content types 54
  template-elements property 21

templates 94
URL.structure 20, 21
web application, packaging 21
web request process 20, 21
web server 15
OpenCms, building
  Ant tasks 44
  project source from CVS, checking 36-40
  steps, Eclipse environment 40
OpenCms dialog classes,
    RSS administration
  actions, implementing 255
  class constructor 251
  column actions, adding 255
  column data, returning 254
  dialog, declaring 250
  dialog columns, defining 251-253
  HTML, adding 259
  independent actions 255
  independent actions, execution handling 257, 258
  independent actions, handling method 256, 257
  multiple actions 255
  multiple actions, implementing 258
  single actions 255
  sorting 251
OpenCms module
  ANT build file 44
  creating, entry fields 52, 53
  module, exporting 51
  module, importing 51
  module events 51
  modules, creating 52-54
  module types 50
OpenCms search index
  configuring 127
  field configurations 128
  Luke 137
OpenCms security
  groups 155
  organizational unit 157
  OrgUnit 157
  overview 153
  permissions 156
  role hierarchy 156
  roles 154

  user 154
OpenCms widget
  getConfiguration method 200
  newInstance method 199
  setConfiguration method 199
OrgUnit
  about 157
  ContentEditors 158

P

page layout
  review 89

R

Real File System. *See* **RFS**
registration code, user
  Java method 172, 173
  new user account, creating 174
  Register.jsp, adding 169, 170
  registerUserAction method 170, 171
resource loaders
  about 21, 113
  invoking 21
  process 113
  types 113
  XML content types, loading 114
RFS 12
roles, OpenCms security
  account manager 155
  administrator 155
  database manager 154
  developer 155
  project manager 155
  root administrator 154
  VFS manager 155
  workplace manager 154
  workplace user 155
ROME 185
RSS. *See also* **RSS feed**
  about 185
  accessing, Java bean used 187
  formats 185
  Jar files, integrating into OpenCms 187
  module, creating 186, 187
  ROME library 187
  RSSReader class 188, 189

RSS administration
  contents, index.jsp file 249
  feed manager class 259, 260
  index.jsp file 248
  new_rsschannel.jsp file 249
  new_rsschannel.jsp file, properties 249
  new RSS channel 265
  OpenCms dialog classes 250
  panel, tasks 246
  panel, viewing 248
RSS client code 187
RSS feed
  channel definition entry field 236
  content caching 190
  design 215
  displaying, in template 189, 190
  feed, creating 237, 238
  Flexcache 190
  formats, Java class 227
  Java class 227-229
  Java code, updating 191, 192
  JSP templates, updating 193-196
  method, retrieving feed entries 229, 230
  structured content type 218
  template 226
  user account, customizing 190, 191
  user account, managing 196, 197
  user preferences, adding to account 190, 191
RSS feed, design
  content data fields 216
  content fields 217, 218
  metadata fields 216
  property values 217
  RSS Channel Definition 215, 216
RSS feed structured content type
  about 218
  annotations 219, 220
  data field definitions 221
  widget, adding 222
RSS feed template 226

S

schema features, structured content types
  about 66
  additional widgets 79, 80
  content, previewing 69, 70
  content creating, model used 70
  content definitions, creating 80-83
  content relationship 68, 69
  explicit content relationship 68
  field, default values 67
  field, mapping 66
  field, validating 67
  implicit content relationship 68
  localization 68
  strong links, content relationship 68
  user interface widgets 70
  weak links, content relationship 68
search code
  CmsSearch bean, subclassing 143, 144
  Search.jsp template 145-151
  search bean, using 141
  search example 140-142
  writing 140
search indexes, Lucene
  analyzer 126
  document 126
  field 126, 127
  field indexing, field 126
  field storage, field 126
  tokenized, field indexing 126
  untokenized, field indexing 126
security, site
  BlogAdmin, adding 163-166
  BlogAdmin account 159
  CommentPublisher account 159
  group, setting up 162, 163
  OrgUnits, setting up 159-161
  resource permissions 167, 168
  setting up 158
  users, adding 163-166
site
  blog site, features 9
  content, developing 23
  deep thoughts blog website, designing 8
  design 8
  developer skills 12
  mockups 9, 11
  page layout, review 89
  security, setting up 158
standard configuration, OpenCms search index

content 130
description 130
keywords 130
meta 130
tittle 130
tittle-key 130

structured content types
acesscontrol/accessentry element 62
attribute, field mapping 66
BlogEntry Content type, creating 55
BlogEntry content type file 63, 65
BlogEntry type 54
configuration files editing, validating editor used 84, 86
content, organizing 87
content type, registering 59, 62
datatypes 55
explorertypes element 61
field, field mapping 66
newresource element 61
parameters element 60
property, field mapping 66
propertylist, field mapping 66
resourcetypes element 60
schema features 66
scope, field mapping 67
syntax, field mapping 66
types, field mapping 66
XSD schema files, rules for creating 55-58

T

templates, OpenCms
blog content loop 97, 98
Blog templates 112, 113
common code elements 100
content loading process 113
creating 94
direct edit provider, Java bean class 108
footer 99, 100
homepage template 95, 96
Java bean class 106
Java Bean class, blogs gathering 108
sidebar 99, 100
template loading process 113
utility methods, Java Bean 109-112
utility methods, Java bean class 109

U

user
login code 175, 176
logout 177
registration code 169

user, OpenCms security
Admin account 154
Export account 154
Guest account 154

user interface widgets, schema features
about 70
AdditionalWidget 79
BooleanWidget 71
ColorPickerWidget 72
ComboWidget 76
DateTimeWidget 71
DisplayWidget 78
DownloadGalleryWidget 72
GroupWidget 78
HtmlGalleryWidget 72
HtmlWidget 74, 75
ImageGalleryWidget 73
LinkGalleryWidget 73
MultiSelectWidget 77
SelectorWidget 76
StringWidget 77
StringWidgetPlaintext 77
TableGalleryWidget 73
TextareaWidget 78
TextareaWidgetPlaintext 78
UserWidget 79
VfsFileWidget 74

user login
about 175, 176
code 175, 176

user preferences to accounts, adding 190

V

VFS 12
Virtual File System. *See* **VFS**

W

WAR file 15
Web Application Resource. *See* **WAR file**
WebDAV

content, importing into project 122-124
site into Eclipse, creating 120, 121
template development 117
WebDAV plug-in, installing in Eclipse 118, 119
Web Tools Platform. *See* **WTP**
widget
creating 223
declaring 201
designing 201
getValues method 223, 224
interface, implementing 223
registering, with OpenCms 213
setConfiguration method 225, 226
widget code
CustomSourceConfiguration class 203, 204
data source, interface 207
getDialogWidget method 205
getSelectedValue method 206
localization, using OpenCms 212, 213
newInstance method 202
SELECT widget 202
setConfiguration method 202
subclassing 202, 206
widget code, datasource
DefaultDS 207
explorer type entry 209
implementing 209
option values, getting 209-211
resource type entry 208
valuelist content type 208
WTP 34

Packt Open Source Project Royalties

When we sell a book written on an Open Source project, we pay a royalty directly to that project. Therefore by purchasing OpenCms 7 Development, Packt will have given some of the money received to the OpenCms project.

In the long term, we see ourselves and you—customers and readers of our books—as part of the Open Source ecosystem, providing sustainable revenue for the projects we publish on. Our aim at Packt is to establish publishing royalties as an essential part of the service and support a business model that sustains Open Source.

If you're working with an Open Source project that you would like us to publish on, and subsequently pay royalties to, please get in touch with us.

Writing for Packt

We welcome all inquiries from people who are interested in authoring. Book proposals should be sent to authors@packtpub.com. If your book idea is still at an early stage and you would like to discuss it first before writing a formal book proposal, contact us; one of our commissioning editors will get in touch with you.

We're not just looking for published authors; if you have strong technical skills but no writing experience, our experienced editors can help you develop a writing career, or simply get some additional reward for your expertise.

About Packt Publishing

Packt, pronounced 'packed', published its first book "Mastering phpMyAdmin for Effective MySQL Management" in April 2004 and subsequently continued to specialize in publishing highly focused books on specific technologies and solutions.

Our books and publications share the experiences of your fellow IT professionals in adapting and customizing today's systems, applications, and frameworks. Our solution-based books give you the knowledge and power to customize the software and technologies you're using to get the job done. Packt books are more specific and less general than the IT books you have seen in the past. Our unique business model allows us to bring you more focused information, giving you more of what you need to know, and less of what you don't.

Packt is a modern, yet unique publishing company, which focuses on producing quality, cutting-edge books for communities of developers, administrators, and newbies alike. For more information, please visit our website: www.PacktPub.com.

Java EE 5 Development using GlassFish Application Server

ISBN: 978-1-847192-60-8   Paperback: 400 pages

The complete guide to installing and configuring the GlassFish Application Server and developing Java EE 5 applications to be deployed to this server

1. Concise guide covering all major aspects of Java EE 5 development
2. Uses the enterprise open-source GlassFish application server
3. Explains GlassFish installation and configuration
4. Covers all major Java EE 5 APIs

Tapestry 5

ISBN: 978-1-847193-07-0   Paperback: 280 pages

A step-by-step guide to Java Web development with the developer-friendly Apache Tapestry framework

1. Latest version of Tapestry web development framework
2. Get working with Tapestry components
3. Gain hands-on experience developing an example site
4. Practical step-by-step tutorial

Please check **www.PacktPub.com** for information on our titles

Managing and Customizing OpenCms 6 Websites

ISBN: 1-904811-76-0   Paperback: 240 pages

A complete guide to set up, configuration and administration

1. Understand the OpenCms web publishing process
2. Learn how to create your own, complex, OpenCms website
3. Develop the skills to implement, customize and maintain an OpenCms website

Building Websites with OpenCms

ISBN: 1-904811-04-3   Paperback: 262 pages

A practical guide to understanding and working with this proven Java/JSP-based content management system

1. Understand how OpenCms handles and publishes content to the Web
2. Learn how to create your own, complex, OpenCms website
3. Develop the skills to implement, customize, and maintain an OpenCms website

Please check **www.PacktPub.com** for information on our titles

Printed in Germany by
Amazon Distribution
GmbH, Leipzig